14.70

*The Metamorphosis of
Greece since World War II*

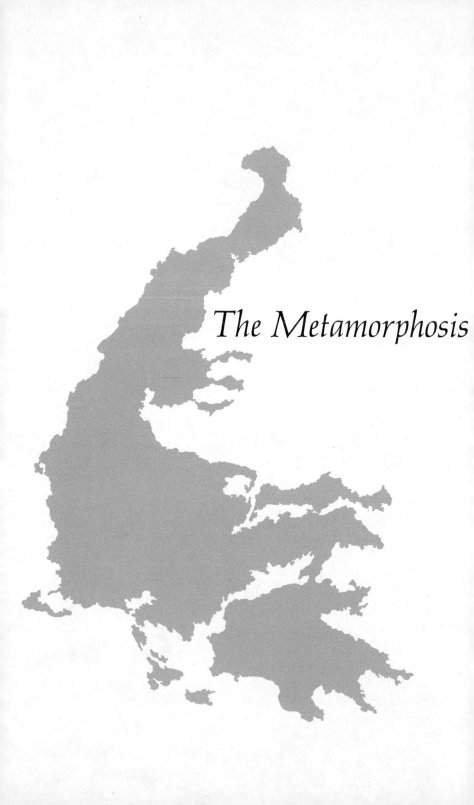

The Metamorphosis

William H. McNeill

f Greece since World War II

The University of Chicago Press · *Chicago and London*

WILLIAM H. McNEILL is Robert A. Milliken
Distinguished Service Professor of History at
the University of Chicago. His many books
include *Venice: The Hinge of Europe,*
1081–1797, and the National Book Award
winning *The Rise of the West: A History of the*
Human Community.

The University of Chicago Press, Chicago 60637
The University of Chicago Press, Ltd., London

© 1978 by The University of Chicago
All rights reserved. Published 1978
Printed in the United States of America
83 82 81 80 79 78   9 8 7 6 5 4 3 2 1

Library of Congress Cataloging in Publication Data

McNeill, William Hardy, 1917–
    The metamorphosis of Greece since World War II.

    Includes index.
    1. Greece, Modern—Social conditions.   2. Greece,
Modern—Economic conditions—1918–   3. Greece,
Modern—Politics and government—20th century.   I. Ti-
tle.
HN650.5.A8M33   309.1'495'07   77-26105
ISBN 0-226-56156-9

Contents

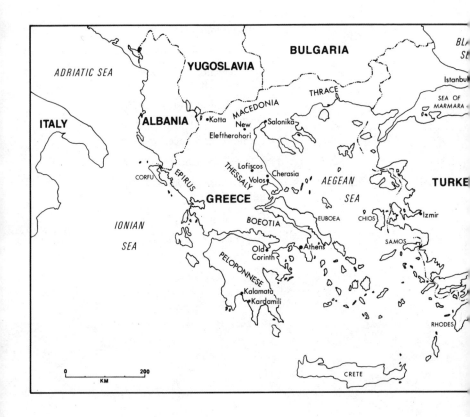

ADRIATIC SEA

ITALY

YUGOSLAVIA

BULGARIA

BLA
SE

ALBANIA

Istanbul

THRACE

SEA OF
MARMARA

MACEDONIA

•Kotta
New
Eleftherohori

Salonika

CORFU

EPIRUS

Lofiscos
THESSALY
Volos•
Cherasia

AEGEAN

SEA

TURKE

GREECE

Izmir

IONIAN

SEA

BOEOTIA

EUBOEA

CHIOS

SAMOS

Old
Corinth

•Athens

PELOPONNESE

Kalamata
Kardamili

RHODES

0   200
KM

CRETE

Acknowledgments

Thanks to a grant from the Rockefeller Foundation that freed me from other duties, I was able to write a draft of this book between May and September, 1976. A preliminary text was then circulated among a number of friends and colleagues whose criticisms, suggestions and corrections aided me in revising the manuscript between January and June, 1977.

I owe a debt of gratitude to innumerable friends and acquaintances in Greece who responded, each in his or her own way, to my questions. This is an old debt, extending in many cases across more than thirty years, and it seems best to allow my informants to remain anonymous lest what I have to say might be confused with what they told me. The fact is that my ideas about Greek society and public affairs are shaped by notions about social process derived from my professional studies; and the Greeks with whom I conversed so freely, since they did not share my education, offered quite different outlooks and explanations for what they saw around them than those I here advance. My informants should therefore never be held responsible for the ideas I set forth. Most of them would find what I say unsatisfactory, if not downright false.

My second debt of gratitude is to professional colleagues, mainly in the United States, who read and criticized my preliminary draft. They, too, hold different points of view from my own in greater or less degree, yet their suggestions were so significant in persuading me to alter and improve the text that I wish to acknowledge their contribution by name: George Anastaplo, W. Bruce Cook, Ernestine Friedl, John O. Iatrides, Halil Inalcik, Kostas Kazazis, William McGrew, John Robert McNeill, Karl F. Morrison, John Petropulos, Evan Vlachos, and not least, my wife, Elizabeth D. McNeill, who accompanied me on my visits to Greece and shared the task of assessing all we saw and heard, both at the time and subsequently when it came to writing things down.

To all of these persons, both those named and those unnamed, I am deeply grateful; but as is always the case, the judgments and even some of the facts recorded in the pages that follow are my own and those who helped me can in no way be held responsible for the end result. Like every book, this is a social product as well as an individual creation; but the society that shaped my sensibilities and conceptual frame is so complex as to defy analysis, since it combines Greek with American and American with European ideas and attitudes, all refracted through a single mind and sixty years of time.

William H. McNeill
Chicago, Illinois
6 June 1977

Introduction
The Greek Scene

The millions of visitors who arrive in Greece each year encounter a landscape that is both age-old and brand-new. The Greek countryside has remained much the same for millennia, ever since cultivators first began to farm the plains and allowed sheep and goats to denude the mountain slopes. In summer, blue sky and even bluer sea embrace a dusty landscape where only a thin cover of drought-resistant vegetation garnishes the rocky contours of hill and mountainside. To be sure, wherever there is enough fresh water to counteract the sun's unrelenting rays, lush vegetation arises; but such places are no more than a series of oases in the barrenness of hill and mountain. In winter, rains descend, and for a few weeks in spring all but the barest slopes burst out in flowering herbage. But grass and flowers soon wither in the summer heat. Only deeply rooted plants, like olive trees and grape vines—traditional staples of Greek cultivation— or the omnipresent scrub oak of the wastelands can retain their greenery without artificial irrigation. Irrigation works have indeed expanded the carpet of summer greenery quite substantially in recent decades; moreover, in parts of the country, on high ground, too steep to cultivate, systematic reforestation has begun to undo the overgrazing of past centuries. Yet these changes, significant though they be for the Greek economy, are not enough to alter the landscape as a whole. Rocky wastelands still separate one fertile plain from another; the sun still burns hot in summer while winds blow bitter cold in winter. Dark cypresses continue to punctuate the skyline like exclamation points. And everywhere the sea is near, even when not in view.

Yet, while almost all of Greece shares these general characteristics, important variations of landscape occur as one ascends the mountains. Lower slopes are often terraced to conserve precious soil. The human labor that went into building such terraces was the work of generations—perhaps of centuries— aimed at extracting the greatest possible returns from a parched and rock-rich land. Higher up, the effects of cooler temperatures and more abundant rainfall begin to show. Where man's hand has not been too destructive, forests appear on higher slopes, yielding in the topmost reaches to Alpine meadows, where fine pasture may be found in the summer months when the snow has melted away. These Alpine pastures, visited by shepherds in summer from time immemorial, have to be matched with winter quarters in the low-lying plains. There, with the permission of the local cultivators, sheep can survive the winter by gleaning harvested grain fields and foraging on fallowed land.

Rainfall is everywhere a limiting factor. In the west where moisture-bearing winds come in across the Adriatic and Mediterranean seas, precipitation is greater and landscapes are correspondingly greener, though here, too, bare limestone ridges often show through. In the lee of the mountains, much drier conditions prevail; and many of the Aegean islands present an almost desert aspect.

Nevertheless, local topography can make all the difference. In landscapes of barren rock, the upwelling of a spring or the run-off from a slope situated so as to intercept rain-bearing clouds can establish an oasis of greenery and fragrance in an otherwise dry and thirsty land. Artificial irrigation, now much expanded, has the same effect. Consequently, whenever one rounds a bend in the road some new vista may open, whether of hill or dale, of seascape or of mountain crag, that alters the aspect of the land in a trice. The small scale of the country is matched by the suddenness with which a traveller passes from one natural zone to another.

Human occupancy of the Greek landscape is very old and had, long ago, by a process of trial and error, come close to exploiting all available resources to the full. Improvements that modern scientific agriculture brought to the cultivation of the plains—eliminating fallow for example—had the side effect of disrupting the age-old equilibrium between summer and winter pastures needed by shepherd communities if they were to exploit the high Alpine meadows effectively. This is testimony to how closely traditional practices fitted the natural environment. Restless search for a way to squeeze just a little more out of the landscape, persisted in across innumerable generations, had, in fact, created an ecological pattern in which there was very little slack.

Yet the natural setting, durable though it may be, does not completely overpower the work of human hands. The barrenness of the slopes is itself the result of ancient overgrazing and subsequent erosion of shallow topsoil. Plato remarked on the phenomenon 2,400 years ago. The effects of these ancient abuses of the natural environment remain as limits to the human occupancy of Greece to this day—and will do so for centuries to come, no matter what regimen of land-use an ecologically more perceptive society may institute. But it is mainly in the towns that the mark of human handiwork may be seen; and it is primarily in the towns that the newness of contemporary Greece becomes apparent.

More than half the visitors to Greece arrive by air, and nearly all of the air travellers land at the Athens airport. There the decor and the arrangements for handling the flow of people and baggage closely resemble those of every other big international airport. The trip into Athens that follows can only reinforce the impression of modernity that the airport conveys. New buildings line the way, almost uninterruptedly, for miles. Many remain in a state of partial completion. One or more stories may be occupied, while other floors remain stark concrete skeletons for years on end, waiting for the day when the owner will have enough money to complete construction. Nearing the center of Athens, if he knows where to look, the visitor may snatch a glimpse of the Acropolis by sighting along suitably oriented side streets. Otherwise, at street level the Parthenon is entirely hidden by new buildings, six to eight stories tall, that line Athens' central streets. These structures have nearly all been built within the last thirty years. They lack character, most having been designed to enclose as much usable space as possible at the lowest practicable cost and with almost no attention to aesthetic considerations.

The growth of Athens is, in fact, the dominating phenomenon of modern Greek society. Ever since 1835, when what had previously been a stagnant provincial town became the capital of the newly independent Greek state, Athens has grown at a cancerous rate, far outstripping all other centers of population. Census records tell the tale:

> 31.5 thousand in 1848
> 179.7 thousand in 1896
> 802.6 thousand in 1928 (Greater Athens)
> 1,378.5 thousand in 1951 (Greater Athens)
> 2,540.2 thousand in 1971 (Greater Athens)

By 1976 the population of Greater Athens was close to three million. Since the total population of Greece was then only a little over nine million, such a concentration into a single urban cluster dominated the entire country to a remarkable degree.

Athens' recent growth rate of about 3.5 percent per annum reflected large-scale in-migration from the rest of the country. In turn, the steady stream of newcomers sustained and required the frenetic building boom that so radically transformed the appearance of the city after 1945. Other outward signs of newness abound. For Athenians today, car ownership matters almost as much as housing, with the result that even the widest streets and avenues jam up with traffic at peak hours of the day, and produce a noxious and all but perpetual smog. In these respects Athens resembles Tokyo and Los Angeles, two other brand-new cities, more than it does such European capitals as Paris or London.

Elsewhere, man-made landscapes in Greece are not quite so new or anywhere near as vast. Only Salonika in the north has shown anything remotely comparable to the new growth rate of Athens; but with 557,360 inhabitants in 1971, it is only a little more than a quarter the size of Athens. Nevertheless, Greek provincial towns and many villages have been largely rebuilt in the past thirty years. Innumerable unfinished structures attest to ambitious plans for the future. One has to travel to remote islands and into the mountains to find outwardly unchanged communities. Some of these have, in fact, been placed under a special regime, whereby new construction not conforming to traditional patterns is expressly prohibited by the government.

The little town of Metsovo is such a community. Perched high in the Pindus range that separates Thessaly from Epirus, Metsovo has a thoroughly old-fashioned appearance. Narrow cobbled streets and walkways run between houses roofed with slabs of light-colored stone. Since the houses straggle up a steep hillside, handsomely patterned stone roofs are much in evidence as one wanders from one level to another through the town. Mule trains still traverse the streets, loaded with wood and wool—traditional export items from this remote but ancient town; and women stand in their doorways wearing the peasant dress seldom seen elsewhere in Greece today. Yet in all this there is already just a hint of artifice. Metsovo is quaint, and has recently become aware of the fact. Community leaders are developing the town into a ski center. They clearly have in mind a model such as Innsbruck, where local architecture and Alpine dress survived and indeed took on fresh life with the arrival of cosmopolitan sophistication.

All the same, outward appearances can be deceptive. Metsovo's quaintness actually contributes to a vigorous modernity, seeking by clever exploitation of limited resources to maintain or increase local prosperity. The people of Metsovo have been doing this sort of thing for centuries. The town was once the center of a far-ranging caravan trade that extended north into central Europe; and even when portage by animal pack-train ceased to be economic, merchant networks among families that originated in Metsovo continued to function in distant cities of Europe. Successful businessmen in foreign parts remembered their ancestral origin generation after generation. Funds for the ski lift that now stands on the slopes above the town came from such emigrés, whose concern for the fate of Metsovo was not lessened by the fact that they live hundreds of miles away in Austria.

It is no less true that the shiny modernity of Athens and other Greek cities does not entirely hide signs of continuities with older Greek traditions and ways of life. To be sure, one has to look for such signs. Those who swarmed into the city from the countryside did so with a fierce intention of winning the right to enjoy the amenities of urban life. This meant a deliberate casting-off of all outward and obvious signs of their village past, insofar as financial resources allowed, and apprenticing themselves most strictly to the fashions of the city. But if one wanders away from the busy central areas of Athens it is not hard to discover small squares and side streets where life retains something of a village flavor. The pattern of life moves slowly: shopkeepers spend many an hour chatting in the café with friends, while keeping an eye out for possible customers. And when a customer does show up, the encounter has something of the quality of a social call as well as of a business transaction. Self-employed and part-time workers abound: not for them the factory whistle or office time-clock; rather, the ageless rhythms of work and rest that characterize village behavior.

Far on the outskirts of town, where recent in-migrants squat on empty land, outward trappings of village life survive practically intact. Humble dwellings, built hurriedly of local materials, are surrounded by small gardens in which kerchiefed housewives bend patiently over their vegetable patches in the back-breaking posture peasant women have always endured. Their menfolk, who work in factories or at various kinds of casual labor in the city, wear city-styled clothing and ride the bus to work. Yet among them, too, odd signs of village ways occasionally crop up. Shiny new dump trucks, for example, often carry across their radiators a strand of blue beads of the sort muleteers have used for centuries to protect their beasts from the evil eye.

Such casual sights suggest that traditional patterns of conduct, passed down through family custom, still pervade Greek society, giving the nation a character all its own. Conscious efforts to escape the village past and its poverty have not meant the repudiation of all village values: on the contrary, the new life in town continues to be inspired, at least in part, by the memories of that rural past, of its harshness, and of rural aspirations for greater material comfort. No newcomer to town supposes that the shift from village living alters ancient rules for getting ahead in the slightest degree. The carry-over from peasant outlook is therefore massive. The wholesale urbanization that has come to pass within a single lifetime makes anything else impossible. As a result, Greek society, politics, and economic behavior differ perceptibly from what happens in lands that do not share the Greek heritage.

Foreigners, and particularly Americans, do not always recognize this fact. Proud of our own accomplishments and sure of the value of American ways of doing things, officials and businessmen have often assumed that Greeks need simply to learn our management skills, whereupon imported know-how will achieve the same results as in the United States or anywhere else. Yet this is not always so. Even when the mighty engine of an impersonal market brings modern technology fully into play, there remains room for personal choices, and such choices sometimes reflect deep-lying traditional values and attitudes, surprising to outsiders who know little and care less about the local past.

This essay aims to illuminate the Greek scene by exploring the continuities and tensions between old and new in Greek life. A first step must be to try to characterize the most relevant aspects of the Greek tradition and to analyze the ways it fitted into the natural and human environment within which that tradition arose and flourished. Accordingly, the next two chapters will be devoted to these themes.

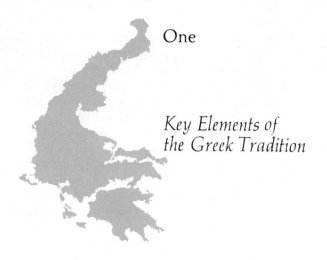

One

*Key Elements of
the Greek Tradition*

The Greek language and the Orthodox Christian faith are the two obvious factors defining the Greek tradition.

The Greek language has a continuous and well-recorded history around the shores of the Aegean, reaching back to Minoan times, when a script now known as Linear B was used to record palace inventories in a language ancestral to classical and modern Greek. Since the days of Homer, more than 2,600 years ago, an unbroken literary tradition records successive phases of the linguistic and cultural evolution of Greek with a fullness, elegance, and depth in time that no other European tongue can equal. Such a rich and varied literary heritage is naturally a source of pride to the modern Greek people; yet it also weighs heavily on the consciousness of the educated elite, since, no matter what their achievements, the culture of modern Greece seems puny beside the classical and Byzantine past, when speakers of Greek gave light to all of Europe, and even to parts of Asia.

Orthodox Christians claim to follow the true faith of Christ, uncontaminated by innovation of the kind that disfigures all other forms of Christianity. Such a self-image dictates rigorous immobilism. Only by keeping every jot and tittle of traditional doctrine and practice unchanged can the Orthodox claim to a monopoly of saving truth be logically maintained. Yet this posture risks making the church increasingly marginal, as ideas and practices unconnected with the Orthodox heritage flood into Greece from abroad.

How then should one understand the Greek tradition? If one fastens upon language and religion as the key elements, the modern nation-state at once appears as an inadequate frame, since significant numbers of speakers of Greek as well as Orthodox Christians (not all of whom speak Greek) live outside the boundaries of the modern Greek state. This is something that should always be kept in mind when thinking about Greece and the Greeks. Forces tending to compel congruence between Greek-ness and the territorial limits of the Greek national state have indeed been strong during the past century and a half. Ever since the country became independent of the Ottoman Empire in 1830, rival nationalisms tended to force previously intermingled peoples into separate, national compartments.

Yet congruence between Hellenism and the boundaries of the modern Greek state was never achieved; nor is it likely to be. The island of Cyprus, with a predominantly Greek-speaking population, continues to exist beyond Athens' jurisdiction. In addition, large numbers of Greeks have always ventured far afield in search of economic gain, and continue to do so. To sustain the resulting diaspora, Orthodoxy remains, as always, universal in spirit, reaching out to the faithful wherever they may be. Membership in a church uniquely and specially Greek, whatever the exotic setting—Australian, American, African, or Asian—obviously helps to maintain a consciously Greek culture and community within whatever alien society serves as host to the diaspora.

Language and religion therefore remain absolutely central, defining and sustaining what it means to be a Greek both at home and abroad. Yet the complexities of the Greek cultural tradition as embodied in language and religion are confusing even to the Greeks themselves, who spend years in school apprenticing themselves to some of its intricacies. The long series of encounters with other peoples—Romans, Slavs, Jews, Syrians, Arabs, Turks, Latin Christians, and the post-Christian world of the West, to name but the more important—makes the literary and religious heritage of Greece a blurred and complex palimpsest. Contradictions between the pagan and the Christian, as well as between the Byzantine and the Ottoman segments of the past, have never been entirely reconciled, and cannot be. Yet in the actual life of a people, rules of conduct and patterns of behavior do, in fact, assert themselves as more or less coherent ways of coping with the world. Moreover, such folkways adjust relatively rapidly to new experience. Anything else would be intolerable, making everyday human encounters too unpredictable and risky.

Hence it seems best to look at actual behavior and the explanations ordinary people give for their conduct if one wants to grasp the living core of the Greek tradition. For this purpose it is wise to concentrate upon what relatively humble and unsophisticated folk do and say. This is so for two reasons. First, such folk by their selection of some elements and facts from the extended repertoire of the high culture perform what an outside observer cannot do for himself: they, in effect, decide by their choices what is primary and of key importance in the high tradition, and what remains passive or marginal, available, perchance, for reassertion at some future time when circumstances may change, but for the time retains merely decorative or historical significance. Second, the culture of cities and the sophistication of highly educated persons, to whom a full range of nuances and contradictions from the Greek literary record remains available, nevertheless build upon core values and assumptions dictated by folkways and village practices. Cities, after all, have always drawn their inhabitants from the countryside. Until about a century ago, cities could not sustain themselves biologically, owing to the intensified exposure to infectious diseases created by urban crowding. Even after this ceased to be true, a continued inflow of country folk to the cities refreshed and sustained older connections between village simplicity and urban complexity.

Another very powerful reason for concentrating attention on rural folk in hope of picking out key elements and ruling principles of the Greek tradition is this: in recent decades, a number of excellent books have been written about Greek rural communities. Careful observation, sympathetic discussion with the members of the community under study, and incisive generalization all come together in works like Ernestine Friedl, *Vassilika: A Village in Modern Greece* (New York, 1962), John K. Campbell, *Honour, Family, and Patronage: A Study of*

Institutions and Moral Values in a Greek Mountain Community
(Oxford, 1964), and Peter Loizos, *The Greek Gift: Politics in a
Cypriot Village* (Oxford, 1975). Fifteen to twenty similar,
though less luminous, analyses of other Greek rural communities exist in the form of doctoral dissertations and journal
articles, or as contributions to learned congresses. These allow
one to assume that the findings of Friedl, Campbell, and Loizos
apply, with only minor modification, to other village communities. My own comparatively superficial observation of six
Greek villages over a thirty-year period also supports the notion
that there really is a core of ideas and practices that informs the
lives of rural folk and deeply affects urban behavior. Let me
therefore try to characterize that core.

The first point that emerges from available accounts of village
life is the centrality of exchange and the critical importance of
the skills of the marketplace in the lives of Greek peasants. From
ancient times, Greek rural life revolved around buying and
selling. Shrewd dealing at the critical moment when supply and
demand are in their optimal conjunction from one's own point of
view is what matters. By comparison, the long hot hours spent
laboring in the fields are less important, though of course they
remain vitally necessary for the success of the year's enterprise.
The fact is that under ordinary conditions, when new crops or a
new technology are not in question, any increase in yield that
more assiduous application of labor may produce is likely to be
far exceeded by the increment a better price can bring to the
family budget.

This elementary fact can be illustrated today in any Greek
village. In June 1976, when I visited Old Corinth, the apricot
harvest was just about to commence; and the upshot of the
year's work and planning depended on how much each farming
family would have to pay for outside labor to help with the
picking, and how much they would get for each kilo of fruit
from their trees. Scabs and other damage to the fruit and, of
course, the amount of fruit each tree carried were also important
variables. These depended on the way the orchards had been
pruned, sprayed, fertilized, watered, and tilled. But such factors
were trivial in comparison to the way the two relevant prices
would be fixed. Individual deals between buyer and seller—deals
that could be broken off at short notice or even with no notice at

all—defined these critical prices and the actual exchange of goods and services upon which the success or failure of the year depended. Each orchard owner was on his own, competing with others for access to available pickers, and competing no less directly for access to truckowners and merchants who would buy the fruit for delivery to Athens, to Germany, or to a local jam factory, as the case might be.

Skill in bargaining for the best possible prices, skill in deciding the exact moment at which to make a deal—knowing when to hold out for more and when to cave in and accept the other fellow's terms—these were the ways to wealth and success. These were also the skills that won the respect of others in the village, even if such respect might be a little grudging. For if one man was able to do even a little bit better than others in such negotiations, it meant that he had somehow outsmarted every-one else. Privacy and deception play a large role in the successful conduct of such negotiations. Deception must be practiced against one's fellows, who, if they crowd round at the critical moment, might spoil the advantageous deal by trying to get in on it too. Deception must also extend to the person with whom one is dealing, for if he were better informed he might be able to conclude a different bargain by contacting others who are also seeking to sell or buy the same goods or services.

The effort to deceive is of course reciprocal. Even after an agreement as to wages or prices has been reached, the parties are liable to harbor anxious thoughts about whether they could not have done better by holding out a little longer. Suspicion of one's contractual partner therefore remains near the surface. Sudden and angry withdrawal by either party is a continual possibility, if either side sees some sign of bad faith or, worse still, if one partner discovers that he could in fact have made a better price by contracting with someone else.

Human relations thus turn upon a struggle, in which it seems self-evident that one man's gain is someone else's loss. The idea that a deal might be mutually beneficial is hard for a Greek to accept. For even if both parties stand to gain, one gains more than the other. Justice is essentially unattainable in such rela-tionships; both sides normally feel that the agreed price does not give them their due.[1] The world itself thus becomes a theater for

1. Cf. Adamantia Pollis, "Political Implications of the Modern Greek Concept of Self," *British Journal of Sociology* 16 (1965): 35 and passim.

perpetual struggle in which cleverness and guile, as well as luck, play central roles in determining success. The humdrum routines of everyday work and the directness of simple honesty take second place, to be exercised, if at all, only when they, too, open the way for successful negotiation in the marketplace.

Such discipline of life is utterly at odds with the routines and outlook characteristic of subsistence farmers, wherever they happen to live. In communities of subsistence farmers, income and status are mainly dependent on the amount of land a family possesses and the assiduity with which the land is cultivated. In such circumstances, work in the fields is the major variable in fixing the level of income a given family can expect. Even if, as usually happened in civilized lands, the harvest had to be shared with landlords acting both on their own behalf and as agents of a distant central government, it still was usually the case that the residue remaining in peasant hands after rents and taxes had been collected was proportional to the amount of the total harvest. Consequently, in a subsistence village economy, hard work paid off perceptibly, whereas prices hardly mattered to the peasants, since it was only the landlords (or merchants acting as their agents) who entered the market by selling part or all of what had been collected as rent and taxes.

Obviously, intermediate rural economies may exist in which peasants enter the market either before or after paying rents and taxes to their landlords. Indeed, the relative importance of market sale as against subsistence consumption for rural cultivators may vary indefinitely. My proposition boils down to this: traditional patterns of Greek agriculture put predominant weight on marketing. Even though villagers always raised some of their own food, the nicety of their adaptation to the variegated natural environment pushed them toward specialization. As a result, they nearly always had to buy important amounts of food (and other commodities) for survival. Traditional Greek rural patterns stood, in this respect, close to one extreme of possible balances between commercial and subsistence agriculture. In this elemental but important way Greek peasants assimilated their life style to that of urban dwellers, who also depended on imported food, secured usually through buying and selling.

Powerful and fundamental though market relationships were and remain for Greek rural society, only a part of human life can be comprehended within commercial networks. Perpetual war of all against all, even if channeled through the conventions of the marketplace, and limited to peaceable expression by law, does not constitute a psychologically tenable way to live. To be sure, in all Greek villages the struggle among individuals is regularly modulated by semiplayful badinage in the coffeehouse. Antagonisms can also be relieved during ritually defined periods of festivity when the struggle for private advantage is temporarily suspended.

But such palliatives are not enough: human beings need additional scope for sentiments of mutuality and solidarity. This the Greeks find within the circle of the nuclear family, and in its extensions through precisely defined artificial forms of kinship. The main form of artificial kinship is that of marriage sponsor and godfather, or *koumbaros*. To be *koumbaros* at a wedding establishes a solidarity with the groom that is more dependable than brotherhood itself since no quarrels over final distribution of the paternal estate can disturb it. Moreover, the *koumbaros* at marriage normally becomes godfather at least to the eldest son born to the new family. This, too, is an important relationship, almost as important as being a father, and provides the youngster with an alternative protector, if the father should die before his children attain maturity and full independence. A parallel system of artificial kinship exists on the female side, so that any one nuclear family normally finds itself surrounded with a clearly defined number of persons from whom help and support can be expected in time of need. In contrast, blood brothers may quarrel and oppose one another without incurring severe moral stigma, though in principle solidarity among collateral blood relations is also to be desired and to be cultivated wherever possible.

The result of such arrangements has been to create in every Greek village a series of small, intense, family in-groups, each with a fringe of connecting and supportive kin. Mutual help and sharing of worldly goods, rescue in time of adversity, and compassion for personal weakness or shortcoming found full expression within the private circle of the family. If a young wife, brought into the bosom of her husband's family, faced a difficult role at first, in due season she could look forward to becoming mother-in-law to her son's bride, and thus begin to

enjoy the perquisites and privileges of a dominant position
earned by years of hard labor and child-rearing.

Mutuality within the family circle and hostility toward those
outside made a tolerable moral universe. An appropriate discrimination of persons permitted expression of a wide range of
human emotions and impulses. It was a universe of polarity, one
kind of behavior being appropriate in some encounters, and a
very different behavior coming into play in others. Male and
female roles were also defined antithetically for the most part,
though for any job that required maximal application of labor in
a defined period of the year, men, women, and children
commonly worked together in the fields, their performance
limited only by muscular strength and endurance.

The centrality of the nuclear family in-group in Greek rural
life rested largely on the fact that all the ordinary operations of
farming could be and normally were performed by the members
of a single such family. Man and wife, assisted by parents at the
beginning of their active career and by children at its close, were
able to carry out all the ordinary farm tasks by themselves.
Work with olives and vines required cultivation with a mattock
and pruning with a knife—both individual tools. Grain fields,
which nearly always played a part in Greek agriculture even in
the best olive and vine regions, had to be plowed. But a light
scratch-plow, that broke the soil but did not turn a furrow, was
universally employed. A single donkey could pull such a plow
through the earth unassisted. A nuclear family could therefore
expect to drive the plow on the strength of its own resources.
Only the very poor, whose land was insufficient to maintain
even a single draft animal, and who normally would have to
supplement agricultural income with wage work of some kind,
were compelled to go to a neighbor to make a deal for help in
plowing. Thus in most Greek villages, most of the time, the
work unit as well as the marketing and consumption unit
coincided with the boundaries of the nuclear family. This
enormously reinforced the power of family sentiment, and made
the difference between "us" and "them," within and without the
family circle, a far sharper line of demarcation than could arise
in societies where such coincidence was not the norm.

Since modern urban life also tends to make the nuclear family
the primary unit of consumption and mutuality, these Greek

rural patterns may not seem particularly surprising. Yet it is worth pointing out that in other parts of Europe such an intensive reinforcement of the nuclear family unit was by no means normal in traditional rural society. Immediately adjacent to Greek lands, for instance, among the Slavs of the Balkan peninsula, nuclear families merged into much larger work and consumption groups, known as *zadruga*, which often numbered a hundred or more persons.[2] In northwestern Europe, also, where a heavy moldboard plow became standard, no single peasant family could ordinarily provide the four to six draft animals required to drag so large an object through the earth. Wherever the moldboard plow came into use, therefore, trans-familial work parties became essential if plowing was to be done at all. Within Greece, for that matter, efficient management of sheep and goats requires the cooperation of more persons than can usually be found within a single nuclear family. Shepherd communities accordingly contrive to establish trans-familial work groups that pool the labor of two or three nuclear families according to an agreed-upon sharing out of the year's yield of milk, cheese, and wool.[3]

Indeed in earlier ages, when death from famine and disease or from violence was far more common than today, serious risks arose from concentrating sentiments of mutuality within such a small unit as the nuclear family. Death of an adult male, when his children were too young to do much work, could be disastrous. The Slavic *zadruga* offered effective insurance against this kind of danger. It retained its vigor as long as sudden adult death remained a common event, and as long as individual ownership of a particular field was not a matter of special moment because supplies of land exceeded the manpower available for cultivation.

In contrast to the *zadruga*, the Greek family pattern was best suited to a society in which land was in relatively short supply and population comparatively abundant. In such circumstances,

2. For discussion of how this difference affected recent political action in Greece and Bulgaria, see Nicos Mouzelis, "Greek and Bulgarian Peasants: Aspects of Their Sociopolitical Situation during the Interwar Period," *Comparative Studies in Society and History* 18 (1976): 85–105.

3. For details, see Campbell, *Honour, Family, and Patronage*, p. 17ff.

even the death of an adult male could be compensated for by contracting with someone from outside to cultivate the family land in return for a negotiated share of the crop. Possession of real property could thus allow a widow and her children to survive, wherever suitably skilled manpower was available on a contract basis to move into the gap created by the death (or disability) of the husband and father. As long as contracting for such services was possible, that is, as long as extra labor was readily available within the community, the narrowing of sympathies to embrace only the nuclear family presumably had positive survival value, whereas the precarious conditions of life inherent in subsistence farming made larger in-groups far safer.

It seems to me hard to exaggerate the central significance of buying and selling for traditional Greek life. This was the really critical activity, even when it occupied only a few days of the year. Everything else was subordinate to the terms of exchange agreed upon; and the welfare of the family, as well as its prestige and repute in village opinion, depended on how skillfully the head of the household made his deals. No wonder, then, that the arts of bargaining developed to a fine point. "What can I gain by making a deal with him?" is the first question that crosses a Greek peasant's mind in almost every encounter.

All the same, there is another and sporadically even more powerful pole to Greek life: the heroic act, entered upon with no thought as to cost, risking life itself for a cause that may be entirely immaterial and of no commercial value whatever. Heroic behavior is, of course, systematically opposed to the calculating conduct necessary for successful buying and selling. Instead of disguising his feelings as a shrewd bargainer must, telling lies or half-truths, and seeming to surrender when actually triumphing, the hero imposes himself upon those around him, either through acts of forceful self-assertion or, alternatively, by accepting risk, privation, and danger that go beyond the ordinary.

Popular appreciation of heroism was and is inextricably connected with the high literary tradition of Greece. Above all others, it was Homer who formulated the heroic ideal, and for all of Europe his poems remain its most powerful, persuasive expression. Needless to say, the Greeks never forgot Homer. In modern times the study of the *Iliad* and *Odyssey*, as well as of other classical writers who express the ancient notion of heroism, constitutes a part of formal education. Moreover, during the long centuries since classical times, other influential literary works reaffirmed and elaborated heroic ideals. The most important of these drew upon continuing popular manifestations of heroic action. Constantly updating its manifestations, they reinforced and revived popular admiration for the heroic way of life. Thus the Byzantine epic *Digenes Akritas* breathes the air of the borderland between Christianity and Islam, where defense of the faith, sword in hand, gave special scope to heroic behavior. The *Erotokritos* of the seventeenth century, and the kleftic songs of the eighteenth and nineteenth centuries, also drew their themes from Christian-Moslem conflict. The latter two attained remarkable popularity among Greek villagers at a time when formal schooling scarcely existed. Propagated orally by recitation and singing, these poems commanded acute attention in an age when competing forms of entertainment were absent from village life. As a result, until the spread of literacy in the twentieth century weakened oral learning, it was commonplace to stud discussion in the village coffeeshop with quotations from and references to these poems, whose lines everyone had heard and often knew by heart.

Saints' lives gave a different but no less pervasive expression to the heroic ideal. These, too, were widely propagated orally in past centuries by preaching. Since the church year was partly built around the celebration of saints' days, stories about the lives of the more prominent saints became almost universally familiar. Several important saints were heroes in the mold of Achilles or Hector, only superficially Christianized. St. George and St. Demetrios, for example, were warriors, and were regularly portrayed as such on church walls.

Yet there was also a more specifically Christian form of saintly heroism. This was lodged in the monasteries, where the most vehement expression of Orthodox Christianity was always to be found. Within monastic walls, spiritual athletes ascended beyond heaven into the living presence of God through mystic experience. This required daring and an ascetic self-discipline as severe as anything expected of worldly heroes. How else could victory over a foe more formidable than any merely human antagonist be won? For the monks set out to defeat the Devil and his legions while winning their way to God. The task was regularly conceived and expressed in the language of heroic encounter and hand-to-hand combat.

Surrounded therefore by the language and aspiration of heroism, both in a worldly and in an other-worldly guise, Greek peasants had somehow to reconcile the pattern of their daily lives with such ideals. Working in the fields, chaffering in the marketplace, worrying about family income and repute: none of this is exactly the stuff of heroism. In dealing with powerful outsiders, in fact, the ordinary man had to defer and submit, seeking the protection or at least the complaisance of power-wielders, even if it meant self-abasement. Such craven conduct amounted to outright betrayal of the heroic style of life: yet this was what ordinary men during their mature years were condemned to do. Heroism simply was not compatible with the realities of farming, of buying and selling, and of protecting the material interests of the family group.

Yet no Greek male could entirely forget what was daily betrayed. Suitably provoked, he often found himself strongly tempted to break away from the manners appropriate to ordinary routines by suddenly assuming a heroic pose. This could take many forms. Strangers were and still are most likely to see such impulses expressed in the form of reckless hospitality, offering food and drink on a lavish scale to persons who may never be able to return the favor, and offering it with no regard for how deeply the expense may cut into the host's available resources. Anyone who travelled in rural Greece before the tourist inundation of the 1960s and 1970s repeatedly experienced the extraordinary readiness of simple villagers to become extravagantly generous hosts, consuming in a day what it took months to accumulate; and all on behalf of a stranger! Such gestures undoubtedly secured status and respect within the village itself: after all, the ability to consume grandly and to give freely proved the host's success as a winner of wealth. But however real the psychic income a generous host might gain through the envy tinged with admiration that his acts aroused among his neighbors, it is impossible to believe that the decision to play the host was not taken spontaneously—seized upon, even, as an occasion upon which the uncalculating behavior appropriate to a hero could safely be given free rein.

Generally speaking, it would appear that honor and respect gained by skillful management in the arena of the marketplace can also be won by exactly contrary behavior. Suddenly giving away in public what had been craftily, hiddenly, and gradually accumulated gave wealth a different but real kind of value. As a result, successful merchants and businessmen, and emigrés who have been absent from Greece for decades, often feel impelled to make some conspicuous gift to their native place. By far the most famous such gift was the purchase of a cruiser for the Greek navy early in this century by a private citizen who had made most of his money abroad. The cruiser *Averof* was named after its donor: more important, it tipped the naval balance within the Aegean decisively in favor of the Greeks and against the Turks during the Balkan wars, 1912–13. No individual has since succeeded in making so remarkable a gift; but the principle behind Averof's gesture remains very much alive. Hundreds of Greek villages boast improvements of one sort or another—a paved square, a public fountain, an icon or even a whole new church, planned and paid for and often named after the donor.

Yet hospitality and gift-giving, however appropriate to the heroic style, are but a small part of the authentic range of heroic behavior. Most Greek villagers and city dwellers have to settle for sporadic and exceptional gestures of this kind. The texture of everyday conduct permits no more; and the pervasiveness of bureaucratic administration in recent times still further restricts the expression of violent, heroic impulses. Revenge, sometimes bloody and brutal, is still condoned, however, when a family's honor has been sexually attacked.[4] Quarrels among men seldom lead to personal violence. Noisy and prolonged exchange of insults may indeed occur in public; and underhanded attempts to undermine a family's reputation by spreading malicious gossip is

4. A man suspected of illicit sexual intercourse risks death or mutilation at the hands of the woman's male relatives; and courts take a lenient view of such acts of revenge. Episodes of this kind are, however, relatively rare, since all concerned understand the drastic consequences that result from infringement of the sexual code of honor. Constantina Safilios-Rothschild, "Honor Crimes in Contemporary Greece," *British Journal of Sociology* 20 (1969): 205–18, recorded a total of 197 cases of such crimes between 1 May 1960 and 30 October 1963. In several instances, wronged women revenged themselves—characteristically by splashing disfiguring acid on the face of the offender.

an even more common way of harming a foe. But physical assault, and the raging recklessness of vengeful heroes, rarely find overt expression in Greek village life.

Monasteries, too, have decayed in modern times to such an extent that this avenue for heroic self-expression has become unimportant. In the eighteenth century and before, holiness attracted wealth, and by the nineteenth century wealth sustained idleness more often than authentic spirituality. As a result, when monastic properties were confiscated by land-hungry nation-states, the monastic calling lost nearly all of its devotees. The old mystical tradition lives on mostly in books.

There are, nevertheless, two niches in modern Greek society where the ancient patterns of heroism find fuller expression. A wilder, freer life than anything fully compatible with bureau-cratic administration persists in remote mountain villages and among shepherd communities. Under the Turks, free villages of the mountains were, in fact, numerically and psychologically important for the Greek nation. Today these villages are rapidly withering away, as emigration empties out communities where farming and herding can only yield a scant living at best. Nonetheless, such communities continue to exist; and in them it is still the case that deeds of heroism in defense of local pasture rights against encroaching outsiders remain a part of ordinary life. Young men between the time that they attain full stature and the time when they assume the responsibilities of marriage are the paladins of such local affrays. Indeed, the status and worth of every young man is in some degree dependent on how well he acquits himself in conflicts with other young men from other communities in disputes over pasture rights. Encroach-ment on a neighbor's pasture land is honorable, if one gets away with it. Repelling intruders is honorable. Physical prowess in battle is honorable. The preferred instruments of combat are sticks and stones: lethal weaponry, which was commonly used in the deeper past, went out of style when the Greek government began hunting down as murderers those who killed their op-ponents. Effective efforts to police the mountains and repress blood feuds became general in Greece only in the 1920s. But scarcely had such measures become effective when World War II broke out, and, as we shall see, the years that followed saw a swift expansion of violence and widened scope for heroic behavior.

The historic freedom of village life in the mountains, therefore, nurtured heroic violence until very recently. Moreover, the
significance of mountain manners is much greater than the
numerical weight of such communities in census returns might
suggest. Dwellers in cities and plains continue to admire the life
of the mountains, regarding it as quintessentially Greek, the true
expression of their nation, largely because it offers a more
perfect, more heroic pattern of life than is possible in the
economically richer but psychologically poorer environment of
cities and plains.

Two circumstances feed this romanticism. One is the fact that
the Greek War of Independence, 1821–30, was fought mainly by
bands of mountaineers, issuing forth from their cramped upland
valleys to descend upon the Turks in the plains. As victors, they
were in a position to define the national traditions of the new
Kingdom of Greece. Moreover, the mountaineers' natural tendency to idealize their style of life was aided and abetted by Lord
Byron and other philhellenes who sought to refresh their own
jaded appetites by finding a living contact with the classical and
Homeric past in the primitive life of the Greek mountains.
Efforts by imported Bavarian officials to construct the new
kingdom on the model of a well-administered bureaucratic state
suffered by comparison from the disadvantage of being unmis-
takably foreign, as well as humdrum and relatively unsuccessful.

A second factor that continues to refresh the idealization of
mountain village life results from migration patterns within and
beyond Greek borders. Life in the mountains was always poor.
A father with more than a single son could not divide the
inheritance and expect his children to start life at even the bare
survival standards of his own household. Emigration was one of
the traditional remedies; as death rates among children and
young men diminished in the nineteenth and more spectacularly
in the twentieth centuries, and as new opportunities opened up
in Greek cities and abroad, the scale of such emigration became
substantial. But emigrants did not sever their familial ties with
the village of their birth. Especially in old age, they often
invested the ways of their childhood with a nostalgic aura of
heroic grandeur—imputing to the mountains all the things that
found limited or imperfect expression in the cramped quarters of
a modern city.

As a result, in modern Greece a literary tradition dating back to the War of Independence was continually refreshed and sustained by word-of-mouth testimony from scores of thousands of mountain-born city dwellers. Urban Greeks, accordingly, continue to set great store by the freedom and heroism of the old life, whether or not their own families can trace any connection to such a past.

Plains villagers, however, only partly share such attitudes. To them, the men of the mountains were at least as much aliens and enemies as heroes, for it was upon the surpluses of the plains that mountaineers depended to make up the deficiencies of their own local resources; and when peaceable means for securing necessary food supplies failed, for whatever reason, the men of the mountains resorted to arms. One can safely assume that farmers of the plains never liked having to share their resources with armed men from the hills; but plainsmen have never been shapers of the national tradition of modern Greece. Certainly, their numerical preponderance has not resulted in public admiration for their market-oriented, shrewd, and unheroic style of life.

The other niche in modern Greek society where freer scope is given to heroic aspiration is the Greek army. In recent decades, the army institutionalized the heroic ethos in remarkably precise, narrow bureaucratic channels. Nearly every young man is drafted into the ranks of the army at the age of twenty-one, or on the completion of more advanced formal schooling. Only a few, physically unfit, are rejected. Service lasts two and a half years as a rule. For peasant boys, the army often acts as a school, teaching them skills which can sometimes be transferred to later life. One such skill is the art of coping with overbearing, even tyrannous, representatives of official, bureaucratic authority. Greek army officers are, after all, not much different from other government employees with whom Greek citizens must do business; and induction into the army is likely to be a young man's first important encounter with officialdom.

Still, the army has a special character of its own. Recruits are invited to view themselves as heroes, ready to die for their country if need be. However drab the daily routines of military training may be, most young men respond positively. Invocations of Marathon and Salamis mingle with no less effective indoctrination concerning battles of the Albanian War of 1940–41, and the guerrilla war of 1946–49. The Byzantine emperor Basil the Bulgar-slayer, together with the hero of the War of Independence, Theodore Kolokotronis, the Turk-slayer, play a role that may be compared with that of the saints of the church. Like icons, they are figures to be invoked as protectors of Hellenism in conflict with its two most feared and hated national rivals.

Such indoctrination has a resonance that Americans, living at a distance from any likely foes, find hard to appreciate. Political relations across Greek borders since the foundation of the modern Greek state have been persistently tense. Since 1897, when Greeks fought a brief and unsuccessful war against the Turks, until the present, every decade either saw active warfare that engaged the whole available manpower of the Greek nation, or at least spawned a crisis acute enough to provoke full-scale mobilization of the reserves. Army training and indoctrination, therefore, has an immediacy and realism that would be lacking in a more peaceful environment. This circumstance, in turn, fosters and sustains the heroic side of the national tradition and self-image.

During the twentieth century, a professional corps of officers (since 1949 about fifteen thousand strong) has become the special guardian of this aspect of Hellenism. Its members stand in self-conscious opposition to the commercial spirit that informs so much of the rest of Greek life; they are disdainful and, at least sometimes, also resentful of the material rewards such conduct brings. Since the 1930s, men attracted to the military (and police) careers were of humble, usually village or small-town, origin. A very few military families connected in some way with the royal court existed in Greece until World War II; but since the death of Field Marshal Alexander Papagos in 1955, no members of such families have played any part in Greek army affairs. Bureaucratic and impersonal patterns of promotion, as realized under the pressure of foreign (mainly American) advisers since 1945, make the military career unattractive to persons of elite status, since they can no longer count on attaining high command by virtue of their family connections. Moreover, army rates of pay are sufficiently modest that only

young men starting life in the lower half of the Greek income
scale are likely to choose an army career.[5]

The result is to create in modern Greece a sharp separation
between the professional military class and other elites. The fact
that the bulk of the Greek army is stationed in the north on the
outskirts of small provincial towns means that most army
officers spend their years of active service far away from the
seats of power in Athens. Within the capital, army headquarters
is removed from the center of the city, and is surrounded by
housing reserved for military personnel. This has created a sort
of special military quarter that is set off from the rest of the city
by invisible but nonetheless real barriers. Army officers are
legally prohibited from taking gainful employment in off-duty
hours, and the regulation seems to be quite effective in checking
interpenetration of civilian and military communities. It would,
indeed, be incompatible with the heroic ideal for officers to enter
the marketplace in the haggling spirit Greeks so often exhibit;
and this difference in ethos, as much as the formal prohibition, is
perhaps what keeps the two segments of Greek life so separate.

The result is that what in rural, traditional Greece had been a
loosely polarized pattern of conduct has become massively
institutionalized in recent decades. The values of the marketplace and its appropriate behavior dominate civilian society; the
heroic self-image dominates the military. What had been the
special preserve and testing ground for young men before
marriage in mountain villages remains a testing ground for this
same age group. But it has become formalized, nationalized,
universalized.

As long as most young men drafted into the Greek army came
from rural communities, the common background and assumptions shared by officers and men were sufficient to withstand the
bureaucratization of heroism required by barracks life. Young
men drafted from the cities, however, are commonly more
critical, and are likely to resent the deprivations implicit in army
life in the north, especially when they come from Athens. This
introduces a divisiveness into the ranks of the army whose
importance is impossible to assess. The officers' reactionary

5. The Greek navy, by contrast, continues to attract a few officers
from the Athenian upper class.

social views and cultural yearning for the verities of their small-town and village past may merely arouse antagonism in the city-bred youths, who are inclined to think themselves cleverer than the officers who are supposed to lead them. Conversely, officers who assimilate city ways may pay only cynical lip-service to the old ideals. The discredit that came to the army in the last days of the Colonels' regime (1974) certainly exacerbated these problems. Whether reaffirmation of old-fashioned patriotism and the heroic rhetoric in which it has long been clothed will in future command enough assent among draftees to maintain army morale remains a secret, subterranean issue that deeply affects the future of the country. No one can possibly tell in advance of some future political crisis just how the army will react. Accidents of leadership have been decisive in the past; the social composition of the army and new strains within it arising from the changing life-patterns of draftees is a new variable whose weight only the future will reveal.

This rift within the ranks of the army is part of a larger systematic weakness of modern Greek society, to wit, the absence of clear and well-defined means of regulating the interaction between civilian and military leadership. The links created in western European nations by aristocratic and courtly domination of professional armies, and the image of the officer and gentleman derived from that linkage, are lacking in Greece today. In traditional mountain life, marriage ended the warrior phase of a man's career; thereafter the obligations of family affairs imposed resort to marketplace behavior as the norm. Only some short-lived emergency or unusual set of encounters were likely to call forth heroic response in later life. But a corporate institution like the army is self-perpetuating. Traditional age-patterns still hold, to the extent that almost all young Greeks wait until after their military service to get married, and treat the completion of their time in the army as a threshold for the assumption of full adult roles. But the existence of a coherent body of professional officers means that a powerful elite does not conform to the traditional age-group pattern for reconciling the heroic with the humdrum. No effective substitute has been discovered. The intersection between military and civil management, therefore, remains an especially delicate one in Greece today, all the more so since both sides of the balance have deep and secure roots in traditional attitudes upon which to draw in time of crisis or challenge.

The ambiguitiy of the relationship is enhanced by the fact that Greek army officers are by no means immune to the ideal of self-enrichment through shrewd exploitation of market opportunities. Usually officers do refrain from buying and selling commodities. But they can sometimes market themselves, that is, arrange affairs in such a way as to maximize their chances of promotion or appointment to coveted positions. Cliques and secret societies, together with intense, pervading intrigue, therefore trouble the personnel administration of the Greek army; and, at the top, where matters of high politics come into play, army officers have always participated in the struggles that define who gets what in the way of power and perquisites of high office.

Heroism, of course, has its own appropriate economic base in the taking of booty and giving of gifts. But a peculiar strain arises whenever military personnel and influence attain decisive authority in matters of public policy. Chances for self enrichment through morally and legally dubious acts multiply as power increases; bribery, whether overt or subtle, becomes an ever-present temptation. Yet such behavior, unless clothed in some ideological garb that disguises favoritism as the defense of Hellenism or some other supernal value, is recognized as being a betrayal of the military ideal of service to the nation. The difficulty of choosing between such conflicting paths was vividly illustrated by the financial corruption—and the anger at it— generated during the recent period of military dictatorship in Greece, 1967-74. But officers' behavior during those years only brought an enduring dilemma to especially acute expression.

The polarity and uneasy coexistence between market behavior and heroic behavior constituted, I believe, the major axis of traditional Greek life, and continue to inform the national experience in our time. Yet it would be less than just not to mention a third, less persistent and dominating but nonetheless real, element of the Greek tradition which also lives on in urban and cosmopolitan circles with no very obvious diminution of its vigor: Orthodox universalism.

Once a year in Greece, the barriers of family in-group feeling are symbolically relaxed when everyone celebrates the risen

Christ at Easter. Lent and Holy Week constitute a suitably serious and sombre preparation for Easter rejoicing; indeed, in many villages of times past, the fasting of Lent was both a religious duty and a practical necessity, since in the spring of the year, before the new growing season had begun to provide new sources of food, there was little left in the larder for anyone to consume. The slaughter of a lamb and its consumption at the Easter feast thus had nutritional as well as ritual significance; and the joy of the occasion, shared by all fellow Orthodox Christians, effectively affirmed and gave powerful emotional expression to faith in the renewal of springtime, the hope of heaven, the solidarity of all Greeks one with another, and the resurrection of Christ.

Orthodox universalism obviously differs in tone and quality both from the heroic pattern of self-expression and from the ideals of the marketplace. Though God saves individual souls individually, it is characteristic of Orthodox theology and feeling to emphasize the salvation of all true believers, and to put great store on ritual as a help on the way to heaven. All human beings are sinful, but all can be saved through the ministry of the church; and it is at Easter, above all other times of the year, that these convictions find public, ritual expression. The nuclear family that normally encompasses the only significant in-group drops its barriers against fellow Orthodox Christians for the Easter festival season, so that for a few days each year sinful humanity anticipates, even if weakly and imperfectly, the openness and mutual solidarity which will be experienced in the Kingdom of Heaven itself.

Because these Christian and Orthodox sentiments usually find expression only on a few days of the year, they seem less important for Greek life as a whole than the other, essentially incompatible attitudes I have already explored. Yet the Easter spirit is real too, and exists in latent form at all times of the year in ways that can sometimes surface suddenly and unexpectedly. This is particularly true in modern times because of the deliberately cultivated confusion that has existed since 1821 between Greek nationalism and Orthodox universalism. In Turkish times, the largest human communities anyone recognized were the Christian and Moslem religious in-groups, though each of these was divided into sects whose members sometimes hated one another more than they distrusted those of completely different religious identity. Building upon this past, Greek nationalists of the nineteenth century strove to identify Orthodoxy with membership in the newly defined Greek nation. The resurrection of Greece as a sovereign state through the War of Independence, 1821–30, has, therefore, been systematically associated with the resurrection of Christ at Easter. Since the revolt broke out in the spring, ritual expression of this association came easily. Patriotic memory fastened on the fact that it was on Easter Sunday, 1821, that the bishop of Kalavryta blessed Greek banners that soon thereafter were carried into battle against the Turks. This event became the symbol of the beginning of the War of Independence, even though hostilities had broken out earlier elsewhere.

Ever since, despite and in addition to secularized forms of patriotic ritual derived from western Europe, celebration of Easter and celebration of the anniversary of the Greek declaration of independence have been linked in popular consciousness.[6] The redemption of souls and the redemption of the nation are both conceived as the work of divine providence; and both become processes of indefinite duration. Indeed, in a sense, the full redemption of Greece and the Second Coming of Christ can only coincide at the end of time. The national struggle is thus perpetual, a part of the human condition, a task never to be completed in present lifetimes.

Such sentiments normally exert no perceptible influence on Greek behavior. But in exceptional circumstances the sentiment of solidarity among Orthodox Christians and the conduct of actual citizens of Greece can converge in practice, approaching the ideal of identity. This, I think, was what happened in the fall of 1940, when John Metaxas, dictator of Greece, rejected an ultimatum from Mussolini with a laconic "Oxi"—that is, "No." When the Italians attacked from bases in southern Albania, the Greek nation responded by merging heroic and Orthodox-nationalist sentiments in a way that surprised everyone—not least Metaxas himself and the foreign observers who had expected the quarrelsome Greeks to put up only a token resistance

6. Independence Day on March 25 is, to be sure, a fixed date in the calendar, whereas Easter moves with the moon, so the two celebrations almost never coincide.

to Italian armed might. But instead of meeting an ill-equipped, tatterdemalion army, riven by quarreling factions and paralyzed by the memory of how Fascist arms had recently laid France low, the invading Italians encountered an excited mass of heroes, ready to attack whenever the slightest chance of success offered itself. The result was ignominious defeat for the invaders, who were soon forced to retreat. Months of stalemate followed, as supplies ran out on the Greek side, and the fervor of the heroic moment ebbed away. But memories of the months of the Albanian war, when for a short time the Greek nation somehow found it possible to bury internal differences and cooperate enthusiastically against a common foe, remain strong to the present. Those who were young then look back upon that time as a precious moment of release from the ordinary limitations and annoying frictions of life. Easter plays exactly the same role in Greek lives each year.

The capacity for abrupt alteration of normal patterns of conduct exists in all peoples, no doubt; but it seems especially significant among Greeks because the elements of their tradition are intrinsically so opposed to one another. Wide variations, even outright contradictions of behavior, can be expected when one of these patterns suddenly asserts itself at the expense of others. This creates an element of unpredictability in Greek affairs—private and personal as well as public—that seems greater than shifts of behavior that other peoples commonly exhibit. Consequently, both remarkable and quite exceptional achievement and no less remarkable self-destruction fall within the range of Greek public life, as the history of the last thirty years amply proves. But before turning attention to events of that era, it seems best to expatiate somewhat on the way tradition interacted with the natural and human environment of the Aegean and adjacent coastlands to create in 1945 a specific and delicate ecological balance, peculiar to the Greek world and, at the same time, fundamentally incompatible with the survival of nation-state sovereignty.

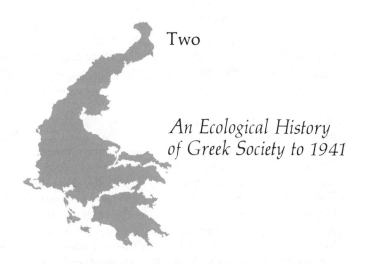

Two

An Ecological History
of Greek Society to 1941

Each of the aspects of the Greek tradition that were sketched in Chapter 1 had a distinctive ecological basis. Survival across time could not have occurred otherwise. Thus, the prominence of market behavior in Greek life rests on geographical facts that made cultivation of specialized crops especially advantageous around the shores of the Aegean and Ionian Seas. The heroic tradition, as we have seen, had its principal basis among shepherds and marginal farmers of the mountainous interior. As for Orthodox ecumenicity, it had its particular locus among the upper classes of the major cities—Constantinople above all—and in the islands of monastic quiet that dotted the Greek countryside. Though often located in wild and remote places, monasteries were closely linked with towns by the fact that after the fourteenth century the higher clergy were recruited from monastic ranks exclusively.

Let me first try to explain why farming for market sale played so large a role in Greek life. The basic fact was that specialized crops brought a bigger return from a given amount of land than could be secured by raising only items for domestic consumption. The reasons for this are both geographic and economic. The two principal commodities Greeks raised for sale at a distance were olive oil and wine. Olives and vines both require long hot summers for maturation; and olive trees cannot withstand prolonged temperatures below freezing in winter. Hence there is a geographic boundary beyond which olive oil cannot be produced—a boundary that does not include all of the present Greek state by any means, but only those (mainly coastal) regions where winter temperatures are mild enough to allow olive trees to flourish. Grape vines are hardier, but only some soils and climates produce a wine good enough to sell at a price that makes vineyards more profitable than grain fields. Hence the limits upon wine production were always more economic than climatic, though the regions where vineyards can produce a commercially profitable wine are climatically defined.

Both to the north, around the western and northern shores of the Black Sea, and to the south, in Egypt, lie grain-rich lands where olives will not grow and where vines cannot produce wine like the best that comes from the Aegean basin. Since these regions are connected with the Aegean coastlands by sea, ships can easily carry wine and oil in one direction and grain in the other; and the cost of such transport is small in proportion to the value of the goods in question. Obviously, for such currents of trade to flourish, someone must produce and be willing to part with large amounts of grain. This has usually meant that local landlords, having discovered the delights of wine and the manifold uses of oil as food, unguent, and fuel for lamps, somehow compelled humbler members of society to raise more grain than they needed for their own support. Such landlords then took possession of the surplus grain and proceeded to exchange it for oil and wine. Once such a current of exchange had become established, other commodities could be swept into the trade net; and the geographic range of profitable exchanges might ramify very widely indeed, east-west as well as north-south.[1] But the fundamental pattern was defined by a north-south axis, allowing oil and wine to be exchanged for grain across climatically defined frontiers.

Terms of trade across this climatic boundary persistently favored the oil and wine producers. After all, grain could be

1. In classical times, before the techniques of oil and wine cultivation had established themselves in regions of southern Italy and Sicily where, nonetheless, climatic conditions were well fitted to such cultivation, ancient Greece also profited from an exchange of oil and wine for grain with these western lands; but by the second century b.c. or before, the spread of oil and wine production to Italian soil made that current of exchange unprofitable. Later still (first century a.d.), the develop-

raised in the Aegean regions; olive oil and good wine could not be produced in the regions with which the Greeks traded. Hence bargaining advantages tended to rest with the Greeks. In addition, production of wine and oil required a wait of several years between the time the vines or trees were planted and the coming in of the first harvest. Such a capital cost was heavy indeed for small producers, and, to make such sacrifice bearable, the price pattern had to favor the man who had waited several years without return. The further fact that both wine and oil carry well, and can be stored for years in jars or barrels without spoilage, also gave those who sold these two commodities a market advantage against dealers in grain whose stock in trade was intrinsically a wasting asset. Rats, mice, insects, and fungi were in perpetual competition with men as grain consumers; and their ingenuity in securing access to human grain-stores repeatedly overcame the obstacles men were able to put in their paths. Hence grain dealers were ordinarily under pressure to sell before losses from spoilage became too great, while wine and oil dealers could afford to wait indefinitely until the price was right.

These simple facts assured Aegean wine and oil producers of a persistent advantage in terms of trade. A plot of land put into olives or vines could usually produce a quantity of oil or wine exchangeable for more grain than could have been raised on that same piece of land—quite a lot more grain. Dense rural populations, living on relatively small plots of land—as little as three or four acres per family was often adequate to keep body and soul together—thus became possible in the parts of the Aegean coastlands where olives and vines flourished best.

The resulting pattern of rural life allowed for abundant leisure. Even with traditional methods of cultivation and harvesting, in which human muscles did all the work, there were many weeks of the year when no useful tasks could be performed in the fields. This was the time devoted to talk about public affairs in ancient times. In ages when direct participation in political

ment of oil and wine culture in North Africa, Spain, and southern France made it impossible for Italy to profit from an earlier pattern of exchange with those lands. The eastward advance of olive and vine culture from the Aegean focus is less clearly recorded, but trees and vines did spread along the north coast of Asia Minor as far as Trebizond, and with them a Greek-speaking peasantry, uprooted only in 1922, came into existence.

decision-making was not permitted to mere peasants, Greek cultivators still used these times of leisure for talk. Conversation, poetry, and speech-making consequently remained highly developed arts among men of Hellenic speech, rural and urban alike.

It is useful, perhaps, to think of wine- and oil-exporting villages as semi-urban communities. The villagers were like townsfolk in depending on imported grain at least for a part of their year's food; and they were like townsfolk in enjoying favorable terms of trade because both offered commodities in comparatively short supply. Finally, these villagers were also like townsfolk in depending on the availability of surplus grain in some distant place.

Social and political conditions were the major variables that determined the availability of grain at a distance. For wine and oil production to flourish in the Aegean coastlands, a complementary region of big estates specializing in grain production had to exist somewhere else within easy reach by sea. Theoretically, stalwart peasants, owning their own fields, could have entered the market of their own free will and exchanged grain for oil and wine and other commodities without dependence on landlords; but such patterns, if they ever existed within the Aegean radius of action, were rare and transitory. A community of peasant cultivators could not be expected to defend itself successfully against professionalized warriors and men of power, who were, of course, the class from which landlords were recruited.

After the fourth century B.C., landlords became increasingly prominent in Greece; and by the time of the Roman conquest (146 B.C.) a landlord class had become dominant everywhere. Yet in olive and vine regions, landlords did not monopolize marketing functions. Even when the rental basis was share-cropping, the cultivator had to go to market with his share of the harvest, for only by so doing could he hope to have access to the grain (and other things) needed to support his family through the year. Grain farmers, by contrast, when landlords and tax collectors had skimmed off their share, had enough left over to feed themselves throughout the year. They therefore had little need to enter the market, save for the occasional purchase of a tool or some other extraordinary object. The Greek wine and oil producer, on the other hand, had to buy and sell to live at all. Hence the great importance of market skills and the centrality of commercial calculations in traditional Greek rural behavior.[2]

Nor were these market skills confined only to coastal regions where olives and vines flourished. In the mountains, shepherd communities produced a surplus of cheese and wool and had male lambs for slaughter each spring. Other specialized crops played important parts in Greek rural economy at different times and in different places, depending on market conditions. From the seventeenth to the twentieth centuries, for example, currants constituted a significant export from the northern Peloponnese because Englishmen developed a taste for what they misleadingly called "plum pudding"; and as the habit of smoking spread in Europe, the coasts of Thrace became the seat of intensive tobacco production during the same centuries.

Grain exports from inland plains, like those of Thessaly and Arcadia, were also sometimes important. Cities and food-deficit mountain villages had to be fed; and when grain supplies from more distant regions fell short, plains dwellers near the Aegean center took up the task of supplying the grain-deficient populations nearby. For geographical reasons, grain farming in Greece was more costly, and restricted in quantity, as compared with Black Sea and Egyptian production; so that when Aegean cities had to depend mainly on grain produced close at hand, the urban population of the region shrank back to relatively small proportions.

Moreover, as happened elsewhere within the Greek radius of action, grain marketing within the Aegean area was nearly always connected with the rise of large estates, managed by landlords or their agents. Whenever and wherever this pattern of life established itself, a landlord-dominated society arose, very like what prevailed in the Black Sea coastlands and in Egypt in the ages when those regions served as major grain exporters.

2. A factor of great importance in reinforcing Greek marketing behavior was the tax policy of the Ottoman Empire. Every Christian was required to pay an annual head tax in cash; and the only way a peasant could do so was by selling something. This meant that in all those places where Turkish authorities were in fact able to collect the head tax from their Christian subjects subsistence farming was impossible. I owe this insight to Professor Halil Inalcik.

Hence there was nothing surprising in the fact that in the eighteenth century growing urban populations provoked the spread of grain-exporting estates in the interior plains of Greece. They were called čifliks. But a society polarized between enserfed peasants and grain-selling landlords never came to dominate the Aegean region, if only because so much of the landscape was unsuited to large-scale cereal production.

Changeable market conditions therefore continually altered the exact mix of goods and services Greek peasants brought to market, but such ups and downs never upset the primacy of buying and selling in their lives, from the time when ancient Miletus first pioneered long-distance trade in oil and wine in the sixth century B.C. until the present. Across the generations, skills of the marketplace were therefore honed to a fine edge. Sharp practices were generally admired; shrewd bargaining paid off; survival itself must often have depended on finding the right trading partner at the right time to provide needed food or services.

Such skills, indispensable in the Aegean center, paid off far more spectacularly towards the periphery of the trade net, wherever expert bargainers came into touch with strangers of different cultural backgrounds, amongst whom the skills of market behavior had not developed nearly as flamboyantly as among Greeks. To keep interregional trade going, someone had to build and man the ships that plied between the Aegean and peripheral regions; someone had to arrange the transport and exchanges in the hinterland so as to concentrate suitable quantities of grain and other commodities of value at the ports where ships came to load and unload; and someone had to distribute Aegean commodities up-country among those who provided the grain. Obviously, Greeks were advantageously situated to play all these roles, and regularly did so in ages when the north-south trade pattern flourished.

The result of these aptitudes was that, whenever a period of commercial expansion manifested itself, Greeks began to move out into regions where their commercial skills found widened scope among strangers of different speech and ways of life. In ancient and medieval times, this sort of commercial diaspora was sometimes accompanied by military and political dominion as well. Thus after Alexander of Macedon (336–23 B.C.) had

projected Macedonian and Greek military force across western
Asia, a swarm of Greeks followed in his wake and took over
governing roles formerly filled mainly by Persians. Greeks
became administrators, soldiers, landowners, and in general
constituted a ruling class in many eastern Mediterranean lands.
Later, after the Romans had come and gone, a Greek-speaking
"Roman Empire" exercised a similar power for almost a
thousand years over shifting portions of the eastern Mediterranean. Greek consequently became the language of government, and presently of the church as well as of commerce.
Greeks today treasure the memory of those times, when Byzantium stood at the forefront of European civilization. When,
after 1453, Turks became rulers and masters throughout the
regions Greeks once had dominated, speakers of Greek were at
first relegated to relatively humble social and economic roles.
Modern Greeks, naturally enough, deeply deplore the Turkish
yoke their predecessors submitted to.

Under the Turks, the Greeks not only lost their role as a ruling
class but had to confront formidable rivalry in commercial
matters from Jews (welcomed in Turkey after their expulsion
from Spain in 1492), and, before long, from Armenians and
Latin Christians as well.[3] But sharpened competition of this kind
eventually succeeded only in reinforcing Greek commercial
acumen.

To be sure, real success in interregional trade required political protection and privilege. This came to the Greeks of
Constantinople in the seventeenth century when the Turks,
having become relatively weaker in war, began to feel the need
of accurate intelligence about western Europe. After the middle
of the seventeenth century, Ottoman Jews failed to keep their
contacts with western Europe sufficiently intimate to be able to
provide this commodity as well as Greeks were able to do. From
the time of the Renaissance, the prestige of western learning was
such that Greeks sent a few of their sons to western universities
for medical and other advanced training. Those who returned to

3. Long before the final conquest of Constantinople by the Turks,
Latin Christians, mainly Italians from Genoa and Venice, had taken a
leading part in the Aegean trade, exchanging wool, metals, and other
western commodities for wine and grain. Cf. William H. McNeill,
Venice, the Hinge of Europe, 1081–1797 (Chicago, 1974).

Constantinople were then in a position to act as skilled inter-
preters of the western world to their fellow citizens—Greek or
Turk as the case might be. This situation allowed the Greeks to
achieve a newly privileged position within Ottoman society after
1669, when a clever doctor, Panagiotis Nicousios, trained at the
University of Padua, negotiated a very advantageous treaty of
peace between Venice and Turkey. Thereafter, Greeks speedily
displaced all rivals as go-betweens for the Turks in their dealings
with the Christian governments of Europe.

Of course only a handful of individuals succeeded in ever
gaining the confidence of Turkish rulers for the conduct of state
affairs. Nevertheless, these insiders found themselves able to
convert their privileged political positions into efficient protection for a host of eager Greek entrepreneurs who began to
penetrate new regions of the Ottoman Empire. The semiautonomous Rumanian provinces of Moldavia and Wallachia, lying
along the northern frontier of the Ottoman Empire, were the
richest and most important areas that thus came under Greek
influence. Vast and fertile regions, formerly used only as pasture, were brought under cultivation when Greek merchants and
estate managers made agriculture profitable for noble landlords
by finding ways to carry the harvest to market. Beginning as
traders, muleteers, rent and tax collectors, Greeks gradually
insinuated themselves into the Rumanian landowning class, so
that in the course of the eighteenth century the cities and courts
of Moldavia and Wallachia assumed a thoroughly Hellenized
appearance.

Other accessible regions offered fewer rewards, and Greek
commercial penetration was correspondingly less spectacular.
Nevertheless, it seems to be true that during these same decades
Greeks became more numerous in inland regions of Asia Minor,
taking up various artisan and (mostly small-scale) commercial
roles in places where there had previously been few if any
Christians. In western Europe, too, vigorous Greek communities
established themselves in such cities as Venice and Vienna, and
smaller outposts of the new Greek diaspora arose in lesser cities
of the Danube valley.

The geographic range and scale of exchanges that sustained
this diaspora expanded abruptly after 1774. In that year, the
Russian government secured the right of free passage through

the Turkish straits for ships carrying the Russian flag; and in the
following years Russian consuls granted Russian registry to
Greek ships quite freely. As a result, for the first time since
Constantinople had become the capital of the Ottoman Empire,
vessels could move freely back and forth between the Aegean
and the Black Seas. Russian vessels (even when owned and
manned by Greeks) did not have to offer their cargoes for sale in
the great capital on the Bosphorus at artificially depressed
prices, which had always before been manipulated in such a way
as to keep provisions cheap for the urban population.

An enormous boom resulted. Grain production in the
Ukraine, organized by the estate agents of Russian noblemen,
got into high gear, and Greek (with some other) merchants
undertook the profitable task of distributing Russian grain
exports around the shores of the Mediterranean. When the
British blockade of French ports during the Revolutionary and
Napoleonic wars drove French ships from the Mediterranean
(1793–1815), the Greeks' most formidable competitor from
western Europe was also put out of the running. As a result,
Greek-owned vessels took on still more new roles (including
blockade-running and occasional piracy as well as peaceable
trade) and reaped some enormously inflated profits.

Ideas and men travelled with the ships and cargoes that
circulated between the Aegean, the Black Sea, and the rest of the
Mediterranean. A large Greek community arose in Odessa, the
major center for the export of grain from southern Russia; and
other Greeks fanned out into lesser centers in the Ukraine and
Crimea where they took on various middlemen's occupations. A
handful even penetrated the Russian court, and the most successful of these, Count John Capodistrias, actually served as deputy
foreign minister to Tsar Alexander I between 1816 and 1822. To
the west, Greek businessmen also flourished in Vienna and
Marseilles, while within the borders of the Ottoman Empire,
Greek traders and churchmen increased in importance throughout the northern Balkans, and probably stepped up the pace of
their expansion into the interior of Asia Minor as well.

Thus, on the eve of the Greek War of Independence, the
Ottoman body politic had come to resemble the old Byzantine
symbol of empire: a two-headed eagle. The Turkish head
controlled military and most public administration, together

with matters of Moslem religion; the second, Greek, head managed some aspects of government but concentrated mainly on commerce and the religious affairs of Orthodox Christians within the empire. In the early part of the eighteenth century this two-headed monster functioned rather effectively. The respective realms of activity assigned to Greek and Turk complemented one another nicely. The Greeks were, in that age, still deeply suspicious of western Christians on religious grounds, and could not forgive the Russians for Peter the Great's apostasy from the true Orthodox faith. Besides that, first the Russians (1711) and then the Venetians (1714) and Hapsburgs (1739) were defeated by Turkish armies and compelled to retrocede territories they had conquered from the Ottoman Empire during the seventeenth century. Thus the Turkish side of public life seemed thriving once again, while the Greeks busied themselves with the rewarding job of organizing commercial agriculture in the Rumanian provinces and elsewhere. Success in this undertaking allowed the provisioning of Constantinople on an ever-expanding scale, thus solving what had in the seventeenth century been a recurrent problem for the Ottoman regime. Such successes sealed, for half a century, a mutually satisfactory arrangement between Greek and Turk, that is, between the Christian and Moslem urban communities of the Ottoman Empire.

It is important, perhaps, to explain that in eighteenth-century Ottoman society the term translated as "Greek" referred to a religious identity. Consequently, speakers of Slavic, Rumanian, Albanian, or Armenian languages who adhered to the Orthodox faith as defined by the patriarch of Constantinople were all "Greek." Amongst this linguistically variegated population an urban elite of Orthodox Christians who were also speakers of Greek occupied almost all the key positions in the church hierarchy, in public administration (insofar as such tasks were assigned to Christians), and dominated commerce and most of the humbler urban occupations as well. Any Orthodox Christian, active or aspiring to become active in any of these roles, found it practical to speak Greek habitually, since affairs were conducted in that language. Hence urban in-migrants of the Orthodox faith, whatever their mother tongue may have been, soon became Greek in the linguistic as well as in the religious sense. As a result, the Greek nation recruited into its ranks a supply of unusually energetic and gifted persons of Rumanian, Albanian, and Slavic origin. (All but a very few Armenians adhered to their own church and therefore kept a separate identity.)

At an earlier time, especially between the thirteenth and sixteenth centuries, upwardly mobile individuals frequently became Turkish by changing their religion as well as their language. This pattern of recruitment to the Turkish nationality dwindled to insignificance when sufficiently ample roles for Greeks opened up in the Ottoman world, so that ambitious Christians no longer felt much temptation to convert to Islam. This was an important factor in weakening the Turkish and strengthening the Greek element in the Ottoman body politic during the seventeenth and eighteenth centuries. Indeed, in those parts of the empire, such as the western Balkans, where the Turkish population was concentrated into towns, their numbers were probably in decline not just relatively but absolutely. After all, until the nineteenth century urban infectious diseases were such as to make townsfolk incapable of sustaining themselves biologically without continued in-migration from the healthier countryside.

Yet the vigor and expansive force of the Greek community within the Ottoman system carried its own nemesis. The middle-man roles which gave the Greeks their most spectacular successes were intrinsically vulnerable. Traders and go-betweens, by the very nature of their activity, create distrust. Conspicuous economic success merely demonstrates that the middleman is cheating those with whom he deals.

Hence the Greeks' economic upthrust, rapid as it was, remained fundamentally dependent on political protection; and Turkish rulers, whose complaisance was requisite, felt absolutely no sympathy with or admiration for the Greek commercial spirit. Government officials might tolerate and connive in Greek market activities. Many were, in fact, personally dependent on deals made with wealthy Greeks; others supplemented their income by taking bribes. But forcible seizure of ill-gotten gains and disdainful rejection of every offer of a share in the profits of skillful wheeling and dealing was always, in Turkish eyes, a tempting and also a fundamentally more honorable alternative.

Nor could Greek merchants expect support among the Christian peasantry of the Balkans. On the contrary, most peasantries
saw the urban middlemen as oppressors quite as alien to their
way of life as the Turkish landlords and administrators were.
What poor man would not feel cheated in dealing with men who
bought cheap and sold dear, sometimes lent money at interest,
and always stood ready to take unfair advantage of an honest
man's moment of utmost need to increase their own wealth?

A second source of instability came from within the Greek
urban community itself. Having won so much, Greek merchants
and men of affairs were sorely tempted to reach for more. In
particular, as contacts with Russia multiplied, they could not
help but wonder whether it would not be possible to use the
might of the Russian Tsar to drive the Turks from Constantinople once and for all, thus opening the way for restoration of the glories of the Byzantine past when Greeks had ruled
from the city on the Bosphorus and set the standard of civilization for all Europe. This was like turning the two heads of the
imperial eagle inward, so that each sharp beak might begin to
strike at the vitals of the body politic that sustained them both.
Such more-than-Promethean suffering was, in fact, provoked by
the degeneration of Christian-Moslem relations within the Ottoman Empire that occurred during the century between 1821 and
1923.

Early in the nineteenth century, the Serbian revolt of 1803
rejected both Turkish and Greek dominion. As such, it proved
the forerunner of a series of other Balkan rebellions against the
Ottoman pattern of ethnic symbiosis. But the Serbian revolt was
confined to a remote frontier region where its implications for
Ottoman life as a whole remained obscure. The parting of the
ways between Greek and Turk that was signaled by the outbreak
of the Greek War of Independence in 1821, on the contrary,
brought the issue of Ottoman viability right out into the open.
Thereafter, neither Muslim nor Christian could really trust one
another, no matter how much Greeks protested their continued
loyalty to the Ottoman regime. With political protection withdrawn, the Greek diaspora, which had expanded its range and
increased its wealth so spectacularly in the 150 years before
1821, began a precipitate collapse. This continued to be the
central, dominating reality for the Greek nation for more than a

century thereafter, reaching its terminus only about 1950, when almost all traces of the eighteenth-century diaspora finally disappeared.

The fate of the diaspora was not, however, identical with the fate of the Greek nation. Indeed, the populations of the southernmost part of the Balkan peninsula and of the Aegean islands, where Greek-speaking rural folk were dense on the ground, seem to have had a hard time in the seventeenth and eighteenth centuries when their urban fellow Greeks were proving so successful further north.

For one thing, the Greek lands were much fought over. Turks and Venetians conducted a long war, 1640–69, in the Aegean; and, as we saw, it was when the Greek, Nicousios, negotiated the Venetian surrender of Crete to the Turks in 1669 that the Greek community of Constantinople made its critical advance towards a politically privileged position. But advantages in Constantinople did not help the Greek peasantry of the south when warfare was resumed in 1684. This time the Venetians conquered the entire Peloponnese. But their administration soon estranged the Greeks, both on economic and on religious grounds. The Venetians taxed more systematically than the Turks had done and Roman Catholic efforts at proselytizing swiftly aroused indignant Orthodox resistance. Not surprisingly, therefore, when war again broke out in 1712, the Turks were welcomed back. Greek rebellion in the Venetian rear made all the elaborate fortifications of Acrocorinth and Nauplion useless, and thus assured an easy Turkish victory.

Organized international warfare did not affect the Greek lands again until 1768, when a Russian fleet, having arrived in the Mediterranean from the Baltic, provoked scattered rebellion on the mainland and in the Aegean islands. Turkish repression of these manifestations of disloyalty was savage but sporadic, for the main Ottoman forces were engaged in the north against invading Russian armies.

In addition to the disruptions arising from these international wars, the Turkish administration of the Greek lands proved to be increasingly incapable of enforcing public peace on a merely local basis. The eighteenth century was, accordingly, the great age of banditry. Klefts issued from their mountain fastnesses to raid the plains; and the Turks, being too few and no longer inclined to the hardships of military life, commissioned other Christian bands—the so-called *armatoloi*—to protect them from the klefts. A single band could easily shift back and forth, depending on arrangements with the local Turkish administrators. Hence in many parts of Greece, two rival armed Christian establishments arose, one of which, at any given moment, was officially legal and the other illegal. But even though the kleft of today might become the *armatolos* of tomorrow, such alternations did not really change the bands' behavior or mode of livelihood. Each, of course, needed the other to justify its existence—hunter and hunted, cops and robbers, hero and rival hero. But whether legal or illegal, these bands lived by exacting food from villagers of the plains; and their exactions, being more akin to plunder than taxation, kept life poor and precarious in the most fertile parts of the Greek landscape.

In such an atmosphere of sporadic violence, Albanians were the ethnic group that flourished best. Tribal and local guerrilla warfare was an age-old feature of life in the barren Albanian mountains; and especially after a considerable proportion of the Albanian population (mainly the northern tribes) accepted Islam, Turkish authorities tended to look upon them as allies against the sometimes suspect loyalty of their Christian subjects. Official toleration of strong-armed violence became in time of war a direct commission to attack Christian villages. The result was a wide-ranging Albanian expansion onto new ground in the course of the seventeenth and eighteenth centuries. Serbs were pushed northward, Greeks southward. Part of Attica, for example, was settled by Albanians on lands that had been devastated in the course of the war against the Venetians, 1684–99. (This was, incidentally, the war in which the Parthenon was reduced to its modern, ruined state as a result of the explosion of a powder magazine the Turks had placed there for safekeeping.) As a result, in villages around Athens the inhabitants continue to be able to speak Albanian to the present. But since, unlike Albanians of the northern tribes, they remained Orthodox Christians, no one (themselves included) thought them anything but Greek. Hence Albanian encroachment on Greek territory in the southern Balkans did not weaken Hellenism, whereas the parallel process in the north, whereby Albanians, adhering to the Moslem faith, displaced the Serbs from the old center of their medieval kingdom, created a separate, Albanian national bloc that endures as an awkward enclave within Yugoslavia to this day.

What perhaps mattered more for rural Greeks was the effort Turkish landlords made to get more profit out of the land they controlled by becoming commercial farmers on their own account. This was, of course, an obvious reaction to the general spread and intensification of marketing networks in which urban Greeks were playing so conspicuous a part. Turkish landlords in the Peloponnese, Thessaly, and Macedonia, who conscripted Greek peasants to grow grain on their estates under conditions approximating serfdom, were doing exactly the same thing that Rumanian and Russian landlords were doing in their lands. But most of Greece is relatively infertile, and the difficulty of controlling a Greek labor force was perhaps greater than was the case with peasants less adept in taking advantage of any lapse of oversight to try to enter the market on their own account. Hence the number of enserfed Greeks working on Turkish commercial estates may never have been very large.

Certain it is that some of the low-lying and potentially rich farmland of Greece was not populated at all in the eighteenth and early nineteenth centuries. The reason for this was the prevalence of malaria in such places. Lands capable of producing good crops of wheat had to be relatively well watered; and this invited malarial infestation. The disease is chronic rather than immediately lethal; but a malarial work force is bound to be inefficient and therefore costly. At the critical moments of the agricultural year, if the manpower of the community finds itself prostrate with fevers, no sort of slave-driving can make the sufferers work effectively in the fields. Muscles enduring the onslaught of malarial parasites are simply incapable of putting forth the necessary effort. Exposure to malaria therefore heightened costs of production, quite apart from the misery of the disease itself and the shortened lives both masters and serfs could anticipate.

As long as the plains of Greece remained thinly populated, cities perforce remained small and unimportant, save where urbanized folk could somehow get hold of grain supplies from far away. The burst of commercial prosperity that came to Greek shipmasters after 1774 made Ukrainian supplies easily available; and a rapid expansion of urban population in a few coastal and island ports—Nauplion, Hydra, and Spetsae above all—registered the new prosperity. Such successes, however, did nothing to improve conditions in the plains of Greece. Abundant shipping may have facilitated marketing of grain produced on Turkish estates in Greece; but it also put Aegean-produced grain into price competition with the cheaper grain from Russia, to the obvious disadvantage of the Turkish landlord class.

Hard times in the Greek plains made the life of the mountain villages correspondingly more important. There, enemies could only approach along narrow access-routes; and villagers could take appropriate action—either intercepting them at some advantageous ambush point, negotiating a truce, or else fleeing towards even remoter fastnesses, as the case might be. Because there was very little food to spare even at the best of times, the parasitism of armed strangers upon mountain communities was seldom important. It was, in fact, young men from mountain villages who supplied the manpower of kleftic and armatole bands. Obviously they preferred not to harrass their own kith and kin, or risk blood feud by attacking a neighboring mountain community. It was easier and safer to rely on contributions wrested from landowners and peasants in the plains. The chronic disorder of the age therefore had the general effect of transferring resources from the plains to the mountain communities of Greece.

The contrary flow of tax money from hill to plain was small indeed. Turkish authority scarcely made itself felt in the mountains. Some communities negotiated a sort of quitrent: the rocky peninsula of Mani, for instance, is said to have owed the Turkish pasha of Tripolis as many gold coins each year as would rest on the blade of a sword. In meeting the obligation everything depended on how the sword was held. In those years when the Maniote chieftains preferred peace to war, the tribute could be delivered ceremoniously on the flat of an unsheathed sword. When they preferred war, the sword blade need only be turned to the vertical to reduce the tribute to nothing. True or not, the story symbolizes the limited liability such mountain communities had to Turkish or any other kind of external authority.

Yet life in the mountains was very difficult. During the eighteenth century, and probably long before then, the population living in mountain villages far exceeded the number of persons who could be supported by local resources. Cultivable land was scarce, and pastures, though extensive enough, were available only for part of the year. Local landscapes were, characteristically, exploited to the limit and sometimes in ways that proved costly over the long run, especially when deforestation provoked damaging erosion.

During the eighteenth century, mountain villagers had to exert themselves mightily to get hold of enough food from afar to supplement what they could produce for themselves. This was of course the identical circumstance that confronted villages in more favored coastal regions of Greece where land put into vines and olives required the regular import of grain. Mountain communities, too, had traditional commodities for sale: cheese, wool, charcoal, and sheep or goats for slaughter. Like oil and wine, these commodities were comparatively valuable in proportion to their bulk and could therefore bear the cost of transport to market, even if it meant travelling across very rough and roadless country for days or weeks. Sheep and goats travelled on their own feet; for other commodities, mules were the normal carriers. An overland trading network, constructed around mule trains, existed throughout the western Balkans in the seventeenth and eighteenth centuries and was, in its way, as complex and technically proficient as was the trade net built around the small sailing vessels that plied the Aegean and Black Seas with such success in the same centuries.

Indeed it is not fantastic to envision a caravan trading network, based on the mountain villages, and a maritime trading network, based on the coastal wine- and oil-producing villages, as converging upon the plains, each offering specialized goods and services in exchange for grain. Inasmuch as the grain-growers were consigned to a passive role in such exchanges, lacking any independent access to means of transport, the two fringes of Greek society were favorably situated to expand their share of available wealth at the expense of the malaria-burdened plains. Assuredly, Turkish landlords and a dispirited peasantry could not match the energy and ingenuity with which Greek mountaineers and coastal populations exploited the opportunities that opened up to them in the course of the eighteenth century. But as the two fringe regions battened more and more

energetically on the plains, the socioeconomic balance between
the diverse regions of the Greek landscape became increasingly
unstable. Impoverished and half-deserted plains meant that
mountain and coastal villagers had to seek further and further
afield for the grain they needed to supplement what they could
produce themselves.

Quite extraordinary linkages across surprising distances resulted from this situation. For instance, a village on the slopes of
Mount Ossa in Thessaly developed a local dyestuff that produced a specially brilliant red. The color became fashionable in
Vienna about 1780, so that for half a century or more, a thriving
trade was sustained between the Hapsburg capital and this
remote village.

Caravan trade could, of course, connect with ports and the
shipping networks as well; and it always had the effect of linking
mountain communities with towns and cities far more intimately
than the distances between them, and the primitive state of roads,
might lead one to expect. Men from the mountains accompanied
the mule trains; and whenever they noticed a role they could
play in intervening landscapes—anything whereby they could
get possession of the needed food that was lacking in their native
villages—they set about playing that role with an energy fueled
by the knowledge that their women and children would go
hungry if they were not successful. The best jobs were seasonal,
for the whole point of working far from home was to be able to
return triumphant in the fall, ready for the time of year when
food would run short in the mountains, that is, in the winter and
early spring months.

A human migration pattern, therefore, arose, which was the
exact reverse of the pattern followed by sheep and goats. At
about the time when shepherds abandoned the lowland pastures
and headed for the high grasslands in the spring, other men
started out from their mountain villages towards cities and
plains, looking for work. Women and children left behind could
provide all the labor needed to cultivate the scant fields available
in the village environs. As summer ended, the sheep started
down from the heights and men headed back towards the high
villages, often carrying on their backs—or on the backs of
mules—the grain they needed to feed their families through the
winter months ahead.

Gainful occupations available to such migratory workers varied greatly from season to season and place to place. Mountain dwellers often became skilled masons and sought out construction jobs of all sorts. They thought nothing of walking several hundred miles to find such work; and news spread by word of mouth allowed hundreds and even thousands of skilled men to gather, as it were spontaneously, at places where some unusually large undertaking was projected. Some villagers found other, bizarre specialities, such as the con-men and professional beggars who learned how to make themselves into pitiable, seemingly deformed creatures so as to extract alms from the gullible; but who were yet able to walk enormous distances— sometimes penetrating deep into Russia—in order to cadge enough money to make it worthwhile to go back.[4] More standard work was helping with the harvest in the plains, for the period of time when grain had to be garnered was brief, and plains villages often lacked sufficient manpower to cut the ripe grain without outsiders' help.

When trade or honest wage-work failed, there was always force. Armed raids into the plains aimed at seizing resources which could not be secured peaceably remained a glorious alternative which came into play often enough in the disturbed times that prevailed after the middle of the seventeenth century. Arms were needed for the protection of caravans, and for the protection of the villages as well. Possession of arms was therefore an important economic resource for mountaineers; and a kind of insurance against starvation. Accordingly, men of the mountains invested heavily in them. No adult male was comfortable without owning a gun and dagger of some kind. The possession of and practice in the use of arms offered yet another job-role to the men of these mountain villages, for they could hire out their services as bodyguards for rich and powerful men of the plains, serve as *armatoloi* to guard the passes, or act as scouts and plunderers in conjunction with an organized army. Both the Turks and the Venetians resorted to such irregulars as a matter of course each time hostilities broke out. Indeed, wartime devastation suffered by the plains of Greece was largely the handiwork of these forces.

4. For details see Patrick Leigh Fermor, *Roumeli: Travels in Northern Greece* (London, 1966), pp. 214–25.

What was happening, therefore, between about 1650 and 1821 was that Greek town populations on the one hand and the fringe of wine- and olive-growing Greek villages along the Aegean coasts combined to batten upon grain produced by serf labor in the broad plains adjacent to the Black Sea, where agriculture was undergoing an enormous expansion. Sailing ships, often quite small, and usually manned by Greek crews, linked these diverse regions into an increasingly close, market-regulated network of buying and selling. Simultaneously, a smaller but numerically significant mountain village community was also able to expand an overland system of exchange in which force and sporadic violence played a larger role than was characteristic of the exchanges by sea. The plains that sustained the growth of mountain village communities were mainly those of Greece itself, though if a mountaineer purchased grain in town, he, too, might tap food supplies deriving ultimately from the Black Sea coastlands.

As far as Greek rural life was concerned, the effect of these twin and interrelated exchange systems was to concentrate wealth and numbers towards the fringes: in the mountains and along the coasts. The plains of Macedonia, Thessaly, and the southern Balkans, having entered into competition with the healthier and broader plains of the Black Sea coastlands, could not prosper. Empty or half-empty plains land, used only for winter pasturage, was therefore a common sight in Greece on the eve of the War of Independence. Possession of the plains, which was all that Turkish landlords enjoyed, became far less valuable than had been the case in earlier times, when alternative sources of grain for the cities of the Aegean region had been less readily available, and when public order had been more effectually maintained.

It is perhaps worth pointing out how the diminished effectiveness of Turkish administration and the shrinking importance of plains agriculture in the southern Balkans went hand in hand. Turkish landlords were losing their grip even before the Greek revolt sealed their destruction in the parts of the peninsula where Christian arms prevailed. Like many another military conqueror, most of the Turks had allowed themselves to be seduced by the sweets of civilization and lived in towns. Unable personally to defend their properties any longer, they were driven to the dubious practice of hiring Christian armed men to guard what remained of their wealth.

But hired guards, whose loyalties stood closer to solidarity with the klefts than to solidarity with their Turkish employers, were an ineffectual substitute for an autonomous, authentically Moslem armed force on the ground. What sustained Turkish dominion until 1821 was the fact that authorities in Constantinople could muster superior force, given enough time and severe enough provocation. When, after months or years, the imperial armies were laboriously brought to bear upon the remoter parts of the Balkan peninsula, they could readily enough prop up or reinstate Turkish authority, even in places where the local balance of forces would not have allowed it to survive otherwise. This happened several times in the eighteenth century; it failed to recur in the nineteenth only because British, French, and Russian intervention against the Turks in 1826 snatched victory away from the sultan's forces.

This, in rough terms, was the position in which the Greek world found itself at the close of the Napoleonic wars. Life-circumstances in villages and towns scattered across many hundreds of miles—from southern Russia to Crete and from outposts in Marseilles and Vienna to Trebizond and Cyprus—had given ample scope and perpetual refreshment to both the market pole and to the heroic pole of Greek behavior. Moreover, the universalism of Orthodoxy, still embracing within its scope most of the Balkan Slavs and the Rumanians, together with almost half the Albanians, remained to bind all Greeks into a self-conscious entity, different both from Moslem Turks and from Latin Christians. As their wealth and education increased, members of the Hellenic community became more and more intensely aware of the diminished stature of their own age when compared to the greatness of the Byzantine and classical pasts. When a few dreamers and schemers tried to correct this defect by summoning the people to rise against their Turkish oppressors in order to restore the integrity of a Christian Byzantium once again, the balance of forces which had allowed the remarkable Ottoman fabric to come into being altered catastrophically. The ultimate result was the destruction of polyethnic Ottoman imperial society. Its death throes lasted more than a century, involving much suffering, hopes repeatedly betrayed on every

side, and economic as well as other forms of retrogression
towards a base level defined by rude peasant life.

Since the aim of the revolutionaries of 1821 was restoration of
the grandeur of Byzantium, the puny Kingdom of Greece that
emerged in 1830 was no more than a sad caricature of what had
been aspired to. It was sovereign only in name, for the three
"Protecting Powers"—France, Russia, and Great Britain—
claimed and exercised extensive authority within the new state.
When they disagreed, as was normal, the diplomatic representatives of the Great Powers looked for and found supporters
within Greece to forward their respective policies. This circumstance reinforced and embittered the factionalism that became
characteristic of Greek public life; it also presented the rulers of
the kingdom with an all but insuperable conundrum. The
problem was this: the Kingdom of Greece could only realize the
Great Idea of its founders by displacing the Turks from Constantinople and as much of that city's hinterland as possible. But
the resources of the kingdom were patently insufficient to
overthrow the Turks without help. Therefore support from the
Great Powers was necessary. A policy of currying favor with
one Great Power alienated the others; and the disaffected Great
Powers were in a position to stir up powerful political rivals to
the existing government in Greece almost at will. Effective
government and successful policy were impossible in such a
situation.

Yet the dream of Great Greece could not be abandoned. It was
the raison d'être of the kingdom. Twice the complex working of
European diplomacy gave the Greeks a few crumbs of additional
territory carved out of the decaying empires of the Levant. Thus
in 1864, Great Britain transferred the Ionian Islands (formerly
part of the Venetian Empire) to Greece; and in 1881 the Turks
were forced to cede Thessaly as a way of compensating the
Kingdom of the Hellenes for the success Bulgarians had achieved
by winning a new state of their own at the Congress of Berlin.
But such accretions of territory fell far short of realizing the
Great Idea. When, in 1897, the Greeks attempted to take matters
into their own hands and fought a war against the Turks, they
met with humiliating defeat and had to turn for rescue to the
Protecting Powers. The dictated peace that ensued imposed
burdensome reparations on the bankrupt government and required the Greeks to cede part of Thessaly back to the Turks.

While the little Kingdom of Greece thus vainly aspired to realize the goals of its founders, the Greek community of the Ottoman Empire living outside the borders of the Greek state faced increasingly adverse circumstances. Distrusted by the Turks and disliked by rival Christian nationalities as well, Greeks found that the old ways of doing business and of providing the Orthodox populations of the Balkans with traditional urban services would not work any more. Overall, therefore, the upshot of the nationality clashes that dominated Ottoman society in the nineteenth century was to impoverish the urban component of the Greek world and to restrict the geographic range within which it operated. Correspondingly, the peasant element of Greek society came more to the fore, even though most peasants also suffered from the disruption of older exchange nets so that their standard of living hovered close to survival level and offered a very unpromising basis for any new growth of commercial or industrial prosperity.

There were, to be sure, some Greeks who successfully transferred the seat of their commercial activity to new ground. By and large, this new diaspora operated in lands under British imperial influence or administration. Egypt was by far the most important focus. Beginning in the 1860s, Greek merchants took a leading part in organizing the export of cotton from that country; and after the 1880s, when Egypt passed under British administration, the port city of Alexandria became a flourishing center of quite diversified Greek enterprises. Other far-flung portions of the British Empire—in India and Africa especially— also saw Greek merchants start new businesses during the course of the nineteenth century; and when Greek shipowners began again to play a significant part in international trade, they got started by taking over marginal operations in the British-centered shipping pattern of the age. What Russia had meant to the shipowners who pioneered the first great flowering of the Greek merchant marine between 1774 and 1815, Great Britain meant to this second flowering, which began about 1890. Such activities spread the tentacles of a new diaspora very far indeed; but except in Egypt, Greek overseas commercial communities remained numerically very small.

A sociologically different emigration set in after 1890, when poor mountain villagers found it possible to extend their accustomed pattern of migration all the way across the Atlantic, seeking work in the United States. These emigrants left Greece as poor rural folk, and it took some time before their children and grandchildren were able to play economic and professional roles in the American environment. Hence until World War II, the American segment of the Greek diaspora remained relatively inconspicuous, being only one and by no means the most massive of a number of other east and south European national groups that had come to the United States at almost the same time.

At the Greek end, however, money sent back from the United States to relatives in Greece became, for many mountain villages, an important supplement to local resources. The emigration to the United States, therefore, helped many such communities to retain a traditional pattern of life until 1941, when remittances from overseas were abruptly cut off by war.

Until then, however, transatlantic migration seemed to be merely a variation on the age-old pattern of going off to look for work in distant parts. The intervening ocean made annual return impossible: to make up for that, money could be sent every month or at some other interval. The emigrants departed with the same intentions their predecessors had always had when they walked off to seek their fortunes. It just took longer to save up enough capital to make return worthwhile. But of course, as time passed, new tastes and ambitions took shape in the minds of the emigrants. Little by little the vision of returning to the ancestral village lost its attraction for most. But before such aspirations faded away, Greek emigrants usually did return for visits, to see their parents, get married, or attend to other family duties. To begin with, and for decades after their first arrival in the New World, Greek villagers therefore carried a private Old World with them across the ocean, and had no expectation of abandoning it permanently. No wonder, then, that Greeks of the United States initially played humbler and more marginal roles in their host society than was in the case in such places as Egypt.

In Asia and Africa, where Greeks acted as large-scale entrepreneurs and capitalists, the emigrants carried forward into the nineteenth and twentieth centuries the pattern of the earlier urban-based Greek diaspora around the Black Sea. Similarly, the migration to the United States (and later to Canada and Australia as well) carried forward into the twentieth century the pattern of temporary proletarian migration that Greek mountain villages had relied upon for centuries to keep themselves from starving.

Those who started from an urban base often brought with them appreciable amounts of capital as well as superior commercial skills. They normally chose to operate in societies where the bulk of the population could not even remotely compete with them when it came to organizing long-distance trade. As a result, financial success was likely to come rapidly and could pyramid into really big business very quickly. Sudden bankruptcy was also possible, for these Greeks engaged, characteristically, in high-risk businesses.

Those who left for the United States, on the contrary, entered American society near the bottom, performing tasks others did not want to do. Learning the language and accumulating even a small amount of capital took time. As soon as these indispensable assets had been acquired, Greek emigrants exhibited a very strong thrust towards entrepreneurial independence. The family was the preferred unit of work, as rural tradition dictated; and a tendency to specialize in food-handling also reflected faithfully the peasant background and biases the Greeks brought with them.

If one tries to look at the phenomenon of the Greek diaspora as a whole in the century and a quarter between about 1815, when the "old" diaspora of the Black Sea and Aegean coastlands was at the height of its success, and 1940, when World War II brought abrupt changes, it seems plausible to suggest that, on balance, Hellenism suffered a massive setback during these years. At the beginning of the period, Greeks were playing a leading role in the life of one of the world's great states, the Ottoman Empire, and from that base had taken over a predominant place in the commerce of the eastern Mediterranean and Black Seas. This was a very considerable world role, and made the dream of restoring vanished Byzantium seem less illusory than subsequent events proved it to be. In contrast, by the end of the period, Greeks outside the borders of the Kingdom of Greece played relatively minor roles in the economic life of parts of the British Empire and in the United States. Even the striking financial success that came to a few Greek families in such fields as shipping and cotton brokerage did not really compensate for the impoverishment millions of others had experienced as a result of the breakup of the older diaspora in Asia Minor and the Black Sea coastlands.

Numerical estimates are really unobtainable. In the Ottoman and ex-Ottoman parts of the world, the question of who was and who was not a Greek became increasingly unclear as the old, relatively straightforward religious definition of Greek-ness gave way to a linguistic definition. But since polylingualism was the normal condition for urban dwellers in the Aegean and Black Sea regions, it became a tricky matter to decide whether a given family was Greek or something else—Bulgar, Albanian, Rumanian, or Russian, as the case might be.

The plain fact was that scores of thousands of persons could alter their national identity by using a different language whenever it seemed desirable to do so. What language to use depended always on circumstances. As peasant masses became politically conscious—a process in full swing between 1870 and 1920—in all the regions of the Balkans and Asia Minor where most of the rural folk spoke a language other than Greek, it became increasingly risky for urban dwellers to use Greek. This meant that the old pattern whereby upwardly mobile individuals assumed a Greek nationality in order to become fully franchised within the Ottoman world came to a complete halt, and was in fact reversed. Partially Hellenized individuals began to shed their Greek-ness. As Greek identity became a liability, only those who held conspicuous positions or had by some past action firmly established themselves as Greek were likely to retain their Hellenic identity. As a result, what had been from 1669 to 1820 a prospering, increasingly confident Greek community became after 1821 a dwindling and beleaguered nationality, whose shift onto new ground in Asia, Africa, and America had not yet attained enough success to counterbalance the throttling of Hellenism taking place throughout the old centers of Greek urban life.

Affairs within the Kingdom of Greece were, by comparison, almost trifling. At the start about eight hundred thousand persons, mostly poor peasants, lived within the new state's borders. Greeks outside numbered at least three times as many, and included wealthy and educated elites of the chief cities of the Aegean and Black Sea coastlands. Most Greeks continued to live

outside the Greek state up to the time of the Balkan wars in
1912–13. Thereafter, the annexation of new territory in the
north combined with massive and much-accelerated disasters
visited upon the old diaspora drove a majority of the Greek
nation within the borders of the Greek state for the first time.
One may indeed argue that the most important thing about the
new Kingdom of Greece as it emerged from the War of Independence was its role in undermining the viability of eighteenth-
century patterns of Hellenic expansion within and under the
aegis of the Ottoman, Russian, and Hapsburg empires.

All the same, however small the initial theater of action, social
changes came rapidly to the people inhabiting the new kingdom,
and followed a pattern entirely at odds with the experience of the
urban diaspora. During and immediately after the War of Independence, a central issue was whether or not leaders of the
revolution would be able to convert their social position into
landownership on the model of the Turkish pashas whom they
had massacred. In the end, the "Christian Turks," as their
enemies called them, failed. This was partly because the Bavarian administrators who headed King Otto's government (1832–
62) distrusted them, and partly because Greek mountaineers,
having destroyed one set of landlords, saw no reason tamely to
submit to a new, self-appointed Christian landlord class. The
result, therefore, was to bring the Kingdom of Greece into the
European comity of nations without a landed aristocracy.
Subsequent territorial expansion did not change this situation
fundamentally, even though the Ionian islands, annexed in 1864,
did have a small Italianate aristocracy of a European type. Its
leaders soon moved to Athens where they played a role at the
royal court and, in a few cases, followed a military career as
European aristocrats were accustomed to do. In Thessaly, too, a
few Greeks were able to purchase estates from Turkish landowners at the time (1881) sovereignty passed from Greece to
Turkey. But a law of 1920 broke up most of these estates; and
even prior to that time, the Greek land speculators who moved
in behind the departing Turks were far too insecure in their new
position to play anything like the role of a European landed
aristocracy.

The absence of this social class in modern Greece had far-
reaching consequences. Manifestations of wealth and power

were rawer in the new kingdom. Families rose and fell far more swiftly than was commonly the case in lands where a long-established landed class provided most of the top military officers, public administrators, and cultural leaders, while systematically snubbing upstarts. In Greece, practically everyone was an upstart; and the pattern of fixed deference and authority, upon which west European state systems rested, was simply absent. Many of the anomalies of modern Greece can, in fact, be understood as the result of an effort on the part of the various kings and a small circle of courtiers to imitate European royal behavior, in a society which lacked the class that as recently as 1914 made European monarchies effective.

Greece also lacked a plausible analogue to the thriving middle class of nineteenth-century western Europe. The handful of towns within the borders of the new Kingdom of Greece that had shared in the eighteenth-century commercial boom fell on hard times after 1821, and the widespread devastation of the war itself made economic recovery slow and difficult. What remained was a peasantry, organized into tight-knit nuclear families, each of which aspired to pursue its own best interest by making exchanges with outsiders according to deals freely entered into and just as freely terminated. For rulers or would-be rulers, such a society was like a quicksand. Pressure at any point met not so much with resistance as avoidance: expectations of deference and obedience on the strength of official position or rank conferred by the king went unfulfilled. The bureaucratic model which King Otto's Bavarian ministers strove to impose upon Greece ran into systematic difficulties from the beginning. The Greek governmental bureaucracy has yet to recover from its inauspicious start.

Yet public affairs and the exercise of power soon found viable forms. At first, power was measured in large part by how plausibly a handful of political men could threaten or actually muster armed force to back up their will. This heritage from the kleftic age soon faded; and after 1843, when a parliamentary system was inaugurated, the tamer method of corralling votes became the standard indicator of power. Votes, to be sure, tended to go to those who were in a position to provide useful services in return—protection, first and foremost. From time immemorial, Greek rural families had found it useful to go to some local big shot for help in handling relations with powerful outsiders. Support from a man of power, who commanded wealth and an armed following—the one initially the reciprocal of the other—gave a better chance of success in all such dealings. That was what the ordinary man needed to make his affairs secure. Such a patron was expected to deal with any and all matters that might come up for his clients; in return, the clients supported him in politics.

Reciprocal relations of clientage and patronage existed also among the men of power, and groupings of such linked person- alities constituted inchoate "parties" from the days of the revolution. The parties were no stronger than the personal understandings that connected individuals in patron-client re- lationships up and down the pyramid of influence.[5] Any demon- stration of the inability or unwillingness of a person to deliver the sort of service his client expected risked an immediate breaking-off of the relationship. At a moment's notice, there- fore, instead of friendship and mutual support, rivalry and hostility might suddenly appear. This fragility ran from top to bottom of the political structure, being an exact equivalent of the economic network that connected the Greeks with one another and with the outside world.

Nevertheless, until the end of the nineteenth century, a small number of political families were able to hold the loyalty of whole villages and regions fairly securely, mainly because, living at a distance from the capital, "their" villagers could not easily find an alternative patron. This gave Greek public life a modi- cum of stability, though the rivalries among such families for posts in the national government frequently provoked sudden kaleidoscopic shifts of alignment amongst the top wielders of governmental authority.

But such volatility, even when exacerbated by the way leading political figures sought and regularly found support from the diplomatic representatives of the Great Powers, did not really have much effect on the life of the country as a whole, nor even on the way government officials impinged upon private affairs. Government remained a skimpy thing, as in the days of the

5. See John A. Petropulos, *Politics and Statecraft in the Kingdom of Greece, 1833–43* (Princeton, 1968).

Turks. Only occasionally did ordinary households somehow collide with officialdom. Viewed from the bottom of Greek society, the function of the political class was to mediate such encounters, putting them on a personal, manipulable basis. Since for ordinary families encounters with officialdom were not very important, politics was not very important either, however exciting it might be as a spectator sport, and however engrossing for those who, once in office, stood to gain a great deal from winning or losing allies and official positions in the game of power.

Little by little, however, professional and mercantile classes attained more prominence, especially in Athens, the burgeoning capital. This group was excluded from the political world of families whose power rested on their ties with rural villages. Western-educated professional men, and their business clients, were impatient, too, with the policy of dancing attendance on the Great Powers, waiting approval for realization of their national goals. This spirit found special lodgment among army officers, whose profession committed them to heroic nationalism. Discontent surfaced in 1908, when the Greek government prudently declined to risk annexing Crete, where a revolutionary movement seeking union with Greece had boiled up under the leadership of a young lawyer named Eleftherios Venizelos. A group of junior army officers, chagrined at the failure of 1897, and humiliated by the weakness of 1908, decided on a coup d'etat. After taking power, they decided to invite Venizelos, the Cretan paladin, to assume the leadership of a new government. His acceptance symbolized an intensified commitment to the ideal of Great Greece, a willingness to take risks, and a rejection of the older political leadership.

Venizelos lived up to his supporters' hopes. He brought many new men into government, and speedily contrived an alliance with the Serbs, Montenegrins, and Bulgarians whereby the three Christian states united to attack the Turks in 1912. Vaguely supported by Russia, the Balkan allies won rapid success. Greek troops occupied Epirus, and another army led by Prince Constantine, the heir apparent, seized the southern part of Macedonia. In 1913, when the victors quarreled over division of the spoils, the Bulgars found themselves at war with an overwhelming array of enemies—Serbs, Greeks, Turks, and Rumanians. A second easy victory consequently allowed the Greek army to take over easternmost Macedonia from Bulgaria. In the confusion, Crete and nearly all of the Aegean islands also joined Greece, so that in two short years the country about doubled in territory and population.

Venturesome policies certainly seemed to have paid off handsomely; and when the Turks lined up with Germany in World War I, Venizelos decided that Greece should go in on the Allied side. The war, he reasoned, would lead to a final partitioning of the Ottoman Empire. When Bulgaria, too, allied with the Germans (1915), Venizelos saw a real chance for realizing the Great Idea. Land annexed from Bulgaria and Turkey, extending through Thrace and along the Asiatic shores of the Aegean, might at last bring Constantinople and all the heartlands of the old Greek urban diaspora under Greek sovereignty. Such a glorious prospect appealed to almost all Greeks; the trouble was that not all of them believed it possible.

In particular, King Constantine, newly enthroned and jealous of Venizelos' fame, believed that Germany would win. If so, to ally with the losing side would be folly. Neutrality seemed the only wise policy, for British sea power in the Mediterranean made active alliance with Germany impossible. Constantine fully shared the ambition of achieving Great Greece. But as a military man, trained in Germany and married into the German royal family, he could not endorse Venizelos' strategy. When the Cretan statesman persisted, the king flatly vetoed a pro-Allied policy. Despite a parliamentary majority, Venizelos resigned and the king soon found another prime minister. In fact, however, he himself had become the leader of a party opposing Venizelos. After prolonged and virulent conflict in Athens, Venizelos withdrew to Salonika and there set up a rival Greek government at the very end of 1916. In the months that followed, a new Venizelist army and administration arose, with the powerful support of the French and British, who had by this time sent an expeditionary force to Salonika and needed Greek help to keep their rear secure.

Allied pressure eventually compelled King Constantine to abdicate the throne (1917), so that the rebel Venizelos was able to return in triumph to Athens. He, of course, turned out to have been right in fundamentals by 1918; but the royalists remained unappeased. Two rival political and military elites had come into existence during the upheavals of 1916–17, and there were not enough positions in government to support them both. Regional and class differences also came into play to embitter politics as never before, though the struggle still remained an affair of relatively few.

Venizelos' enemies got their great chance when he failed to win title to Constantinople for Greece at the peace conference. Without that peerless capital, Great Greece could not become a reality; and the acquisitions the Greek prime minister was able to bring back from Paris—eastern Thrace and the right to occupy Smyrna and its environs on the coast of Asia Minor—seemed trivial by comparison. Elections in 1920 consequently returned royalists to power. King Constantine came back from exile; and in the hope of trumping Venizelos' ace by securing firm title to territory in Asia Minor, the new government undertook active military operations against the Turkish nationalists, who had meanwhile repudiated the terms of the peace treaties. Lacking firm Allied support (Constantine, after all, had shown himself no friend of France and Britain), the Greek army soon overreached itself and suffered disastrous defeat (1922). In the weeks that followed, scores of thousands of Greeks fled before the advancing Turks, who were resolved to allow no Christians to remain within their country. When a treaty was eventually negotiated, in 1923, systematic exchange of Christians and Moslems was agreed to. The final destruction of the eastern half of the old Greek diaspora resulted. Simultaneously, Greek soil was cleared of Turks except in western Thrace, where in return for an undertaking by the Turks to leave the Greeks of Constantinople and eastern Thrace undisturbed and in possession of their property, the Greek government agreed to let villages of Turkish peasants retain their traditional way of life.

The settlement after World War I also cleared Greeks out of Bulgaria. Simultaneously, many but not all Slavs were evicted from the Greek part of Macedonia and sent to Bulgaria. In addition, the Russian Revolution had the effect of persuading many Greeks to flee from those areas of the Ukraine where they had lived; for the sort of middleman's work in which the Greek community specialized was exactly what the Bolsheviks hated most.

Hostilities did not come formally to an end for Greece until 1923; and these exchanges of population, supervised in some measure by the League of Nations, continued until 1927. In the few years of peace that ensued, the country went through bitter travail. Fitting more than a million refugees into the texture of Greek society was an enormous task. A handful of them brought urban skills and even some capital with them. But few were ever able to regain the level of life they had known in their homes in Asia Minor, Thrace, or Russia. Most refugees arrived penniless and in rags, and had to huddle in temporary camps that sprang up around Athens and other cities. Eventually, about half were assigned farmland, divided up into lots judged just sufficient to sustain a single family. These settlements were concentrated mostly in northern Greece, where Turks and Slavs had formerly lived. Some of the land was very fertile; and pioneering work by the Rockefeller Foundation transformed what had been desolate malarial plains into relatively healthy places to live in. All the same, starting up in unfamiliar surroundings and with minimal capital was difficult at best. Memories of how much better things had been before the war remained vivid. The refugees for whom no land could be found faced even harder conditions. By slow degrees, various urban occupations took shape for them; and what had begun as temporary camps gradually turned into shantytown suburbs. Whether in town or country, chronic discontent was the natural result. The refugees became a radical, or potentially radical, element in Greek politics, wherever they were to be found.[6]

On the political scene, coup followed coup as the two rival political and military elites sought to capitalize on the rancorous spirit which the defeat of 1922 left behind. Greece became a republic in 1924, but this failed to bring stability. Nevertheless by the end of the 1920s the worst of the crisis had passed. Venizelos, restored to power, even made pacificatory gestures towards the Turks.

Then, the world depression set in (1930), and fresh political upheavals followed in its wake. After a couple of abortive coups

6. D. Pentzopoulos, *The Balkan Exchange of Minorities and Its Impact on Greece* (The Hague, 1962), offers a detailed and dispassionate account of the way the refugees were incorporated into Greek society.

failed to prevent royalist victories, Constantine's son, King George II, returned to the Greek throne in 1936. He soon abandoned the effort to govern the country on a constitutional basis. The first elections after the king's return produced a Parliament evenly divided between Venizelists and anti-Venizelists; a handful of Communist deputies held the balance of power. This was unacceptable to King George, so he appointed an army general, John Metaxas, as prime minister despite the fact that he had almost no support in Parliament. Metaxas therefore ruled as a dictator from the beginning, and soon began to toy with fascist ideas. Nevertheless, it was his regime that led the country during the successful initial phase of the Albanian war. Metaxas died before surrender to the invading Germans brought a squalid ending to what had begun so gloriously. When the German victory became certain, King George II and a tattered remnant of his government went into exile under British protection (1941); while a rival Greek administration took over in Greece itself under German and Italian direction.

In the years of Axis occupation and civil war that followed, Greeks experienced what now seems clearly to have been the nadir of their modern fortunes. Outright starvation afflicted the towns in the winter and spring of 1941–42, since there was simply not enough food in the country to feed its inhabitants. The mountain villages experienced severe privation, not just in 1942 but throughout the war years. The one thing that kept hope bright was the heroic self-image that all Greeks cherished of themselves and their nation: an image that events of the Albanian war, suitably remembered, had refurbished handsomely. Yet such hopes and memories did not prevent Greeks from bearing arms against one another during and after World War II; and the fact that the Greek government in exile ranked officially among the victors at war's end did little to establish a basis for secure public administration, and still less for social and economic reconstruction.

The balance of this book will undertake to describe some of the highlights of the transformation that has come to Greece since World War II. It is a success story for the most part, and stands in striking contrast to the tangled tale of disappointed hopes and poignant disaster through which the Greek people had passed between 1821 and 1945.

Three

Public Affairs since 1941

The years of Axis occupation, 1941–44, brought the cities and mountain villages of Greece to the verge of starvation. In the winter of 1941–42 thousands died in the streets of Athens from lack of food; thereafter, wheat imported by the Swedish Red Cross (with Axis and Allied permission) provided Athens and other major cities with a minimal food supply; but in the mountains food shortages continued at crisis level throughout the occupation years. The result was predictable. In mountain villages where local food production could not feed the inhabitants, young men took to arms as a way of finding food: and since there was no shortage of guns in Greece (many soldiers simply carried their rifles back home when the Greek army disintegrated in the spring of 1941) armed bands of mountaineers, living outside the law, soon became formidable.

From the beginning, recruitment to such bands depended on political as well as economic circumstances. The fact that most of Greece came under Italian occupation made continuation of the resistance seem natural. Why should a despised, defeated army of macaroni eaters lord it over the land unchallenged? In addition, a living tradition sanctified guerrilla action. As recently as 1905–12, Greeks had struggled with Bulgarian guerrilla bands and Turkish gendarmes for dominion over Macedonia, and before that klefts and *armatoloi* had chased one another across the Greek landscape for centuries. In 1941 and 1942, young men in remote mountain villages had grown up to the tales old men told of what they remembered about such bands. To go and do likewise in a new time of patriotic crisis therefore seemed natural and proper.

Recruitment accelerated when a coalition of leftist parties, known as EAM (National Liberation Front), undertook to organize a guerrilla army, called ELAS (National People's Liberation Army). The acronym was doubly effective, since when pronounced it was indistinguishable from the formal Greek name for the country, Ellas. Patriotism and service with ELAS thus easily blended, even when the influence of the Communist party in both EAM and ELAS became unmistakable.

EAM/ELAS also recruited manpower in the cities, and some politically committed, comparatively well-educated young men did achieve conspicuous leadership positions in guerrilla ranks. But the mainstay of the fighting forces remained the unmarried youths from mountain villages who joined up less in response to political ideals than because life at home in their parental households had become unendurable. The fact was that to have grown sons lounging at home when there was not enough food to go round was unacceptable to old and young alike. Young men were supposed to be breadwinners. Traditionally they had always departed in the spring, going to seek work in distant places, or else following the sheep to the high pastures, and returning in the fall with whatever increment to family resources their months of work had allowed them to accumulate. Joining an armed band was, in effect, a simple variant of this age-old pattern. For when peaceable work was impossible to find—as assuredly was the case in 1941–44—a man with a gun could still expect to feed himself by demanding a share of the harvest from peasants of the plain. With luck, he might even lay hands on a little extra booty to take back home. Since such actions were also patriotic and heroic, this avenue of escape from the futile idleness of mountain villages became irresistible. A ready supply of hardy manpower was thus assured to any political leaders who chose to step forward. EAM seized the opportunity energetically and resolutely, beginning in 1942; and in ensuing months achieved ideological consolidation and military coordination of something over sixty thousand guerrilla fighters.

Indirect but persuasive evidence to support this interpretation of the dynamics of the Greek guerrilla movement of World War II comes from the fact that Yugoslavia was the only other country of Europe to generate an active guerrilla resistance in the early years of the war. Yugoslavia was also the only other country of Europe to have food-deficit mountain villages like those of Greece, where the same heroic tradition prevailed. Elsewhere resistance fighters became active in the field only when German power was about to collapse. The special combination of circumstances existing in the western Balkans was needful to sustain armed bands early in the war, when defeat of the occupying powers was only a hope, not an obvious certainty of the immediate future.

Greeks commonly reject this view of their recent history. For conservatives, it puts the Communist-led resistance of 1942–49 too close for comfort to the series of heroic national uprisings against the Turks upon which Greek patriotic tradition has long been nurtured. Leftists, who might be expected to take satisfaction in these continuities, prefer to believe in the unadulterated force of political ideology as an explanation for the Greek resistance during and after World War II. Yet having actually visited two guerrilla bands in 1946 whose members were almost entirely drawn from nearby mountain villages and whose motivations fitted the description given here, I am quite convinced of the accuracy of this analysis, despite the fact that I have no documentary evidence to back it up.[1]

Everyone, however, agrees that by the end of 1942 a powerful guerrilla movement had come into being in the Greek mountains. From that time onwards, the bands, in effect, competed with the urban communities of Greece, and with the Italian, German, and Bulgarian occupying forces, for access to the shrinking food surpluses produced in the villages of the plains. By 1944, the bands had clearly won the competition. Athens and other Greek cities increasingly depended on food imported by the Swedish Red Cross. Supplies from the rural hinterland

1. Satisfactory evidence probably can never be found; ELAS men took noms de guerre to make vengeance against relatives less likely. This makes tracing origins difficult. Moreover, propaganda systematically obscured the traditional basis of recruitment into ELAS ranks, since after all, it was nobler to fight for freedom than to be using guns to feed oneself. Memoirs are therefore untrustworthy evidence.

hardly reached the towns any longer. Political and military control of the plains villages had passed into guerrilla hands, except in the immediate neighborhood of Athens.

Greek, Italian and German efforts to check the process were ineffective.[2] Severe but sporadic retaliation achieved nothing, even when it involved the destruction of entire villages or the slaughter of all the men in a mountain community. Such terroristic acts simply hardened the spirit of resistance, and not infrequently drove adult men, whose homes had been burnt, into the guerrilla ranks. Urban control of the hinterland depended on a system of mechanical transport—one that could carry men and goods between towns and villages. Such transport almost disappeared from Greece: what remained was preempted for German military use. The corollary was loss of control by the towns of the countryside. The guerrilla bands were not seriously hindered, for they depended on more primitive but also more indestructible forms of transport: human legs, supplemented, sometimes, by animal pack trains. Another way to describe the bands' conquest of the plains would be to say that mountain consumers came down to the plains in armed pursuit of the food they needed for survival, whereas city folk, fed from overseas, remained *in situ*, more and more cut off from the Greek hinterland.

As in Yugoslavia, it was the Communist party and associated leftist groups that principally profited from this situation. Other politicians in Greece preferred talk: and though several army officers and other would-be national heroes did try to assume leadership of armed bands, they never were able to compete with the Communist-led and organized resistance forces. The reason for Communist success was mainly this: Marxist doctrines appealed powerfully to the young, and there were in

2. The Bulgars, however, were able to prevent Greek guerrillas from disturbing their occupation of Thrace. This apparent anomaly confirms my analysis of the social dynamics of Greek guerrilla action, since no significant number of Greek-speaking food-deficit villages existed within range of the coastlands annexed to Bulgaria. On the contrary, local mountaineers (across the prewar boundary) spoke Bulgarian. Some of them settled on lowlands near the coast, seized from their former Greek owners. Such provocation produced no Greek guerrilla, however, until the very last weeks of the war, when Axis defeat had become obvious to all concerned.

Greek cities a significant number of young men, often educated beyond the primary level, full of vigor and ambition and quite unable to find any worthwhile occupation. As in the mountain villages, life at home for such young men was difficult and unsatisfying, not least because ordinary urban existence offered so little chance for expression of the heroic values which urban Greeks had not forgotten. A significant number of such persons were therefore ready and eager to respond to the party summons to resistance against the Axis occupiers, even if—or just because—it meant rough living in the hills among rude villagers whose educational level was far below their own.

The Greek Communist party had previously been a small organization, frequently riven by doctrinal disputes, and, since 1936, officially illegal. Its top leadership accepted directives from Moscow, at least as long as they did not drastically conflict with party interests. From the late 1930s, instructions coming from the Comintern in Moscow had commanded a policy of popular front against Fascism; and in the circumstances that confronted Greece after 1941 this fitted the interests of the Greek Communist party very well. As in Yugoslavia, therefore, the wartime policy of the KKE (Communist Party of Greece) emphasized national solidarity against the Fascist invaders.

KKE did not act alone. It was only one of five leftist parties constituting EAM, the political and propaganda front that organized resistance to the Axis. All who would help were welcome, and in fact many Greeks who had little sympathy for Communism took part in EAM activities. Rival resistance groups could never get far, for EAM's open, broad-front policy made it illogical to refuse cooperation, and had the effect of calling into question the patriotism of those who did refuse to take part in EAM activities. By 1943, British agents in Greece became alarmed at the pro-Russian posture EAM/ELAS had assumed and did succeed in helping one rival guerrilla force to survive ELAS attacks. But when the German forces withdrew from Greece in October 1944, this organization, known as EDES (Greek Democratic National League), controlled only a small region in the remote northwest. Military preponderance in all the rest of the country rested unambiguously with ELAS.

The balance of forces that emerged within Greece after the German withdrawal was anomalous. ELAS counted as part of the Allied forces; certainly it claimed, and with justice, to have led the Greek resistance against the Axis. Yet the cities of Greece had not come under ELAS control during the war. Sketchy ELAS "reserve" units had been constructed under the eyes of the police during the Occupation, but no more than that was possible. Naturally enough, all those elements in Greek society that disliked or dreaded the prospect of social reform and/or revolution, as promised by EAM/ELAS, had gravitated into the cities; and in Athens, at least, these groups remained firmly in control during and after the German withdrawal. The issue, from an EAM point of view, was how to complete the ascent to power by seizing control of the cities from "collaborators" and other corrupt social elements without sacrificing access to the food and other supplies coming from Allied sources upon which the survival of the city populations depended. From the point of view of the established urban elites of Greece, the problem was how to find an efficient outside protector until such time as the normal urban control of the rural hinterland could be re-established. The swing group in the Greek population was the villagers of the plains, whose reaction to having to contribute food to guerrilla bands was like that of any peasantry subjected to arbitrary taxation: outwardly submissive, but inwardly resentful.

Under the circumstances, the policy of those who controlled delivery of food and other supplies to the cities of Greece from abroad was critically important. This function devolved, initially, upon the British armed forces with only token American participation. Official British policy had wavered during the war between support for EAM/ELAS and support for the urban elites that were being challenged by that insurgent guerrilla force. Early in the war, British agents had favored ELAS as the most effective military force available to harrass the Axis occupation regime. Later, suspicion of the postwar political ambitions of EAM/ELAS mounted in British circles and official policy hardened against handing Greece over to Communist-led, pro-Russian and antimonarchical leftists.

Prime Minister Winston Churchill, who took personal control, at critical points, of British policy towards the Greeks, was particularly strong in support of King George II, whom he regarded as a bulwark against Communist takeover in Greece.

Moreover, because King George's government had rallied to the British side in 1940–41, Churchill felt a sort of personal obligation to him, and believed that the least he could do was make sure that the Greek king returned to the throne he had occupied before the war. Churchill may have known that this meant undoing a political revolution already consummated in most of the Greek countryside; but the doughty British prime minister was not intimidated by such a task, believing that a firm British lead would suffice to reverse the balance of forces within the country.

Churchill had another reason to suppose that his policy could be made to prevail in Greece. As early as May 1944, the British and Russians had agreed to a tentative definition of spheres of influence in the Balkans that assigned Greece to Great Britain. The United States decried spheres of influence but somewhat reluctantly went along with the deal. Suspicion of British imperialism was then quite as lively among American officials as any distrust of the Soviet Union. Instead of spheres of influence, the United States was committed to creating a new world order, in which legal process conducted through a well-designed international organization would make war obsolete. Plainly, an indispensable prerequisite for any such scheme was continued harmony among the world's great powers, that is, among the principal allies of the war; and it was because harmony with Russia and Great Britain was necessary for success of the larger American purposes that President Franklin D. Roosevelt made no objection to the British claim to preeminence in Greece.

As a matter of fact, Great Britain had long enjoyed a special influence in Greek affairs. In 1941, King George II and his government had accepted British protection by fleeing before the advancing Germans, going first to Crete, then to Africa. Later still, King George took up residence in London while his government moved to Cairo. This geographic separation reflected growing polarization of opinion in Greece and among the Greek exiles over the role of the monarchy. King George claimed the right to return to Greece regardless of public opinion. Indeed, royalist theory held that the stabilizing institution of monarchy was needed in Greece precisely because popular opinion was liable to go to extremes and might at a given moment commit the country to some sort of radical action that would cost the nation dearly in the long run. Since 1915, however, this royalist argument had been vitiated by the king's role as leader of a political party. This made it practically impossible for the monarchy to preside over all the rival groupings of Greek politics in anything like a neutral, moderating fashion. Another complication was that as the war years passed, supporters of the monarchy within Greece became more and more liable to the charge of collaboration with the Axis occupation forces, while the elements of the Greek nation supporting the resistance became vociferously republican.

This situation presented Great Britain with a delicate diplomatic problem. British agents close to the Greek scene realized how difficult it would be to restore the monarchy against the expressed will of all the elements in Greece that had opposed the Germans most actively. A government in exile returning with little or no organized support within the country risked failure. Some kind of agreement between EAM/ELAS and the government in exile was needed to head off revolution and/or civil war.

British efforts to prevent such a denouement moved ahead rapidly in the spring and summer of 1944. A "Government of National Unity" was established in May, headed by George Papandreou, a former aide to Eleftherios Venizelos, and a man of unusual eloquence and high personal culture. He was also a great egotist and shrewd bargainer, yet was never able to unite all the fragments of the Venizelist party behind him since two other would-be heirs stubbornly disputed the succession. One was Sophocles Venizelos, son of the great Venizelos; the other was Themistocles Sofoulis, an older man, who felt that seniority conferred on him the right to lead the Venizelist party. There was, in fact, no such party: it had long since split into quarreling groups of politically ambitious men, none of whom controlled a party machine remotely comparable to the network of local committees, together with youth and women's groups, that gave EAM its tangible, grass-roots strength.

Papandreou's principal support, instead, came from the British ambassador to the Greek government in exile, who allocated seats in the new cabinet across the entire political spectrum. Five seats, a quarter of the whole, were assigned to EAM; and that body was invited to nominate the individuals who would fill these positions. Until September 1944, the EAM seats remained vacant; but then five men were secretly flown to Egypt from Greece and were sworn in as ministers, filling out the cabinet and giving the Government of National Unity at least the appearance of representing all varieties of opinion. This fragile creature was the government that returned to Greece in October 1944, when the Germans pulled out of Athens; this was the cabinet that had to face the problems of relief and reconstruction in a devastated land where the war years had effectively split the country into two rival sociopolitical communities, divided one from the other by deep suspicion and by not a little bloodshed. The issue was quite simple: either the city elites of the war and prewar years would somehow survive and succeed in extending their power over the rural hinterland of Greece once more; or a Communist-led rival elite, relying on the strength and morale of armed men from the mountain communities, would extend its dominion into the cities and thus become ruler of all of Greece.

The Government of National Unity tried to paper over the issue by bringing representatives of each of the rival elite groupings into the cabinet of ministers. But juxtaposition could not resolve the collision. No government could have brought healing to the divided country at once; and Papandreou's cabinet lacked cohesion, could not agree on policy, and had no administrative machine at its command anyway. Like a cork tossed on stormy seas, registering the impact of wind and water, the so-called government of Greece was without significant weight or momentum of its own.

The EAM ministers who joined the government in September did so only after consultation with Russian diplomats in Cairo. Russia thus lived up to the agreement with Great Britain. But Russian policy puzzled and offended the leaders of EAM/ELAS, and angered the rank and file. Their wartime effort had been directed towards a world in which they would exercise dominion, punish the sins of those who had collaborated with the Axis, and establish justice and equity in ways only vaguely spelled out but deeply believed in. ELAS veterans, having suffered hardship and danger for years on end, generally distrusted anyone who had not shared their war experience. Since military preponderance and administrative control of almost all the country fell automatically into EAM/ELAS hands with the German retreat, there seemed small reason to defer to orders coming from the so-called government in Athens if such orders conflicted with the ideas and convenience of local EAM committees. The network of these committees, set up throughout the country during the resistance, offered a skeleton upon which a new national administration might swiftly have been built.

In most of Greece, the tattered and demoralized remnants of the wartime collaborationist administration offered no effective counterweight. In Athens, however, police and administrative services did carry on from the occupation regime, however fumblingly; and Papandreou's government had, in addition, the armed support of a brigade of Greek troops equipped and trained in the Middle East and made up of persons who had fled from Greece during the war. As a result of two mutinies and subsequent political purges that had occurred in 1943 and 1944, this armed force was firmly, even fanatically, opposed to EAM. These brigades constituted, with a handful of British troops, a small but real counterweight to the preponderance of ELAS. EDES, the other armed group rivalling ELAS, turned out to be far more fragile than anyone expected. When ELAS attacked in December 1944, EDES collapsed in a matter of a few days.

A key item in the situation was an agreement between the Greek government and Allied Forces Headquarters, Caserta (Italy), whereby supreme command over all Greek armed forces was conferred upon a British general named Ronald Scobie. Theoretically ELAS thus came under Allied command; but when, at British urging, the Greek government decided that ELAS should be disbanded and disarmed in order to prepare the way for the creation of a new Greek national army to be recruited by conscription, the hollowness of the agreement became apparent. Such a shift involved radical redistribution of power in the country; and not unnaturally, those who had but recently graduated from the hardships and dangers of guerrilla life were quite unwilling to abandon what they had so recently won. Various efforts at compromise failed: and when the British insisted that a firm time schedule for the disarmament of ELAS and the recruitment of new National Guard battalions be adhered to, the quarrel flared into open war.

At first, neither side expected to resort to force. When the EAM ministers resigned on the night of 1–2 December 1944, they thought the cabinet would collapse, whereupon new negotiation would produce a government more responsive to EAM/ELAS wishes. The British, for their part, were convinced that Greeks would never dare to attack British troops directly. But as the stakes mounted, each side proved mistaken. Two days after the resignation of their ministers, EAM/ELAS staged a great demonstration in the central square of Athens. When the crowd broke through restraining cordons, the Athens police opened fire and killed or wounded a dozen or more demonstrators.

In the ensuing tumult, nearly all the pillars of Papandreou's authority crumbled away. EAM leaders then decided to seize power by organizing attacks on police stations and government buildings. A few hours before these attacks were launched, however, a handful of British soldiers were assigned to guard the doors of a number of key government buildings in central Athens. This gesture blunted EAM's scheme, for, to begin with, ELAS troops in Athens were instructed not to fire on British soldiers. After the RAF had been ordered to strafe ELAS strong points in the city, however, this ban was lifted; and for the next five weeks the heart of Athens witnessed a nasty house-to-house battle. The British patched together a narrow perimeter in the very center of the city, and held a small beachhead in Piraeus as well. ELAS brought in reinforcements from the Peloponnese but at first used their main field forces to attack EDES in Epirus rather than directing them towards Athens. By the time EDES had been defeated, it was too late to tip the balance in Athens, for in the meanwhile the British had brought over battle-hardened troops from Italy in such numbers as to assure victory.

When large-scale fighting broke out in Athens, public dismay in Britain and disapproval in the United States became intense; in Russia enigmatic silence prevailed. It seems certain that the Russians gave no encouragement whatever to the Greek Communists either before or during the fighting in Athens. Stalin was holding to his bargain with Churchill (reaffirmed and extended in October 1944) knowing full well that he was likely to have similar difficulties in bringing suitably obedient governments into office in his own sphere of influence. Indeed, it seems probable that the high-handedness of British actions in Greece pleased Stalin, for it offered precedent for what he expected to have to do himself in countries like Rumania.

In the absence of active support from outside, the intrinsic disproportion between a guerrilla force and a regularly supplied modern army soon asserted itself. By mid-January ELAS had to withdraw from Athens and Attica to secure a truce. Before that time, political negotiations had blunted some of the force of EAM's cause. The question of the king's return had been settled: he would not come back until after a plebiscite had been held to determine the people's will as between monarchy and republic. In this way the sovereignty of democratic opinion as against the theories of an overriding royalist legitimacy were vindicated; and most Greeks who had sympathized with EAM could believe that as long as the king was not there to obstruct democratic political processes, elections could be counted on to see the legitimate aims of the resistance put into practice.

As a matter of fact, the fighting in Athens provoked acute strains within EAM's ranks. Many sympathizers were dismayed at the initial decision to resort to force instead of relying on negotiation. Others were appalled at the bloodthirstiness ELAS demonstrated by executing several hundred "traitors" and taking thousands of hostages, more or less at random, from among the Athenian upper classes. In the provinces, too, some EAM committees discredited themselves by acts of violence. More important, food and fuel were desperately short. The fond hope that economic conditions would somehow get better when the Germans left and EAM took over proved completely untrue, not just for collaborators and those who could plausibly be painted as such, but for the rank and file, including persons who had supported the resistance movement.

Thus when the agreement of Varkiza, signed in February 1945, prescribed once more the disbandment of ELAS and its replacement by new conscript National Guard battalions, this time there was no concerted refusal to obey. Relief supplies from abroad could only be expected to reach the Greek countryside if a government acceptable to the Allies existed in Athens. Winter was bad enough; spring was always the shortest time for food. In many communities help was required, and urgently, if starvation were not to set in. Under the circumstances, then, further armed resistance to British-imposed political ground rules seemed futile, and was, in fact, not attempted. Some sixty thousand ELAS men turned in their weapons as required; and though rumor held that their best weapons were hidden in secret caches, for the present at least the shift from an EAM/ELAS administration based on armed mountaineers to an Athens-based administration backed by the British army and by the food it could bring into the country, went swiftly ahead.

As this shift of power proceeded, however, new armed bands came into action. In nearly every community there were persons who had been frightened or hurt by EAM/ELAS, and who saw a chance of revenge from the moment armed preponderance passed into new hands. Accordingly, in many communities, rightist violence replaced leftist violence; and National Guard battalions did little to check the trend. The ideal of a nonpolitical army and neutral police force, though professed by British advisers and paid lip-service by Greek officers, was in practice unattainable. A virulent distrust of EAM and all it stood for dominated the Greek gendarmerie, most of whose members had served through the occupation period; and the Greek prewar officer corps, called back into service to command the new National Guard battalions, was also strongly anti-Communist.

The army, unlike the gendarmerie, had available two cadres of officers: those of republican opinion whose commissions dated back to the Venizelist days; and those of royalist conviction, whose commissions dated back to the time of Metaxas. Republican officers were older, and often lacked up-to-date professional skills. With few exceptions, they had been out of service since 1935, when an unsuccessful republican coup d'etat had paved the way for a drastic purge of army ranks. Hence the conservatively minded, anti-Communist leaders of the Greek brigades that had come back from the Middle East could and did argue that strictly professional considerations required them to appoint younger officers, who happened to be royalist—or at least anti-Communist—to the command of the new armed forces. Efforts by republican ministers to insinuate their old friends into the army met with rebuff; for British military advisers as much as the Greek General Staff wanted to avoid blatant politicization of the new army. After December 1944, taking veterans of the ELAS resistance into active service was not considered by anyone in authority.

The result, faithful to the past and fateful for the future, was to give the officer corps of the newborn Greek army a pronounced political coloration. Intense anti-Communism was the keynote: but this expanded into a number of other politically significant propositions. Thus, it became an article of faith that Communism in Greece was a Slavic plot aimed at undermining Hellenism. Further, all EAM/ELAS sympathizers were labelled Communist, despite the fact that most of them were not members of the KKE. This in turn made leftists of any sort into traitors to the nation.

Such views were not necessarily conservative: officers coming from humble social backgrounds did not usually admire or sympathize with the upper classes of Athens; and the canny behavior of capitalists and rentiers, systematically seeking reinsurance for their wealth by negotiations with any and every political movement and party, did not win the respect of most Greek officers. On the contrary, insofar as they took heroic ideals to heart—and most of them did—their nationalism and anti-Communism was potentially radical in the same way that prewar fascist movements had been radical. For the moment, however, this dimension of the officer corps' mentality remained hidden. Instead, the great majority of Greek officers accepted as self-evident the royalist claim that only a king could provide constitutional protection against Communist infiltration of the electoral process. Many ordinary Greeks, dismayed at continued disorder and desirous above all else of seeing improvement in their economic circumstances, were inclined to concur.

The time between February 1945 and March 1946 sufficed to bring about a sharp reversal of the political balance within Greece. This was facilitated by the fact that most Greeks were still peasants, and, for them, politics remained essentially an alien affair of the mighty. When asked to vote, ordinary men voted for whoever seemed in the best position to repay the favor by providing efficient protection. Given the way ELAS dissolved as the gendarmerie and new National Guard advanced and given the political views that dominated the new armed forces, prudent voters did not need much persuasion to decide whom to support at the polls. Conservatives had might on their side—obviously. Therefore, it was right to vote for them and absurd to do anything else—unless, of course, some previous act or local quarrel had made commitment to the left irretrievable, in which case heroic defiance of the mighty became the necessary or preferable path.

Had an election been held while ELAS controlled the country-side, there is no doubt that the same peasant shrewdness that brought victory to royalists in March 1946 would have brought victory to the left. The psychology of the people made any other result impossible. Whoever held power securely in his hands could count on winning a "free" election. The concept of politically neutral police and army, though piously professed on occasion in Athens, was completely alien to reality and to the minds of Greek voters. It was because the ministers in Athens and their British advisers recognized this fact that the struggle over control of the armed forces had to be settled by force. There was no other arbitrament both parties would accept; and once force had swung to the side of the royalists, the apparent predominance EAM had enjoyed in 1944 and early 1945 melted away far more rapidly than the leaders of EAM or anyone else had thought possible at the time they signed the Varkiza agreement in February 1945.

The new aspect of Greek public affairs was demonstrated in September 1946, when a plebiscite on the form of government resulted in a 69 percent vote for monarchy. The fact that the left urged its supporters to abstain from the plebiscite deprived this endorsement of some of its force, though, of course, the tactic of abstention registered the fact that the leaders of the left antici-pated defeat. From the right's point of view, the plebiscite amply authorized King George's return to his palace. A duly elected government supported by a suitable parliamentary majority completed the political reconstruction of Greece.

But the mere fact of having successfully extended a military and administrative net throughout Greece from the Athens base did nothing to restore a viable social structure and economy to the country. Though mountain men no longer controlled the plains villages, they somehow had to have food—or guerrilla activity would surely recur. But surpluses available in the plains were insufficient to feed the urban population of Greece, let alone the food-deficit villages in the hills. Short-run famine was headed off by massive import of foodstuffs under the auspices of UNRRA (United Nations Relief and Rehabilitation Administra-tion). Efforts to distribute rations equally throughout the country were not perfectly successful. But UNRRA did, for a few months, forestall the prospect of immediate starvation in the hill

villages of Greece, as well as in the towns. This form of aid was
scheduled to end in 1947; and what little could be accomplished
towards long range reconstruction by that date proved grossly
inadequate.

Damages of the war years were far too severe to permit any
sort of automatic and spontaneous resumption of prewar social
and economic life—even if that life had been satisfactory enough
for the majority of the people for them to wish it restored. The
war had impoverished Greece so much that the country could
not possibly support the urban-based administration and professional armed forces that were needed for internal security. Only
subsidy from Great Britain kept the government going. Tax
income fell drastically short of expenditures, provoking run-
away inflation. This inhibited economic recovery, so that the
Greek urban population, having little to offer the peasants in
exchange for grain, remained, as during the Occupation, stubbornly dependent on food delivered from abroad as charity.

An unmistakable sign of impending crisis was the resumption
of guerrilla activity that became apparent in parts of Greece by
midsummer, 1946. The poverty of the Greek hill villages remained insupportable unless or until jobs appeared in the cities
and plains to allow the villagers to make good the local food
deficits they confronted each year. Hence manpower for a new
guerrilla force was at hand for the asking. Bands would probably have appeared even without any political cause to justify
taking up arms again. But political causes were not lacking.
ELAS men and EAM/ELAS ideals were still around, even if
sadly discredited in the cities and plains villages of Greece. In the
hills government control was fainter; the weight of village
opinion backed heroes of the resistance—their own sons for the
most part—and circumstances all but required the village youths
to search again for food by force of arms. When, therefore, Tito
and his Communist colleagues in the Balkans decided to assist
the KKE in another round of guerrilla war, they found many
Greeks ready and willing to go along. Veterans of ELAS, who
had retreated into Yugoslavia rather than submit to Athens in
1944–45, needed only to appear in their native villages and
summon their younger brothers and other relatives to take up
arms for a new band to spring into existence almost overnight.
Supplying such bands with suitable arms was more difficult.

Caches from 1945 were insufficient; capture from the gendarmerie and new National Guard battalions was dangerous; and
delivery across the Yugoslav and Albanian borders was slow.
All the same, by the late summer and fall of 1946, new armed
bands were in being, harrassing gendarme posts in remoter
villages, and once again asserting the armed power of the left in
Greek public life.

The elected government of Greece was quite unable to cope
with such a challenge. The government's only idea was that
private initiative ought to swing into action to restore the Greek
economy to a viable level, as it were automatically, once the
political system of the country had been restored. But the
top-heaviness of the instruments of law and order—and their
manifest ineffectiveness—assured continued economic malfunction; and economic malfunction, in turn, fueled the renewed
guerrilla.

This vicious circle was more than the British had bargained for
when they claimed responsibility for Greece in 1944; and early in
1947, the new Labour government decided to stop subsidies to
the Greek government and armed forces. They so informed the
United States; and after some weeks of hurried consultation,
President Harry Truman decided in March to urge Congress to
take up the British role by appropriating enough money to
restore Greece to working order, and thereby stop the advance
of Communist revolution in Europe. Turkey was linked with
Greece in Truman's message to Congress, for there, too, Russian
demands for concessions in the Straits and along the Armenian
border seemed to threaten Turkish independence, unless American support could convince the Turks that it might be safe to
resist Russian demands.

From the very inception of the Truman Doctrine, there was
systematic discrepancy between the military and the civilian
aspects of the proposed American program. Because the U.S.
Congress shrank from endorsing naked military action, economic rehabilitation was emphasized in the public debate. The
basic assumption was that, to be able to enjoy a secure and
stable democratic political system, a country like Greece must
first solve its economic problems by developing new productive
resources. This would then permit a rising standard of living;
and a rising standard of living would in turn sustain rational and

moderate debate about public affairs. Such a solution would be good in itself. It would also discredit the Communist appeal to revolution as the only effective response to economic backwardness and political malfunction.

The whole idea was fundamentally shaped by American New Deal rhetoric and experience. What the Truman Doctrine meant for most Americans who cared about foreign questions at all, was that something like our own national experience of the 1930s would be projected upon Greece. That country, obviously, was disorganized and depressed, as the United States had been in 1932. Details were no doubt different, but the remedy of resolute governmental action in the economic sphere to regulate and stimulate private enterprise seemed applicable, if only the needful will and the know-how were brought to bear. Will, know-how, and a suitable infusion of capital were what Americans figured they could provide. Confidently, the mission to administer the Greek Aid Program, authorized by Congress in May 1947, set out to demonstrate American efficiency by achieving results.

Familiarity with local traditions and history were judged irrelevant: the problems were technical, economic, military. Experts in each field could be expected to cope with matters falling within their competence. Local differences had nothing to do with the way fertilizers, the profit motive, and military hardware worked if properly applied—or so the Americans assumed. What was needed, therefore, was expertise and action, goodwill and intelligence, a little time and a few hundred millions of dollars to pay for vital capital installations. Then Greece could be expected to carry on, grateful no doubt for American help in time of crisis, but in essentials once more free and independent, newly democratic and securely prosperous.

Only so could the superiority of the American way of life over Russian communism be demonstrated: only so could the larger vision of world peace and international security through law be vindicated; only so would the poor and oppressed of the world see clearly that it was preferable for them to turn towards freedom and democracy, American-style, and turn their backs upon the siren song of Russian communism. The stakes, in short, were huge: and to begin with, in American eyes, there was no incompatibility between the Rooseveltian vision of postwar peace and freedom and the purposes of the Truman program in Greece and Turkey. It was just that temporary weakness in those two countries, and their geographical position on the fringes of the Russian sphere of influence in eastern Europe, required emergency assistance.

Yet, from the very start, there was an element of deception involved. The Turks wanted weapons. Turkey had suffered no war damage and needed economic rescue far less than Greece did. And, as anyone familiar with Greek affairs had to admit, in Greece, too, military matters took precedence as long, at least, as the guerrilla bands in the hills inhibited large-scale, long-range economic planning and reconstruction. Peace had to come before economic reconstruction could get very far; but if the Greek Communists chose to fight, and got sufficient encouragement and assistance from across the northern borders, then only a large-scale buildup of the Greek national army could be expected to overpower the guerrillas. This, of course, is what happened; but in March 1947, it was not yet clear that events would follow such a course; and it was assuredly not on the basis of such a future that the Truman program of special aid for Greece and Turkey was approved by Congress in May.

Uncertainty mounted in Greece in the spring and summer of 1947. The bankruptcy of the government that had emerged from the elections of 1946 was evident. The cabinet, headed by Constantine Tsaldaris, lacked the ability to cope with the economic and social distresses of the country. British support tapered off; American aid was not assured until May nor delivered until August. In the meantime, government morale came close to cracking.

Greek political leaders responded in completely traditional fashion, seeking to profit from the discomfiture of the governing party by constructing a new parliamentary coalition that would bring new men to power. Greek Communists played the game to the hilt, feeling that what had escaped them so cruelly in 1944 was now once more within their grasp, if they only played their cards right. The party had been reorganized after the failure of 1944. New leadership, loyal to the Comintern, took over from the discredited, more home-grown types who had led the resistance; and even though EAM had disintegrated during December 1944, when the other parties and leaders withdrew from the wartime popular front, the Greek Communists continued to call for a broad anti-Fascist coalition, aiming at a people's democracy of the sort then governing all of the countries under Russian influence in eastern Europe.

Full records of Communist deliberations about Greece have never been published and are unlikely to be. Nevertheless we can be sure that in 1946 and 1947 Tito's prestige was riding very high, not only within Yugoslavia but in Communist parties of eastern Europe generally. The Communist recipe for the Balkans as laid down in the 1920s had been federation: only so, Marxists argued, could the distractions of rival nationalisms be laid permanently to rest, and a broad enough base be secured for modern industrial development. Tito and his partisans took this prescription seriously. They reorganized Yugoslavia into six federal republics, and initiated moves towards extending the federation to include Albania and Bulgaria as well. Rivalry between Tito and George Dimitrov, leader of the Bulgarian party, was manifest in debates as to whether Bulgaria should join the new federal state as an equal of the Yugoslav federation, or as equivalent merely to one of the constituent republics of the new Yugoslavia. But when this matter was referred to Stalin, he vetoed further movement towards federation of any kind.

Stalin's decision presented Tito and his followers with a dilemma. Tame acquiescence involved abandonment of their ideals; defiance involved the abandonment of a cardinal principle of communist discipline—obedience to a single, internationally defined line of policy. Tito solved this dilemma by deciding to back the Greek Communists in a renewed effort at guerrilla war. This had many charms. Even Stalin could hardly oppose an act so clearly aimed at forwarding the common interests of the Communist movement. Success might allow the incorporation of "Aegean Macedonia" (that part of Macedonia that had fallen to the Greek state in 1912–13) into Tito's new Macedonian republic. This would round out historic boundaries, tie Slav Macedonian national feeling more securely to Tito's regime than hitherto, and simultaneously secure access to the Aegean through the Vardar valley and the port of Salonika. No wonder, then, that Tito allowed the "hard-core" ELAS veterans who had taken refuge in Yugoslavia in 1947 to return to Greece in the spring and summer of 1946, hoping that fraternal cooperation with the Greek Communist party might permit a decisive step towards the realization of the Communist program of Balkan federation.

How much Greek Communist leaders knew about Tito's problems with Stalin and Dimitrov remains unclear. They realized that if they came to power in Greece with Tito's aid, they might have to pay a very high price: the cession of most or all of Greek Macedonia and Thrace. There is no doubt that they did not want to pay such a price. They therefore preferred to seek power by clever exploitation of the weaknesses of rival Greek parties, without having to depend too much on Tito's dangerously fraternal offers of help.

In any event, until July 1947 the Greek Communists avoided an all-out appeal to arms. They kept the guerrilla alternative alive, but restrained the newly formed bands from energetic action. Just enough predation to supply themselves with food and remind Athenian officials of their existence was what the KKE Central Committee seems to have recommended; and this, being what the average youth from the hill villages wanted anyway, was exactly what happened. Meanwhile, the Greek Communist high command tried to negotiate a deal whereby they might enter the government, secure control of suitably powerful ministries, and thus avoid resort to the guerrilla alternative and to the closer dependence on Tito such a policy would entail.

The man with whom the Communists principally negotiated was Themistocles Sofoulis. Aged, ambitious, and shrewd, Sofoulis saw in the political constellation of late 1946 and early 1947 a chance to become prime minister again, even though the Liberal party he headed held only a handful of seats in Parliament. Papandreou and other center politicians were discredited by their recent failures: the right, in power, was visibly demoralized; it was Sofoulis' turn. He argued that he and he alone was in a position to bring the guerrillas in from the hills by instituting a moderate, politically unbiased government. This obviously called for an understanding with the Communists, and Sofoulis did indeed seek such an understanding. Who offered what has never been divulged; but by July 1947 the effort had failed. Sofoulis publicized a statement denouncing both the Communists and the government for political intransigence; and by September he reaped his reward by becoming prime minister of a ragged coalition that remained in office through the bitter months of renewed guerrilla war.

In July 1947 the American Aid Mission began to arrive in Greece, though the first shipments under the Truman program came only in August, and full-scale operations waited until 1948. Simultaneously, the top leaders of KKE secretly took to the hills, where they set out to increase the scale and coordinate the movements of previously separate bands so as to make a more organized army than before. KKE newspapers continued to appear in Athens until October, when the party was again declared to be illegal. By then the so-called "third round" between Communist-led, hill-based guerrillas and an Athens-based Greek armed force had become unambiguous. This time both commanded enthusiastic foreign backing. The struggle became correspondingly more intense than in 1942–44 or 1944–45, when the scale of supply from outside the country for the contending forces had been far smaller than came to be true between 1947 and 1949.

By the time the Americans settled in, the situation in Greece had already made the economic side of their aid program inoperative. The biggest single item in the American economic blueprint for Greece was the construction of a national electric grid, based on new hydroelectric and some lignite-burning power plants. But the regions of Greece where water power might be tapped were of course located in the mountains where the guerrillas were strongest. Such long-range projects therefore had to wait. On the other hand, the urgency of doing something about military supply and training was far greater than had been anticipated. In view of opinion at home, Americans were reluctant to shift from economic to military aid. But investments in roads and docks, trucks and communications obviously could serve both military and civilian purposes. Accordingly, in the first stages of the American aid program to Greece, a great deal of what was formally counted as economic aid took the form of improving facilities for transport and communications. These were, in fact, initially used almost entirely by the Greek army.

Another change altered the character of the American aid program for Greece in the course of 1948. The Marshall Plan, proposed in June 1947, and approved by Congress in December, was extended to Greece in April 1948. What had been a short-term emergency affair, dependent on annual appropriations, thus became part of a European Recovery Program that was expected to last for four years, until 1952. This made instant results less urgent. On the other hand, the fact that Greece found itself convulsed by an intensifying guerrilla war made Marshall Plan operations there utterly different from programs elsewhere in Europe.

There was another important peculiarity: the Greek national government was quite incapable of the sort of independent economic and social planning that had gone into the definition of Marshall Plan goals in countries like Britain, France, or Italy. Managerial deficiencies of the Greek government and the heavy costs of war made the remarkable economic recovery, that soon became evident in western Europe, impossible in Greece— and this despite an application of American money and expertise which, on a per capita basis, was more intensive in Greece than anywhere else.

For a long time Americans underestimated the difficulty of bringing the guerrilla war to an end. The most effectual means the Greek government found for checking the spread of Communist bands' power was to remove the inhabitants from villages within easy range of their raiding. This deprived the bands of recruiting grounds, supplies, and information. But it was very costly. By war's end about one-tenth of the entire population of the country lived in refugee camps on the outskirts of a few cities. American economic aid supplied these refugees with food, but many of them remained idle, since the cities were already suffering from massive unemployment. Nevertheless, the systematic emptying out of hill villages did permit the Greek army to eliminate guerrilla activity from the south and central parts of Greece by the early months of 1949, confining resistance, thereafter, to an area immediately adjacent to Yugoslavia and Albania. There the mountains remained firmly in guerrilla hands until the final campaign. Supplies from across the border made up for the very slender economic base the guerrilla bands were able to control within Greece itself.

In effect, therefore, the policy of removing villagers from the penumbra of guerrilla power had the effect of denying the guerrillas the chance to dominate the Greek countryside, as they had been able to do under the Occupation. After mid-1947, when the removal policy was started, the villages of the plains remained firmly within the perimeter defended by the Greek National Army. Control from Athens over almost all of Greece therefore remained effective; and the war took on much more the character of an international collision than had been the case in 1942–44. Food coming from abroad, and paid for by American aid, not only supplied the cities but also sustained about seven hundred thousand refugees brought down forcibly from the hills. Massive infusion of outside aid thus upset traditional relationships between city, hill, and plain fundamentally and, as later developments were to show, lastingly.

In spite of numerical preponderance, the Greek National Army found it difficult indeed to dislodge the Communists from the mountain fastnesses adjacent to the border. Commanders of the "Greek Democratic Army," recognizing the changed conditions of their existence, took pains to construct carefully prepared defenses on the slopes of Mount Grammos and other nearby peaks. When, in 1948, the Greek National Army attacked, the result was bloody repulse. Heavy weapons could not be brought to bear in such terrain; and the defensive advantages were enormous. Of course this worked the other way as well: the guerrillas, too, were quite unable to mount any sort of offensive against the Greek National Army.

The resulting standoff might have lasted for a long time had not political crisis within the Communist world intervened. The critical matter was the quarrel between Tito and Stalin that came into the open in June 1948. This presented the Greek Communists with a dilemma. They needed help from both Tito and Stalin and no doubt tried to avoid making a definite choice between them. But eventually KKE came out against Tito, whereupon he retaliated by closing Yugoslav borders to the Greek guerrillas.

This immediately simplified the strategic problem facing the Greek National Army; but before the Athens forces could seal off the Albanian frontier, which had become the only source of supply for the Greek Democratic Army, another disaster hit the Greek Communists. On March 1, 1949, the KKE mouthpiece, the so-called "Free Greek radio," operating from Rumanian soil, broadcast a formal endorsement of the familiar Communist plan for an independent Macedonia. The policy was aimed at Tito. Appeal to Macedonian nationalism, it was hoped, might further disrupt the Yugoslav federation and bring Tito down. Probably Bulgarians were the architects of this policy. For the KKE, it spelled disaster. Every soldier in the Greek Democratic Army who heard the statement (and the Greek National Army radio quickly picked up the theme and hammered it home unceasingly) recognized that victory for the Communist cause would mean dismemberment of Greece. This was not what most of the men in the guerrilla army were fighting for. In their own way nearly all of them were patriotic Greeks too, and were not ready to assist actively in the partitioning of their country. A few Slavic-speaking Macedonians may have welcomed the prospect of an independent Macedonia, but such persons were relatively few within the guerrilla ranks and had always been distrusted by the Greek majority.

Hence by the spring of 1949 when the Greek National Army was ready for a new attack, the morale of the guerrilla forces had collapsed. Resistance was minimal. The Greek army swiftly cut off the guerrilla supply lines into Albania, whereupon a small core of the once formidable guerrilla bands, abandoning their dug-in positions on Mount Grammos, fled across the Albanian border to safety. The war was over; and on October 16, 1949, the KKE radio formally admitted the fact, declaring that hostilities had been suspended.

Oddly enough, the American military mission that had supplied the Greek National Army, supervised its training, and accompanied Greek troops on operations, did not recognize the central importance of political morale for the way the Communist "insurgency" had been suppressed in Greece. Instead, they credited the victory to their own know-how and Greek readiness to accept instruction. Many American officers, having served in Greece, came to believe they had a technique that would allow them to put down Communist guerrilla uprisings in any part of the world. British success in Malaysia and American success in Greece only pointed up the French failure in Indochina. American officers, therefore, felt it would be easy to move in and show the world how to stop the Communists in Southeast Asia too. This opinion, based on a self-serving misinterpretation of what had happened in Greece, was one of the factors that sucked the United States into the morass of the Vietnam War.

For the time being, however, American soldiers thought they had accomplished their mission in Greece. The war being over, it was time to go home and let things get back to normal. Initiative passed, in other words, into the hands of the civilian element in the United States Aid Mission, whose task was to put Greece back on its feet within the two years of the Marshall Plan period that remained. The task was daunting. Greece was as impoverished in 1949 as it had been in 1944. Ports and roads had been built; otherwise, long-range, productive investment had been postponed. Economic aid had mainly gone into feeding the refugees and meeting the budget deficits the Greek government faced each month.

But just as American soldiers knew, or thought they knew, how to define goals and then meet them, so also American economists and businessmen, who staffed the civil side of the aid mission, believed that they knew how to devise a solution for the problems of Greece. With sufficient determination, they might yet be able to get the country onto a self-sustaining basis by 1952 when the Marshall Plan was scheduled to come to an end. What was needed was to cut down unproductive government expenditure, reduce the army, dismiss unnecessary civil servants, and in every possible way shift resources from paying bureaucratic salaries into productive investment. Rigorous tax collection and mounting productivity would then allow the government to balance its budget, and Greece might at last be able to manage on its own as a genuinely independent, democratic state.

To carry out such a program a strong government would be needed: a government able to undertake unpopular policies that would pay off only in the long run. In addition, technically competent civil servants were required: men who spoke the language and could handle the concepts of post-Keynesian economics. To achieve such results in a mere two years was no doubt difficult; but the Americans' mood was shaped by their experience of the New Deal and war years, when seemingly "impossible" goals had in fact often been attained more or less on schedule. Why not in Greece as well?

As a matter of fact, some aspects of the American blueprint for social and economic reconstruction were carried through with remarkable success. This was generally the case in the agricultural sector, for instance, where the Americans had the age-old patterns of Greek peasant family enterprise working for them. When a new technique, a new crop, new seeds, or some other novelty could be shown to pay off on an individual family basis, Greek peasants were not slow to accept the innovation, and proved apt pupils in learning whatever new procedures or skills were required.

Often, initial suspicion and conservatism had to be overcome. In prewar Greece, peasants had sometimes lost their land by going into debt. Consequently, any novelty that required borrowing, even when terms were very advantageous, had to overcome initial skepticism. But all that was needed to start a general stampede towards a new technique or crop was for someone in a village nearby to succumb to the arguments of an agricultural extension agent, try the new thing, and find that it paid off. Then, behold, next year most or all the farmers of the community sought to do likewise. Sometimes, of course, this created marketing problems. In the absence of storage and distribution systems, enhanced production could lead to sharply lowered prices and sudden collapse of profitability. But despite such local miscalculations, in the nation as a whole, peasant readiness to pursue anything new that promised to help the family budget led to rapid upgrading of agricultural production. Simple things, like making fertilizer available at prices and on credit terms that made the debt easy to pay off, often doubled or tripled yields. High-yield seed for wheat had almost as great a result. Irrigation required much greater capital investment; but where it could be instituted, the increase in yields was even more spectacular, and a possibility of developing a broad range of new crops opened at once. In 1950–52, the long-range potentiality of agricultural change had only begun to manifest itself; but food production had already surpassed prewar levels at a time when industrial and mining production lagged far behind.

Another early success was the relocation of the wartime refugees. The displaced hill villagers were rounded up and sent back to their homes, willy-nilly. Positive inducements took some of the edge off this sort of high-handedness. Sums were granted to families for repairing damaged houses; sheep and draft animals were distributed to those who needed to restock their farms. Equally important, to bridge over the time before normal income could be expected from the land, wages were paid to the villagers for work on public improvements—above all, for the construction of roads that would assure access to every inhabited place by wheeled vehicle. The Greek army and government were anxious to make sure that no communities on the Greek mainland should exist beyond the reach of army transport. Villages that had been perched high in some cleft of rock, accessible only by mule track, were therefore not reoccupied. In such cases, the villagers were employed to construct entirely new communities for themselves at some accessible site within the limits of their village lands.

Another government policy of great import for village life was to assure communication with Athens by installing in every village square a loudspeaker, permanently tuned to the Athens radio. News and music, entertainment programs and official pronouncements thus flowed freely into every village of Greece, with the result that an urban, national outlook gained ground as against older local and narrowly familial points of view. The new roads also had the effect of linking the villages of Greece with the world beyond as had never previously been possible. Ramshackle buses, usually owned and managed privately, often by the driver himself, began to visit even exceedingly remote communities once or twice a week. Indeed the bus system ramified so widely that it became possible to travel to Athens in a single day from a very large proportion of the villages of Greece, and for a price that was not prohibitive for ordinary villagers. Even the most distant communities on the mainland were no more than forty-eight hours away from the capital, once the road system had been completed; and all villages became correspondingly closer to provincial towns and market centers.

The effect was to deprive village life of its old-time local autonomy. Communication overcame distance as never before. Moreover, the drastic experience of the wartime refugee camps meant that women and children, as well as men, had glimpsed something of the great world beyond the village. Even after they were compelled to go back, the old ways and the old limitations on life could no longer simply be taken for granted. Restless discontent with renewed poverty was one result. Readiness to try almost anything to escape such poverty was a corollary, even if it meant that young women were now ready to imitate young men by emigrating from the village in an effort to find a better life somewhere else.

Before, women had always stayed home: and by staying home had maintained unbroken the tradition of the hill communities. When they ceased to be willing to remain in the places where they had been born, the long-range survival of these food-deficit communities became problematical. Women had traditionally led extremely hard lives in Greek hill villages. Their wartime existence in refugee camps had given hundreds of thousands of village women a glimpse of much easier ways of life; and nothing could erase such impressions from their minds thereafter. Hence the wartime experience laid the ground for farreaching disruption of traditional life-patterns in the hill villages of Greece; but this, of course, was not yet apparent in the early 1950s when the government repopulated these villages by sending the refugees back home.

The other field in which the American planners met solid success was in the construction of a national electric grid, fed by power stations located at hydroelectric sites or where lignite beds provided suitable fuel. Construction of dams and power stations took time; and it was not until 1955 that the scheme, approved in 1950, came into operation. By that time, electricity generated in Greece was 5.7 times as great as in 1939, even though only 384 communities were as yet connected to the national grid. There are about two thousand villages in Greece; and in the ensuing fifteen years electricity came to nearly all of them as the national power grid continued to expand to new regions and to develop new power plants to meet new demand.

The arrival of electricity with its capacity to activate machinery of many kinds—electric lights, refrigerators, washing machines, power tools, pumps, and the like—constituted, in fact, a second wave of modernization in Greek rural communities that followed about a decade behind the revolution wrought by new communications in the immediate postwar years. The effect was to transform rural life within a single generation. Village existence became far more comfortable, approximating to urban standards. Yet, paradoxically, increased familiarity with city ways provoked restlessness among the young who found village life restrictive and boring when weighed against the freedom and glamor of the city.

Aspiration for the excitement and comforts of city life was, of course, nothing new in Greece. But in the early 1950s the refugee residue from World War I still clogged the towns. Years of economic dislocation during World War II meant that an enormous proportion of the urban population was unemployed or underemployed. Finding productive occupations for these people was far more difficult than reviving and expanding village productivity. To be sure, starting up old factories and refurbishing run-down machinery by bringing in spare parts offered no problems. By 1950 this had been done. But getting private capital to invest in new industrial plants was quite another matter; and here the American aid mission met with little success, despite the fact that their blueprint for putting Greece back on its feet required substantial expansion of industrial and commercial activity.

This difficulty was not, however, the real American failure in Greece. Eventually industrial-commercial expansion did occur, more or less along the lines impatient Americans had hoped for. But before this vindication showed itself, two fundamental anomalies of the U.S. plan for Greece, as originally conceived, had become painfully apparent. First of all, reform of the Greek government proved beyond American capacities. The American ambassador's efforts to manipulate the cabinet that emerged from elections held in 1950 proved futile. To be sure, the Americans unseated one cabinet and imposed another, but General Nicholas Plastiras, whom the Americans put in as prime minister, proved unable (or unwilling) to carry out the sort of far-reaching, radical administrative changes the American experts judged to be needed. Those experts expected Plastiras to generate the sort of public support that had sustained the American New Deal. But the left-center politicians grouped around General Plastiras had no idea of social reform or governmental modernization à l'americaine. Rather, their assumption was the same as that of politicians on the right: that Greek society and economy should operate autonomously and as usual, while politicians also should act as usual, that is, manage public services in such a way as to reward friends and punish enemies, and thus create a network of clients who could vote them back into office when elections became necessary.

Such attitudes were entirely incompatible with the wholesale restructuring of public expenditures and taxation that American advisers wanted. Even when cabinet ministers promised to cut expenses and raise taxes, they dragged their feet when it came to action, and found good and persuasive reasons why the reforms the Americans judged to be essential would not work in Greece. It is hard to doubt that the Greeks were usually right in pointing out flaws in American proposals for reform. Radical restructuring of the Greek economy could not be carried through as long as the governmental administrative machine remained democratic, that is, responsive to special pressures and traditional values. The centuries-old habit of seeking and finding favors through personal channels of patronage and friendship tore gaping holes in any kind of government-decreed general regulation designed to control economic processes. From a Greek point of view, such regulations, whenever they happened to interfere with individual and family self-interest, were obstacles to be overcome, not rules to be obeyed. In such a world, American nostrums for the economic ills of Greece—a stiff progressive income tax, for instance, to distribute wealth more equitably— were simply unworkable. The more formidable the regulation, the more energetic the effort to escape its incidence and the greater the occasion for bribery. Irritable condemnation of the inefficiency and corruption of Greek politicians and civil servants was a poor substitute for thinking through the defect of the original American blueprint, which had naively assumed that Greek society was essentially the same as United States society, and needed only a few pointers in order to duplicate the American New Deal.

Failure to make the Greek government into a pliant instrument for American ideas about social engineering was a bitter enough pill for the experts of the Economic Aid Mission to swallow; but their coup de grace came from half-way round the world with the outbreak of the Korean War in June 1950. Ironically enough, that was undertaken by the United States in defense of the vision of a peaceful postwar world, where international conflicts would be regulated according to law by the United Nations. But if one of the essential preconditions of success for such a policy—general concurrence among the Great Powers in defense of democratic and legal processes among nations—was invalid, then, of course, the whole ideal came tumbling down. After so many muted clashes between Communist and non-Communist forces in Europe and elsewhere, the outbreak of the Korean War seemed to show that a global struggle between the ideals of the Soviet Union and those of the United States could not, after all, be avoided. The principles of the United Nations, the search for world order through legal process and public discussion, to which the United States continued to profess its loyalty, required active armed defense. To create armed forces strong enough to deter attack seemed the only realistic policy. Military plans and preparation would have to take precedence over alternative public concerns.

In such a situation, to expect Greece to disarm in order to balance the government's budget no longer seemed sensible, especially since it now appeared that the United States might soon find itself wanting military allies in Europe very badly in case of a Soviet attack. But unless the Greek army were drastically cut back, all hope of making Greece economically self-sustaining within the limits of the Marshall Plan years had to be abandoned. Not only that: the entire original concept of the temporary and emergency character of the American aid program had to be given up. If Greece were to keep a strong army indefinitely, American aid would also have to continue indefinitely. The NATO treaty of April 1949 had foreshadowed ongoing American involvement in European affairs. Simple logic called for a similar prolongation of the relationship with Greece, even though, or perhaps especially because, the prescription for social and administrative reform, which had inspired the aid mission, had proven so imperfectly suited to the realities of the Greek scene.

The changed climate of world affairs put primacy back into the hands of the military as far as American actions and policy in Greece were concerned. How much it might cost to keep a Greek army in being hardly mattered to either Greek or American army officers; what concerned them was planning and preparing what would be needed to face various imagined patterns of attack from the adjacent Communist lands. The idea that every young man should serve in the armed forces and learn how to play his part in war was fundamental to both Greek and American military mentalities. Only so could the full strength of the nation be mobilized; only so could a kind of rough justice be meted out to all classes of society; and only so could the professional officer class find secure employment. The size of the

Greek army was thenceforth determined not by any sort of economic calculation or by the financial resources of the Greek government but depended simply upon the number of young men reaching draft age each year. American aid could be counted on to supply any shortfall between Greek resources and what was required to keep the resulting force (roughly fifty thousand men) under arms and reasonably well supplied with up-to-date weaponry.

The ideal of making Greece independent, and capable of standing on its own feet in the international arena, was tacitly abandoned; instead military planning began to treat Greece (and Turkey) as part of a larger whole—the NATO alliance. No longer was it the American New Deal that provided the model for U.S. official action in Greece; instead World War II trans-national patterns of military administration and planning took over. Greek sovereignty was, of course, seriously compromised by such a development. The Greek army became a state within a state, having more important relations with the American armed forces and NATO planners than with other branches of the Greek government.

Many and complex sympathies bound Greek and American military men together in the years that followed. The anti-Communist ideology that inspired NATO and made the entire enterprise of preparedness against expected attack worthwhile was something both military elites shared fully. Indeed the Greeks could feel that they had seen the truth first and experienced Communist aggression more painfully than the Americans, who had initially been blinded by their wartime association with the USSR.

The heroic self-image that sustained Greek army officers was also shared by their American counterparts, along with a certain disdain for civilians, whose pursuit of wealth and ease contrasted unfavorably with the leaner military ideals. Finally, American army personnel were often persons with a social background and life career very like that which predominated among the Greek officer class. The officers of both armies usually came from the humbler ranks of society, often with a rural or small-town background, and preserved, self-consciously, a special reverence for old-fashioned virtues and ways of life.

Within the limits created by these basic commitments, it seems fair to say that Greek as well as American officers wanted to have a nonpolitical army in Greece. Invocation of professional criteria for promotion and appointment to key command positions was a useful way of excluding outsiders from the delicate matter of determining just who should control the armed forces of the country. Politicization would mean the creation of rival cliques within the ranks of the army; with that, awkward decisions as to which faction to support would confront every Greek officer who was not already committed. It was far more comfortable to have only one set of superiors, one set of criteria for advancement, one pattern of behavior to which to conform. Learning how to manage the complicated new machineries of war the Americans brought into Greece, and exploiting the potentialities of new communications systems designed to survive even atomic attack, offered an adequate challenge for even the most ambitious Greek officers. And every year thousands of new recruits had to be imbued with proper attitudes, taught how to soldier, while others, after their basic training, had to be fitted into existing field units, taught various specialties and exercised in the field each summer and fall so as to be ready should attack from the north suddenly become a reality.

Such an army and outlook assumed a stable social order. Drastic reconstruction of government and society of the sort American economic experts had envisaged for the years 1950–52 was incompatible with the kind of military planning that took precedence after 1950. What was needed was a government that could keep things quiet in the rear while the soldiers did their duty in the front line of any future conflict. Not change, therefore, but stability and a firm assertion of traditional, national values were what defense against the Communist danger seemed to require.

American official policy changed accordingly. Soon the U.S. Embassy, which had once backed the center-left in hope of forwarding social change in Greece, began to look kindly upon efforts to use Field Marshal Alexander Papagos, commander-in-chief in both the Albanian and in the guerrilla wars, as a figurehead around whom patriotic Greeks might gather. Papagos lent himself to this idea and, following his retirement from the army, entered politics by founding the Greek Rally. Like General de Gaulle in France, whose example did much to

shape Papagos' outlook, he sought to emphasize the difference
between his following and that of other Greek politicians by
rejecting the name of "party." But elections in September 1951
did not give the Greek Rally an absolute majority, and Papagos
refused to consider entering a coalition with anyone who had
not submitted to his leadership by joining the Rally. Plastiras,
accordingly, again became prime minister, but without his
former backing from American officials.

New elections held in November 1952 turned out differently.
This time, under American pressure, the electoral system was
changed from a complicated proportional pattern to the majority system long familiar in the United States. On this basis,
Papagos' Greek Rally came in with 49 percent of the vote and 82
percent of the seats in the new Parliament. A stable government,
sympathetic to the needs of the Greek army and NATO planning, had finally been achieved. It set the style of Greek public
life for the next decade.

American aid patterns in Greece also underwent basic rearrangement in 1952. In February, Greece and Turkey became full
members of NATO, despite some reluctance on the part of
western European governments. NATO plans and command
structures were correspondingly enlarged to include the eastern
Mediterranean. The Marshall Plan terminated in the same year,
as originally intended. Until 1962, whatever additional American aid might be needed to keep Greece strong and stable was
delivered under the terms of the Mutual Security Act, and
treated as part of NATO planning and requirements.

Papagos proved to be a rather haughty prime minister,
unwilling to engage in the wheeling and dealing that character-
ized Greek politics. For a while, his government was dominated
by a brilliant and ruthless radical of the right, Spyros Markezinis. As minister of coordination, Markezinis was responsible
for the main lines of economic policy. He used his office to
inaugurate a more general dependence on market forces than
had previously been attempted. Various barriers to import and
export were removed, and in 1953 an obedient Parliament
passed a law guaranteeing foreign investors against nationaliza-
tion of their property. At first, the effect of such liberalization
was masked by continued inflation of the Greek currency; but in
1954 a revaluation of the drachma established an exchange rate

of 30 drachmae to \$1 which, as it turned out, lasted unchanged for twenty years. Gradually, confidence in the value of the drachma returned: private bank deposits began to accumulate, allowing new scope for private investment, and the former reliance on gold coins for all major transactions became less and less important. The first large-scale investment by a foreign corporation came in 1954, when a German firm signed a contract for exploitation of nickel mines near Lamia; and in the same year a French company made a contract with the new Public Power Authority of Greece for the construction of an additional hydroelectric plant.

Before his decisions began to bear fruit, Markezinis quarreled with Papagos and resigned; but his economic policies stood. In the ensuing months, the marshal's increasing ill-health inaugurated a period of watching and waiting as the problem of succession became obvious. Then, when Papagos died in October 1955, King Paul (who had succeeded his brother George II on the throne in 1947) chose a hitherto relatively obscure politician, Constantine Karamanlis, to form a new cabinet.

This choice was a great surprise at the time, and remains puzzling in retrospect. It was fateful too, since Karamanlis remained in office until 1963, a longer tenure than any Greek prime minister before him had ever enjoyed. Before his surprising designation as Papagos' successor, Karamanlis had been minister of public works in Papagos' cabinet. As such he had an opportunity to drive ahead with road building, for which abundant American funds were available. He undoubtedly made his mark in this capacity, and it was a highly personal mark, for Karamanlis differed from the usual Greek politician in a number of fundamental ways. Born in Macedonia near Serres in 1907, Karamanlis was the son of a village schoolteacher and tobacco grower who took an active part in the last phases of the guerrilla struggle among Greeks, Bulgars, and Turks for control of that disputed land. Trained as a lawyer, he remained an outsider in Athens, and cultivated a blunt manner that underlined his humble provincial origin.

Shrewd, aggressive, and confident of his abilities, which were indeed of a high order, Karamanlis personally shared the provincialism characteristic of patriotic Greeks. Having grown up in a superheated atmosphere of struggle between Greek and

Bulgar for control of the Macedonian hinterland, he accepted the equation of Slav and enemy of Hellenism as self-evident.

Karamanlis was not really interested in political ideology. Communist doctrine probably seemed to him merely a convenient tool taken up by an eternal enemy: no more than a device (like the ill-fated Exarchate, which had divided Orthodox Christians into rival segments after 1870) to split Greeks into warring factions and so permit alien Slav victory. The proper response was therefore to close ranks, keep a watchful eye out for traitors, and defend the sacred cause of Hellenism—if necessary, at risk of life itself.

Perhaps Karamanlis owed his initial appointment as prime minister to American backing. His practical achievement as a builder of roads was the sort of thing Americans admired, and his abrupt manner was the very antithesis of the doublespeak of Greek politics which so often enraged Americans. Yet the king also had to concur; and a man of Karamanlis' background was a strange choice for the palace to have made, since he lacked the connections with Athenian upper-class life that normally made for acceptability at court.

His most important qualification for political leadership, however, was the congruence between his views and those that animated the officer corps of the Greek army. Like Karamanlis, the leaders of the army came from simple backgrounds. They had risen to positions of authority by virtue of technical expertise, just as Karamanlis had done. As long as Karamanlis remained in office, therefore, shared backgrounds created a broad band of sympathy between civil and military leadership. In this respect, Karamanlis was a true heir to Papagos, and the comparative stability of Greek public life from 1952, when Papagos was elected, until 1963, when Karamanlis resigned, reflected this elementary but fundamental fact.

Yet there were flaws in the system. Dissent and difference of opinion about domestic policy looked like treason to those who set out so self-consciously to man the battlements of Hellenism. But in a society growingly diverse, where urbanization and economic deveopment began to assume unprecedented velocity, the ideal of a united community, in which everyone shared the same public attitudes, became increasingly removed from reality. Nevertheless, Karamanlis and a good many other Greeks,

reflecting their peasant and Orthodox backgrounds, were reluctant to admit the possibility of systematic differences of opinion
within the nation. The ideal of a shared national life, in which all
Greeks ought to stand shoulder to shoulder against the threat
from outside, was more attractive than the admission that no
such tight-knit primary community of like-thinking men existed,
or could exist, under conditions of modern urban life.

Because that ideal held such power over their minds, it seemed
right and proper to Karamanlis and his followers to use the full
resources of government to support those who did live up to
their national tasks and, correspondingly, to subject those who
betrayed their duty to the nation to all lawful penalties. Identification between party advantage and the sacred cause of the
nation is not, perhaps, an unusual posture for public men to
assume in democratic states; but in Greece, during the years
when Karamanlis headed the government, this identification
was heartfelt and genuine in unusual degree. It was an article of
faith.

Such self-assurance, not to say self-righteousness, would have
been unattainable by anyone who had not, like Karamanlis,
ascended from a village origin to the heights of power so rapidly
as to carry along all the basic attitudes and assumptions of his
village upbringing. What Karamanlis and the men who followed
him faithfully wanted was to project the familiar structure of
village life onto the national scene. This meant letting everyone
attend to his own business, as each peasant family attended to its
own affairs, while sharing, as Greek peasants normally did, the
risks and burdens of local self-defense if and when some neighbor
threatened the village by challenging pasture rights or any other
collective resource.

Initially Karamanlis probably modeled his behavior as prime
minister on the way Marshal Papagos conducted himself in that
office. Papagos was a professional soldier and an aristocrat—a
rare phenomenon in Greece—with close, though not always
harmonious, personal connections with the royal court. He
deliberately carried the manners of military command into
politics. Parliamentary representatives had to vote as instructed
with no backtalk, or else be read out of the Rally. Papagos got
away with this unprecedented highhandedness, partly because
of his personal prestige, and partly because he had such a large

majority after 1952 that he could afford to shuck off even such a figure as Markezinis and still retain a secure majority. Oddly enough, when the upstart from Macedonia attempted to dominate parliamentary deputies in the same way, it worked. Karamanlis' domineering manner offered the deputies a drastic choice between submission and rebellion; and in the event, the great majority chose to submit, transferring to Karamanlis the obedience they had become accustomed to offer to Papagos.

To be sure, Karamanlis' authority was not consolidated all at once. He became prime minister in October 1955 and promptly set about organizing a party of his own, called the Greek Radical Union (ERE) in preparation for new elections that were held in February 1956. The new party inherited many deputies from Papagos' Greek Rally, which disappeared; but most of the established political figures who had clustered around Papagos refused to follow Karamanlis and went into opposition. As a result, ERE won only 55 percent of the seats in the new Parliament; but the voting bloc Karamanlis secured stood firm behind him and provided a satisfactory basis for a vigorous administration.

The ERE deputies were well rewarded for their support. By applying to the prime minister's office, they could get things done—a decision made, a favor granted—instantly and authoritatively. In the years that followed, this pattern of patronage consolidated Karamanlis' power. His party remained entirely personal, and soon became almost indistinguishable from the apparatus of official administration. This gave the regime a sort of momentum that was difficult to resist. A government intervening in more and more kinds of economic activity had more and more favors to grant and decisions to render: and since these systematically favored supporters of the ERE, massive vested interests soon accumulated behind the ruling party.

On top of this, the liberalized economic policies inaugurated by Markezinis, and the investment in infrastructure that had been made with the help of foreign aid, began to pay off in spectacular rates of economic growth. As more and more individuals contrived to improve their standard of living, the business of personal enrichment became more fascinating than politics. To be sure, the old pattern continued to operate whereby any government decision favoring one person created a dozen enemies and one lukewarm friend. But the increasing number of ways to earn more money and live better distracted those who had been disappointed by official decisions from the sort of fierce vindictiveness that had, in earlier times, sufficed to overthrow one cabinet after another in rapid succession.

The spectacular character of economic upswing can be best grasped from a few simple statistics. The average annual income in Greece was officially calculated at 4,775 drachmae in 1951; it had risen to 12,926 drachmae by 1962, that is, money income increased a little more than 2.7 times in eleven years. Prices lagged far behind, for the drachma remained stable in relation to the dollar after the revaluation of 1954. Naturally, the increase of living standards was not uniform. Rural incomes rose only from a calculated average of 3,036 drachmae in 1951 (63 percent of the national average) to 7,800 drachmae in 1962 (56 percent of the national average). But when increases were so great, everyone felt the improvement, even if some benefitted more than others.[3]

This expansion of incomes was primarily a result of innumerable small-scale, individual enterprises seizing upon some new possibility and making the most of it. The sector that expanded most rapidly was manufacturing: but the average number of employees per manufacturing establishment remained no more than four persons. In other words, family-scale enterprise predominated in manufacturing as well as in service occupations and agricultural work. The efficiency with which the Greek nuclear family could pursue gain, by a combination of hard work, shrewd exploitation of market opportunities, and rigorous saving for the future, lay behind the Greek economic miracle, which, in its way, was just as spectacular as anything happening in Germany.

Nevertheless, it remains true that the enhanced scope for family enterprise depended on large-scale fundamental investments, all of which were made with the active participation of the state. The Greek government's basic tactic was to try to create on Greek soil the necessary infrastructure for modern

3. These figures come from Nicholas Vernicos, "L'Economie de la Grèce, 1950–70," (Thèse pour le Doctorat d'Etat des Sciences Economiques, Paris, 1974), typescript, p. 116. This is a very incisive work, and richly deserves publication.

commerce and industry. The American aid program had made a
start in this direction; and in the years after 1952, the government continued to expand electrical generating capacity, to
improve storage and sorting installations for Greek agricultural
exports, to build roads and develop banking facilities. This was
done partly with loans and grants from foreign governments
(mainly the United States) and partly by making deals with
foreign private corporations.

A second important official policy was to channel private
capital into the construction of new factories producing goods
that otherwise would have had to be imported. The idea was
that such import substitution would help the balance of payments. Insofar as the result was to guarantee privileged access to
the national market for newly constructed high-cost factories
making low-quality goods, the policy in effect taxed Greek
consumers for the benefit of owners and employees of the new
enterprises. To check this tendency, which became very pronounced, Karamanlis' government arranged in June 1961 for
Greece to become an associate of the European Economic
Community. The resulting treaty prescribed a twenty-year
period of adjustment, during which time Greek tariffs would
gradually be brought into line with those of the EEC countries
and all protection against goods manufactured within the Common Market countries would be withdrawn. This agreement was
later suspended and only recently (1976) renewed; whether
hitherto protected Greek industries can adjust to the full weight
of German, French, or Italian competition remains to be seen.

A third important aspect of governmental policy under Karamanlis was the encouragement of migration. The government
welcomed the fact that as job opportunities began to open in
Greek cities and abroad, emigrants started to cascade down
from the hill villages. The scale of movement became truly
enormous. Athens grew from 1.37 million in 1951 to 1.85 million
in 1961; in 1960 statistical sampling showed that no fewer than
56 percent of the persons living in Athens were in-migrants.[4]

4. Eva E. Sandis, *Refugees and Economic Migrants in Greater Athens*
(Athens, 1973), pp. 180, 183. Another calculation found 218,000
in-migrants to Athens within a five-year span (1956–61). Cf. Evan
Vlachos, "Urbanization and Development: The Case of Greece," *Rocky
Mountain Social Science Journal* 6 (1969): 137.

Other towns and cities lagged far behind Athens; only Salonika showed somewhat comparable expansiveness, with a 25 percent increase of population between 1951 and 1961.

Emigration abroad also grew during these years, though the full cresting of the flood tide from the villages came only in 1965, when 117,167 persons left Greece to seek their fortunes in some foreign land. Between 1951 and 1961, however, net emigration from Greece amounted to a comparatively modest 207,497 persons, or about 3 percent of the total population of the country. Most of them went overseas to the established centers of Greek emigration in the United States, and to new ones in Canada and Australia.

Job opportunities within Europe became important only in 1957 when an agreement for sending Greeks to work in Belgian coal mines was concluded; but conditions of work in those mines were so severe that this did not attract many emigrants. Far more significant was an agreement signed with the Federal German Republic in 1960 whereby the two governments undertook to facilitate the emigration of Greeks to work in German factories. The agreement specified that rates of pay would be equivalent to German pay scales for similar skills, and living conditions would be regulated by official inspectors.

But German pay for unskilled labor was a veritable bonanza by the standards of Greek village life. Accordingly, beginning in 1961, massive emigration set in which sometimes emptied out whole villages and led to a perceptible drop in Greek agricultural production. Disruptive side effects of this movement were felt mainly after Karamanlis resigned from office in 1963, however. It is best, therefore, to reserve consideration of the impact of this precipitous emigration until later.

Up through 1961, the effect of migration was to give rural families a new hope of solving the hill villagers' age-old food problem. If young men and women could find work at a distance, in Greece or outside the country, then their remittances could be used to buy food from the plains. It thus became possible to secure peacefully all the food village families needed. Indeed, in more and more cases, those who remained behind found it possible to feed themselves from local resources, in which case remittances could be used for various improvements to the family house and property. An upward drift of living standards from the rock-bottom survival levels that had so long prevailed in the mountain villages thus began to assert itself; and with this, the prominent and precarious role those communities had played in Greek public life for centuries began to fade.

The cost was real enough, for half-empty villages, in which only the aged and the very young remained behind, were lame human communities. If too many people left, such villages ceased to be viable. But, at least to begin with, community costs seemed trifling in comparison to the release from personal frustration and restless anxiety about where next month's food was coming from.

This was a fundamental change in the dynamics of Greek society. The pattern that had sustained guerrilla action 1942–44 and 1946–49 swiftly weakened and by the early 1960s had all but disappeared. The new critical social sector was rather to be found among the host of migrants, whose new patterns of life in Athens and other communities did not always satisfy the hopes that had inspired the move in the first place, and always tended to detach the individual or family from the web of village life that in earlier times restrained and gave meaning to every important personal act. Given the massiveness of the migratory movement of the 1960s, it is not strange that a new kind of political-social crisis began to manifest itself in that decade, in spite of the fact that—or indeed just because—the economic advances of the preceding years had been so great.

The public crises that came to Greece in the 1960s were also shaped, in part, by the changing structure of foreign affairs. The mind-set Karamanlis brought to office was attuned to struggle against Communist subversion and infiltration from the north. But as time went by, the plausibility of such a vision of reality weakened. Communist governments soon found themselves distracted by internal and external rivalries, just as bitter and far more complex than the quarrel between Tito and Stalin had been. By 1960, the Chinese had begun to reproach the Russians with treason to revolutionary principles; and Albania, making good its independence from both Yugoslavia and the Soviet Union, became China's vociferous European ally. Rumania, too, was attracted by the Chinese alternative and also won effective independence from Russian supervision. Hence the notion of a single, worldwide Communist plot to expand Russia's power lost plausibility, and the willingness of west European nations to put large resources into preparation for attack from the east diminished. Doubts about the use of atomic weaponry multiplied in western Europe, especially after the confrontation in October 1962 between the United States and the Soviet Union over Cuba. Consequently, NATO planning ran into rough weather.

Ironically, the two poorest members of the NATO alliance, Greece and Turkey, continued to supply the full contingents NATO planners assigned to them. The armed services of both these countries had become so dependent on supplies and subsidies from abroad as to be almost independent of budgetary control by their respective governments. Yet this became a dubious asset to the NATO alliance as frictions between Greece and Turkey mounted over Cyprus, where an armed agitation for union with Greece attained critical momentum in the mid-1950s.

Cyprus was then still governed by Great Britain. The British had annexed the island from the Ottoman Empire in 1914, abrogating an earlier protectorate which dated back to 1878. Earlier still, the Ottoman Turks had conquered Cyprus (1573) from the Venetians; and in the ensuing three hundred years a Turkish minority developed on the island (totaling about 18 percent). Nearly all the rest of the Cypriots were Greek-speaking Christians.

As early as 1950 the Greek government suggested privately to the British that justice required transfer of Cyprus to Greece. Initially the British government turned a deaf ear, so the Greeks of Cyprus conducted an unofficial plebiscite to prove that the overwhelming majority of the island's inhabitants wanted union with Greece. At this time, the Turkish minority of the island remained indifferent to Greek political agitation; and the government in Ankara paid no particular attention. After 1955, however, this situation changed. As Greek nationalist organizers began to penetrate the villages of Cyprus and initiated armed actions against all who failed to rally to the cause, the Turks of the island also began to stir; and presently Ankara began to take an active interest in the fate of their fellow nationals.

Anti-Greek feeling was just as near the surface in Turkey as anti-Turkish feeling was in Greece. Accordingly, antagonism mounted swiftly. In 1955, as a kind of tit for tat, paying back the

Greeks for acts of violence against Moslems in Cyprus, the Turkish government staged riots in Constantinople directed against Greek shops and other properties. In the following months practically all Constantinopolitan Greeks fled from the ancient Byzantine capital. NATO cooperation between Greek and Turkish armed forces became impossible; sporadic fighting broke out in Cyprus between the two communities; and war scares became almost annual events each summer as the newspapers of each country unleashed violent propaganda campaigns.

American dismay at such a quarrel between the NATO allies was genuine enough; and after the fiasco of its attempted invasion of Suez in 1956, the British government no longer wanted responsibility for the island of Cyprus. But finding an arrangement that would be satisfactory to both Greeks and Turks, not only in the island, but also in Athens and Ankara, was well-nigh impossible. In 1959 a patchwork treaty was contrived whereby Cyprus was to become independent, with elaborate guarantees written into the constitution for safeguarding Turkish minority rights. Such a plan postponed, perhaps forever, the hope of making Cyprus part of Greece; but under heavy pressure from Britain and the United States, Karamanlis nevertheless accepted the proposed treaty.

Such a policy grated against the nationalist sentiments which had previously helped to keep Karamanlis in power. He became vulnerable, as never before, to the charge that he was merely an American puppet, responding to secret instructions from the CIA. The plain fact was that the constellation of international affairs that had prevailed in the early 1950s, when NATO was new and memories of the guerrilla war were still fresh, had altered; and the attitudes that justified the internal as well as the foreign policies of Karamanlis' government had become archaic.

The changed complexion of the international scene was soon registered domestically. In 1958 some key members of ERE resigned and Karamanlis decided to call new elections. Gerry-mandering of electoral districts allowed Karamanlis' party to win a larger proportion of parliamentary seats (57 percent as against the previous 55 percent) on the strength of a diminished share of the popular vote (41 percent as against 47 percent two years before). A weakened right, as registered by this election, confronted a resurgent left, for EDA (Union of the Democratic Left) became the largest opposition party, with 26 percent of the seats in Parliament. Modeled on the wartime EAM, EDA was an association of leftist political groups in which Communists played a conspicuous role, despite the fact that the Communist party remained illegal in Greece.

The left, naturally, was jubilant. Men of the right concluded that the old danger of Communist takeover was as insidious as ever. Some of them felt that the electoral process, even as managed and manipulated by Karamanlis' party, was an undependable means of holding Communist subversion in check. Secret, politically motivated societies of army officers seem to have taken on new life in reaction to this election. Veterans of the war against the guerrillas readily believed that another round of anti-Communist struggle was close at hand. Center politicians, and all those of the right who had refused to submit to Karamanlis' leadership, drew a rather different conclusion, to wit, that unless they could bury their differences and unite into a single voting bloc, they would never be able to unseat Karamanlis.

In the course of the next three years, accordingly, George Papandreou put together a new Center Union party which included almost every Greek politician who had quarreled with Karamanlis and who was not ready to consort with Communists in the EDA. The party lacked cohesion. Submission to Papandreou's leadership was almost as galling to many of its chief figures as Karamanlis' ruthless assertion of personal authority was to those who followed ERE. But the sweet scent of victory at the polls kept the Center Union together, for continued trouble in Cyprus made the government vulnerable.

When new elections came, in October 1961, Karamanlis' supporters were almost desperate. Many of them viewed the Center Union as a stalking-horse for the EDA; and indeed EDA leaders made some efforts to concert tactics with Papandreou's party in the hope that victory for the Center Union would bring in a more evenhanded administration when it came to dealings with the left. Fearing defeat at the polls, therefore, the government mobilized all available forces, including police officers and other public officials, who set out vigorously enough to urge voters to support Karamanlis. Simultaneously, secret societies of the right, sometimes acting in collusion with local police officials and army officers, made various threats against those whom they regarded as traitors to the nation. The election results reflected these activities: Karamanlis' party won 50.8 percent of the seats in Parliament, whereas the Center Union came in with only 33.6 percent of the vote and 33 percent of the seats. The left shrank to a mere 14.6 percent of the vote and 12 percent of the seats.

This result might have confirmed Karamanlis' power had not the underhanded means used to win the election been so blatant. As it was, Papandreou challenged the legitimacy of the official tally and soon publicized so many irregular episodes that the election result was in fact effectually discredited. To drive his attack home, Papandreou decided to use his formidable oratorical talents to rouse the people's resentment through a series of mass meetings.

Conditions in the larger towns and cities of Greece, where these meetings were held, had become volatile by the early 1960s. Thousands (in Athens, scores of thousands) of recent migrants from the villages were finding urban life hard and lonely. Papandreou's political agitation offered them an establishment to hate and an excited crowd of fellow citizens with whom to identify. Moreover, many of the newcomers to the towns and cities of Greece had lived previously in poor mountain villages where the guerrilla movement had found its main support. Political tradition therefore inclined them to oppose the established regime; and the difficulty of making a satisfactory life in town, entering at the bottom with no special skills and without any capital to start with, reinforced such inclinations. Papandreou's attacks on the government therefore found responsive hearers in Athens and other towns; and the fiercer his attacks, the more warmly he was received. The emptying out of hill villages had thus removed one form of social instability only to enhance a different but scarcely less formidable challenge to the existing pattern of government and society.

The tone of the agitation was unabashedly jingoistic, for, according to Papandreou, Karamanlis' great crime, aside from the elections, was betrayal of Cypriot Greeks at the behest of the Americans. This removed the old difficulty whereby social protest had been identified with treason to the nation. Instead, it was now the rich and well-to-do, the men of power and privilege, who were charged with betraying Hellenism. Small wonder, therefore, that depths of long suppressed emotion boiled powerfully to the surface of Greek public life. Papandreou's campaign tapped hitherto hidden levels of personal frustration and social dislocation. Not the hill villages but the cities of Greece had become the locus where discontent with the status quo found its most critical expression. This was a new constellation of public affairs; a heady one for the silver-tongued Papandreou, who felt, naturally enough, that he was leading the people towards vindication of truth and justice, not to mention the defense of democratic principles and national self-determination against the evil forces of entrenched privilege, American imperialism, and extralegal violence.

Karamanlis tried to conduct the government as though nothing had happened. In 1962, for instance, he agreed to the biggest deal yet for bringing private foreign investment to Greece. By its terms, the Standard Oil Company of New Jersey undertook to build a refinery and a group of other chemical factories in Salonika. By the time all the plants had been constructed, many millions of dollars had been invested in Greece; but from the start, both Papandreou and the EDA criticized the terms accorded to the American company as being far too generous.

Conceivably, the government could have weathered such attacks indefinitely if Karamanlis had not also quarreled with the royal family in the spring of 1963. His relations with the Palace had never been intimate, and they became positively inimical when the prime minister collided with Queen Frederika. The queen was an energetic, self-assertive woman. Her husband, King Paul, suffered from cancer, and by 1963 had relinquished his royal functions in all but name. Frederika reached out for more and more authority as Paul's grip on affairs weakened. The immediate issue was money. She wanted an increased civil list; Karamanlis was unwilling to agree. Frederika felt outraged. Her demands rested upon a personal vision of the proper deference royalty should receive from commoners, and the role of lavish display in shaping the public consciousness. The result was a direct clash of wills between two strong personalities, neither of whom was accustomed to yielding.

Karamanlis was also, no doubt, tired and irritable after so many years in office. He may also have felt the force of an argument fashionable in circles around the American Embassy, to the effect that what Greece needed was a change of government. According to this view, any party, left in power too long, was liable to corruption and needed the tonic of having to renew its ties with the voters during a period of exile from the seat of power. The fact that Democrats had recaptured control of the White House in Washington in 1960 after eight years out of office gave topicality to such a doctrine; moreover, some of the persons around President John F. Kennedy were personal friends of Andreas Papandreou, son of George Papandreou, and former chairman of the Department of Economics at Berkeley. Andreas Papandreou had returned to Greece in 1959 to head a Center for Economic Planning funded by the Ford Foundation; but as his father's assault on the government gained headway, Andreas abandoned academic and theoretical studies in order to enter politics as his father's lieutenant. The Center Union, while bearding American imperialism in public, could therefore claim the sympathy of one element in American officialdom, even if, as seems certain, the United States military mission continued to prefer the straightforward anti-Communism Karamanlis and his supporters represented.

Given these circumstances, it is not altogether surprising that Karamanlis resigned as prime minister in June 1963, even though his majority in Parliament remained intact. Two events precipitated this action. One was the May 28 murder of Gregory Lambrakis, a prominent left-leaning politician. His murderers proved to have close enough connections with officers of the gendarmerie and with some persons active in the prime minister's office in Athens to embarrass the government seriously. Soon thereafter, Karamanlis and Queen Frederika quarreled openly about whether or not the queen should visit London, where Cypriot Greeks could be expected to make her visit the occasion for public demonstrations against Karamanlis' government. Rather than face the double opposition of the Palace and the Center Union, Karamanlis decided to resign. Not relishing the role of opposition leader, he decided to leave the country, and went off to France.

His resignation ended an era of Greek public life and inaugurated four years of intense perturbation during which Papandreou and his followers challenged the prevailing distribution of power in Greece only to suffer sudden setback at the hands of a self-appointed junta of army officers who seized control of the country by coup d'etat in April 1967.

The first election after Karamanlis' resignation, held in November 1963, resulted in a paper-thin victory for the Center Union. But with only 46 percent of the seats in Parliament, George Papandreou could not hope to conduct a government without depending on support from the Communist-tinged left. This he was unwilling to do. Instead he demanded new elections, which were held in February 1964. This time the Center Union came in with a clear majority, winning 52 percent of the popular vote and 57 percent of the seats in Parliament. Papandreou thus at last entered office with an unquestioned majority, only to face a series of embarrassing due-bills he had accumulated during his heated electoral campaigns.

A satisfactory solution in Cyprus proved as impossible under his leadership as it had been under Karamanlis. The establishment of an independent Cypriot government in 1960 had the effect of splitting the Greek community in Cyprus between those who remained loyal to the ideal of union with Greece and others who found independence increasingly attractive. When, to no one's surprise, the cumbersome constitutional settlement broke down (1963), fighting started up again between Greeks and Turks. Soon the Greek government found itself constrained to accept a United Nations peace force for Cyprus (1964). Yet Papandreou did not altogether betray the patriotic rhetoric that had helped him come to power. His government, for instance, sent army officers secretly to Cyprus, where they were expected to work for the cause of union with Greece. He also explored, vainly, the possibility of getting Russian support for the Greek cause. Such actions failed to resolve the Cyprus question in the only way that would have satisfied Greek national feeling. Instead they backfired by provoking Ankara to evince an ever stronger interest in the Turkish Cypriots.

Domestic promises of a new and better deal for the poor and dispossessed of the land were also difficult to honor. Policies for radical income redistribution which Andreas Papandreou declared necessary for a healthy development of the Greek economy ran headlong into the tangled interplay of special interests and personal ties that bound Greek politicians to the existing economic order. Andreas was eager to push ahead, even if it meant offending powerful individuals and contributors to the party's finances. Other Center Unionists were totally disinclined to act on such principles, and were, indeed, appalled when some of Andreas Papandreou's followers showed signs of really undertaking a deliberate effort to restructure Greek society and economy.

Andreas Papandreou's ideas were essentially the same as those that had inspired the American aid mission between 1948 and 1950. Like the American experts who had prescribed social transformation as the cure for Greek ills in the late 1940s, Papandreou had acquired his leading ideas from economic doctrines taught in American graduate schools during the 1940s, when Keynesianism was new and the flexibility of a managed economy first dawned on eager theorists.

Despite his Greek ancestry, the young Papandreou had little appreciation of the peculiarities of the Greek scene. When Greeks refused to behave as American economists thought men should, everywhere and always, he was tempted to dismiss such behavior as a sign of backwardness or a demonstration of personal or institutional corruption that would have to be swept away. A brisk, self-confident group of young, American-trained Greek technocrats clustered around him. Their affectation of intellectual and moral superiority deeply antagonized other leaders of the Center Union party. George Papandreou, the party leader, found himself torn between pride in his gifted, abrasive son, and the need for maintaining party unity.

When Andreas Papandreou's theoretical ideas and the practical dictates of party politics coincided, action was relatively easy. Thus, for example, as had been promised, the government raised salaries for civil servants and set price supports above world market levels for a wide variety of agricultural commodities in an effort to bring peasant incomes more nearly abreast of urban pay scales. In addition, George Papandreou initiated a much-needed overhaul of the Greek educational system and renegotiated the agreement with the Standard Oil Company of New Jersey so as to require the company to make a larger investment on somewhat less favorable terms than before. A

trade agreement with Bulgaria opened the possibility of profitable economic relations with Communist-ruled lands; and efforts to open up markets for Greek products in other east
European countries followed quickly, though without achieving
any very spectacular results.

Such policies did nothing to reassure the Greek right, but the
mounting intensity of political disagreement did not check
economic development. As before, small-scale family enterprise
was the prime mover, though a number of new, larger-scale
factories, employing scores or even hundreds of persons, also
began to come into operation. These remained, nonetheless,
exceptional, often foreign-owned or financed by the government. More important was the sudden spurt in emigration
which took hundreds of thousands of Greeks to Germany,
where high wages and encounter with the conditions of a fully
modern factory economy provided ex-peasants with a dizzying
and entrancing vision of a world of ease and plenty hitherto
inaccessible to them.

This new diaspora numbered just under half a million by the
mid-1960s. Unlike the diaspora overseas, Greek *Gastarbeiter* in
Germany found it relatively easy to return home for visits
during their paid holidays. Circulation between Greek village
and German factory was therefore a continual process. Indeed,
when the first pioneers returned in second-hand cars they had
actually been able to buy on the strength of a year or two of
wage work, the effect on their home villages was galvanic.
Almost every person of working age, and especially the young
who would otherwise have to wait long years to accumulate the
wherewithal to set up a family of their own, sought to go off to
Germany. In many villages the result was socially disruptive,
but the incidence of catastrophic departures was quite irregular.
Other villages, even close by, saw no one leave for Germany,
their inhabitants preferring emigration routes into Athens or
Salonika. And in still other cases, peasants kept open older paths
to the United States, Australia, and Canada.

The total effect of the massive emigration of the 1960s on
Greek society and economy remains highly controversial. There
can be no doubt that, measured by material standards, millions
of individuals benefitted greatly. Perhaps there were long-term
psychic and social costs involved that had not become fully

apparent, even in 1976. From the Greek government's point of view, the loss of jurisdiction over so many Greek citizens seemed deplorable. On the other hand emigrant remittances, by shoring up the balance of international payments, helped to keep the government's credit sound and the drachma comparatively stable. Financial stability, in turn, was prerequisite for the continuance of the country's economic growth.

Disagreement starts when one considers the effect of the subtraction of productive labor from the Greek economy due to emigration. By the mid-1960s, labor shortages became manifest. The supply of extra harvest hands, once overabundant in every part of the country, fell short or disappeared entirely. In towns, servants started to be hard to come by, and the extravagant uses of labor which a persistent surplus of semiemployed and unemployed persons had encouraged in times past began to erode. Striking increases in productivity resulted; and higher wage rates, in turn, by making extra workers more costly than before, tended to push employers towards more economical patterns of staffing their enterprises. Greece, in short, changed during the 1960s from a country where the available labor force exceeded job openings to a country in which some of the least remunerative customary occupations were no longer being filled. A drastic drop in the birth rate, beginning in the 1950s, indicated that this would be an enduring change. Perhaps the transition from a labor surplus to a labor deficit society would have occurred eventually in Greece even without large-scale emigration—though this, surely, is far from certain. What is certain is this: massive emigration in the 1960s hastened the transition enormously. According to one calculation, no fewer than 850,000 persons, or 25.9 percent of the entire Greek work force, emigrated between 1951 and 1970.[5] No wonder, then, that labor shortages arose!

Nationalists soon began to worry about what would happen if the Greek countryside emptied out. Where would recruits for the army come from, if hardy peasant lads were no longer available

5. Vernicos, "L'Economie de la Grèce," p. 591. Since many Greek emigrants returned to Greece, the net emigration during this twenty-year period was only about 666,000 persons; but that figure equalled 21 percent of the active work force of the country—a very considerable loss.

in their accustomed numbers? How could Turkish and Slavic rivals be held at bay by a nation that allowed its most energetic citizens to seek their fortunes abroad in such numbers as to weaken the muster of potential soldiers at home? Andreas Papandreou's answer was to raise wage rates and find new jobs at home. The way to achieve such results, he argued, was by a government-regulated redistribution of incomes within Greece.

This remedy frightened the possessing classes, but as long as the Greek army remained firmly within the mold fixed for it since 1944, conservatives could feel, quite correctly, that the Greek officer corps constituted an effective check on any really radical efforts to remodel Greek society along the lines Andreas Papandreou advocated. A second pillar of the establishment was the Palace. King Paul's death in March 1964 brought a young, athletic, and inexperienced monarch, King Constantine, to the throne. His relations with the top generals and admirals (Constantine was himself a skilled sailor) remained cordial and close; and high-placed habitués of the Palace taught the king that he had the duty to override any transitory popular mood that might threaten the long-range interests of the nation.

As long, therefore, as king and army remained capable of vetoing radical social change, conservatives could sleep well in their beds at night. When, however, early in July 1965, Andreas Papandreou was accused of trying to tamper with the army by encouraging the formation of a secret society of junior officers sympathetic to his aims, the stakes were instantly raised. Before the case could come to public trial, George Papandreou dismissed his minister of war, a conservative member of the Center Union party, and the person directly responsible for army discipline. He claimed the right to take over personal direction of the War Ministry, even though his son was the principal person accused. This, King Constantine refused to agree to, and, in an angry scene, Papandreou either resigned or was dismissed by the king, despite the fact that his party, the Center Union, had a majority in Parliament.

In the following weeks the king and a coterie of politicians around him used all available means to splinter the Center Union; and since there were plenty of ambitious men in its ranks who were intensely jealous and distrustful of Andreas Papandreou, this was not a very difficult task. Eventually, by promis-

ing ministries and other favors, enough deputies were seduced
from the ranks of the Center Union to form a new majority in
Parliament. The apostates from Papandreou's party, plus the
voting block constituted by Karamanlis' old party, now headed
by Panagiotis Kanellopoulos, made a bare majority of one. Not
until September was the new arrangement defined; by which
time, in effect, the right had managed to climb back into power,
aided and abetted by the Palace, and supported behind the
scenes by the army and police.

Amidst these heated intrigues, the American Embassy tried for
a "low profile" so as to escape reproaches of those who lost out
in the scramble for power. The policy was a failure. Practically
all Greeks came to believe that secret CIA actions played a
decisive role in the way the results of the election of 1964 were
thwarted. Popular opinion probably exaggerated the effectiveness of American secret initiatives, whatever these may have
been. But ironically, what so many Greeks came to believe was
and remains politically more important than the truth about
whatever it was that the CIA did—or refrained from doing—in
Greece.

Papandreou, once more in opposition, blamed the apostates,
the king, and the Americans for what had happened, and took
up again the congenial task of challenging the government's
legitimacy by fomenting popular indignation against the power
brokers who had so blatantly frustrated the popular will. A
series of large-scale strikes and demonstrations attested to the
intensity with which the poorer urban classes responded to
Papandreou's agitation. Nearly everyone believed that elections,
scheduled for May 1967, would result in a new victory for the
Center Union party. To some it also looked as though Greece
were approaching a revolutionary situation: and a few among
Papandreou's followers welcomed such a prospect. Diminution
of the rapid rate of economic growth which had prevailed under
Karamanlis became apparent in 1965–66. This exacerbated
political instability which in turn constituted a major reason for
the economic slow-down that Greece experienced. A classic sort
of vicious circle thus began to manifest itself. Rightists reacted
by preparing countermeasures, though what exactly lay behind
the many rumors that circulated in Athens about an impending
coup d'etat, to be organized by the king, by a group of generals,

by the CIA, or by a combination of all three, has never become public.

George Papandreou himself only wanted to hold office once again. He remained a conservative at heart, and definitely shied away from encouraging para-revolutionary action of the kind his son was toying with. This is proven by the fact that he made a secret deal with his principal political rival, Panagiotis Kanello-poulos, according to which, after the election, the two leaders would cooperate to set up a government to oppose extremists of both left and right. Such planning was cut short by the fact that on April 21, 1967, a clique of hitherto obscure and relatively junior army officers (mostly colonels) seized power by a coup d'etat, inaugurating a revolutionary government of the right.

The Colonels' coup came as a surprise to everyone who had not been privy to the small secret society of like-thinking army officers who contrived it. Their success depended on the acquies-cence of General Spandidakis, chief of the General Staff, whose confirmation of an order to activate a NATO plan for counter-ing Communist revolution was what gave the conspirators their initial hold on power. The young king subsequently also decided to accept an interim government which contained a window-dressing of civilian ministers. General Spandidakis, no doubt, shared the distrust of the electoral process that inspired the Colonels to their coup d'etat; and the king, if forced to choose between revolutionaries of the right and revolutionaries of the left, probably preferred the former. At the same time, it is only fair to recognize that at the time these two individuals made their fateful decisions, they seemed to have little alternative. Having fallen into the hands of armed, determined men who cut them off from all communication with others, both king and general found themselves effectually stripped of rank. They became in fact no more than two isolated human atoms facing ruthlessly superior force.

Only gradually did the personalities and power relationships among the officers who contrived the coup emerge. Their intentions were likewise initially unclear. The patently false claim that they had acted only to forestall a Communist plot to seize power was matched by very radical words. On the day of the coup, the anonymous new rulers of Greece proclaimed:

"Who are we? We belong to no political party and are not

disposed to favor one political group over another. We belong to
the working class and we remain on the side of our brother
Greeks who are least well-off. We are activated solely by
patriotic aims and we hope to abolish deprivation, to cleanse
public life ... and to create a healthy basis so that the country
may quickly return to a normal parliamentary life.... Our
essential object is social justice, equitable distribution of income,
the moral and material resurrection of all society and particularly of the peasants, the workers, and the poorest classes."[6]

The man who eventually emerged as dominant among the
conspirators, Colonel George Papadopoulos, as well as his
principal collaborators, were all born into peasant or humble
small-town families. All had entered cadet school in the late
1930s, when General Metaxas was seeking to create a new,
disciplined Greece on a fascist model. Their political ideas harked
back to the Metaxas era; and in a far cruder way than Karamanlis,
they also yearned to recreate on the national level the spontaneous social discipline and egalitarian freedom of village life.

Their ideal was to live in a world where all Greeks thought
and felt alike, conforming to an orthodoxy that was national as
well as religious. In such a world, and only in such a world,
could every Greek be perfectly free to pursue his personal and
private affairs, because shared values and rules of life would
keep conflict to a minimum and prescribe proper solutions to
hostile personal encounters when they did occur. And only in
such a world, they felt, would all Greeks be ready and willing
spontaneously to rally to the defense of their country against
any and every danger from outside. Indeed, the internal discord
they had found so distressing in the public life of the 1960s was
itself a proof that outside influences were nefariously at work
undermining the national solidarity and Orthodoxy of the Greek
people. It followed that anyone who resisted the Colonels' effort
to restore the wholeness of Hellenism was consciously or
unconsciously a tool of evil foreign influence. All such opponents, by definition, stood in urgent need of correction, either

6. Extracts from the full text as printed in Marc Marceau, *La Grèce
des Colonels* (Paris, 1967), pp. 77–80. For a fuller account of the
Colonels' professed purposes, see Richard Clogg, "The Ideology of the
Revolution of 21 April 1967," in Richard Clogg and George Yanno-
poulos, eds., *Greece under Military Rule* (London, 1972), pp. 38–58.

through persuasion or, if need be, by force. If they were real Greeks, the Colonels believed, they would soon see the error of of their ways and willingly return to an acceptance of true Hellenism.

The peasant and Orthodox background of such ideals is clear enough. Village life had in fact been so well defined by custom that the sort of spontaneous agreement the Colonels yearned for had been pretty much of a reality when it came to judging individual behavior. Similarly, ever since patristic times, the Greek Orthodox church had demanded meticulous doctrinal uniformity among the faithful in matters of theology. On the other hand, when it came to human conduct, owing to the sinfulness of humankind, the church had reserved the ideal of perfect unanimity for the Kingdom of Heaven. Thus the Colonels, in effect, were asking the Greeks to bring the patterns of behavior appropriate to the Kingdom of Heaven down to earth in order to preserve a profoundly endangered Hellenism.

The endangered "Hellenism" they so strenuously sought to preserve was a technologically up-dated simulacrum of the society they had known in early childhood in remote villages and small provincial towns of Greece. The Colonels would not admit that technological up-to-dateness was incompatible with the village past. They were technocrats themselves: men who owed their positions to skill in managing modern instruments of war, especially communications systems, intelligence systems, and counterintelligence systems. Admiration for the wonders of modern technology and an unambiguous aspiration for more and more machine miracles were just as much a part of their lives as was the yearning for the village past. They saw no incompatibility between their two ideals, even if, to an outside observer, it seems self-evident that high-level technology, and the intensified communications technology brings, were exactly what had hastened the disruption of traditional village ways of life.

Failure to face up to this inherent contradiction was a fundamental weakness of the regime the Colonels established. The resulting ambivalence manifested itself in practice from the start. Yet there was another ambiguity almost as important. Being professional military men, the Colonels set great store by the heroic element of the Greek tradition. Karamanlis' regime had, in effect, allowed the market pole of Greek behavior to attain dominance at the expense of the heroic and Orthodox aspects of life. What the Colonels set out to do, therefore, was to redress the balance.

They were never really clear as to whether the heroic took precedence among these ideals. In one sense it did: for the men fitted to guide the Greek people towards the promised land of unanimity were soldiers—that is, aspiring heroes, who had chosen the hard, disciplined life of the army in preference to softer civilian careers. In moments of emergency, like that facing the country in 1967, unanimity under such leadership was the appropriate attitude for all true Greeks. This, in fact, was what justified their seizure of power. But once in office, Colonel Papadopoulos and his fellow officers faced a painful dilemma. Power tended to corrupt exactly those qualities that justified its exercise. A military elite that mixed too much with the grubby defilement of everyday economic management was in danger of losing all trace of the heroic asceticism that qualified it to show the way towards the necessary moral reformation of Hellenism. From the start, the new rulers of Greece therefore proclaimed their intention of turning government back to civilian hands as soon as possible. But the conditions that would permit such a transfer of power without again endangering the ideals of the regime were never stated clearly, and, given the intrinsic contradictions of that ideal, could surely never have been attained.

Here, then, lay a second glaring defect of the Colonels' ideology. The heroic basis of their claim to power was liable to tarnish with too much immixture in politics and administration. Yet once in, how to get out? Only if civilian attitudes could be altered to assure unanimity behind a government sympathetic to all that the Colonels stood for, would a return to "normal" be possible. But in the meantime, the army was being strained and the heroic pattern of life was being stained by too close contact with wealth and the opportunities for self-enrichment inherent in the exercise of political power. Personal corruption and enrichment, restrained at first, assumed growing importance as years went by. Such behavior eventually discredited the grander, patriotic claims the regime had begun by proclaiming.

Yet in the first months, the Colonels' pronouncements commanded considerable resonance among the Greek people as a whole. Even when measured by the sterner test of practice, they were able initially to arouse considerable latent sympathy, although outright supporters were few and usually inarticulate. Certainly many in Athens and a majority in the villages agreed with the Colonels in detesting Communism, atheism, long hair, and short skirts. The Colonels' dislike for the rich and wellborn, who had been running affairs in Athens, was also widely shared in Greece; and their ambivalence towards the self-made businessman—admirable, but only so long as he knew his place and recognized the superior claims of national and heroic behavior—mirrored the mingled jealousy and admiration Greeks normally reserved for those more successful than themselves in exploiting the possibilities of self-enrichment in the marketplace.

The Colonels demonstrated their attitudes in these matters by launching a vigorous campaign against tax evasion as soon as their power was secure. As a result, during the first eight months, tax income increased by 25 percent.[7] The rich who got caught in the Colonels' net won little or no sympathy from their fellow citizens even when methods of assessment and collection verged on extortion.

But, not surprisingly, a policy of squeezing the rich opened innumerable paths to corruption. Tax collectors demanding more could be bought off. Bribes merely had to be carefully disguised and suitably escalated to match the larger tax bills being presented. But since an arbitrary element entered into almost every decision about back taxes and penalties for tax evasion, the chances for buying new privilege were simply multiplied by the severity of the initial assault on old privilege. Ironically, too, the persons who were best situated to evade taxes were those who had enjoyed similar advantages before. Having access to ready cash was what mattered; and since the Colonels were not interested in initiating large-scale property shifts within the country—indeed as dedicated anti-Communists they regarded such a policy with holy horror—an array of artful tax dodgers soon formed around the new wielders of political power. The naive and fierce initial effort to right injustice thus swiftly faded away into bureaucratic routine, leaving things just

7. C. L. Doumas, "Crisis, Revolution and Military Rule in Greece," *Southern Quarterly* 6 (1968): 269, 278. This figure may have been inflated for propaganda purposes, but there is no doubt that the campaign against tax evaders did bring substantial returns.

as before. But for the first year or so, this result was not yet apparent, and public sentiment cheered the government on in its effort to squeeze more taxes from the rich.

Even the aspect of the Colonels' policies that roused the greatest protest abroad—imprisonment of political opponents and heavy-handed censorship of the press—met with acquiescence. Anathema against heretics was the Orthodox response to disagreement; the Colonels' practice of exiling heretics to small islands, where they lived under police surveillance, was no more than a modern example of that traditional practice. On the other hand, torture of suspects went beyond anything Greek tradition could approve, and for that reason the regime always strove to conceal such acts.

The new military masters of the country were thus able to appeal to a wide spectrum of support in their early days. Certainly, there was no effective resistance within Greece, despite the fact that politicians of every stripe and the entire Athenian upper class were dismayed to find power in the hands of such crude and unknown men. But the majority of the nation, and especially the peasants, rather enjoyed the discomfiture of the old elites, and shared enough of the Colonels' attitudes to remain indifferent to appeals from abroad for active resistance against the new tyranny.

Traditional foci of discontent remained completely quiescent. No stirrings of the old guerrilla spirit in the hill villages could occur, partly because the population pressure in those communities had been so effectually reduced in the preceding decade, and partly because the ideals the Colonels voiced had a special resonance for those very communities, whose hard and heroic way of life was in fact endangered, if not already destroyed, by the forces of modernity the Colonels so deplored. Social radicalism, traditional in the mountain villages, was in fact far more accurately mirrored by the Colonels' initial assault on the rich than by anything Marxist doctrine had to say. Among farmers of the plains, cancellation of debts owed to the Agricultural Bank, decreed in 1968, enhanced the government's acceptability. Indebted peasants welcomed what amounted to a direct gift. Some, who had paid their debts punctually, grumbled at the unfairness—but they were few.

The critical sector of Greek society was in the towns, where so

many newcomers crowded together. The regime was not una-
ware of this, and took steps to ingratiate itself with the wage
earners and salaried groups of the cities by decreeing, from time
to time, across-the-board pay increases for private as well as
public employees. Such increases ran ahead of the rise in the cost
of living, and yet fell short of increases in productivity. What
wage earners perceived, therefore, was a distinct improvement
in their standards of living by gift of the government. This
compensated for the suppression of the right to strike and the
government's high-handed takeover of labor unions. Unions had
never been strong in Greece, and labor leaders, who were always
embroiled with Communists, had never commanded much
working-class loyalty. From the employers' point of view,
acceptance of government-decreed wage escalation was an acceptable alternative to having to face strikes and threats of
strikes that had boiled up so strongly in 1966. Suppression of
strikes, in turn, facilitated the continued upthrust of the GNP;
and this, in its turn, permitted upward wage adjustments and
real increases in living standards.

The principal locus of the new regimes's support, however,
came from the ranks of the army. The government demonstrated
its sympathies by raising pay rates and introducing a multitude
of new perquisites and privileges for the officer corps. Military
standards of living, which had lagged behind civil incomes under
the preceding regimes, now shot ahead. This excited considerable jealousy among the professional classes of Athens, who
could not afford the cars and new houses that suddenly bur-
geoned among army officers.

Having defied the military chain of command in seizing
power, the Colonels initially faced a delicate problem within the
ranks of the army itself. How could they rightfully command
officers senior to themselves? And how prevent a new coup by
some ambitious circle of still more junior officers? This dilemma
was much relieved when King Constantine undertook a counter
coup d'etat in December 1967, summoning his generals to
overthrow the upstarts in Athens. The Colonels, adequately
forewarned, easily forestalled the king's effort to unseat them.
The government allowed the young monarch to leave Greece,
creating a regency to exercise royal power. Papadopoulos and
his colleagues also set out to purge the army of all senior officers

who had been in touch with the king, which meant, in effect, getting rid of all officers senior to themselves in the ranks of the army. Rapid promotion for more junior officers was a not unwelcome by-product of this policy, which created an army (and police force) that was outwardly (and probably inwardly) well satisfied with the new government.

Abroad, the Colonels faced far more intractable problems. European governments and public opinion, soon stimulated by energetic propaganda among Greek emigrés, disapproved of dictatorship and reproached the Greek government for its imprisonment and occasional torture of political opponents. European disapproval took more tangible form in December 1969 when Greece withdrew from the Council of Europe in order to prevent expulsion. The agreement for associating Greece with the European Economic Community was also suspended; and radio broadcasts in the Greek language, especially those coming from Germany and Great Britain, made it a point to disseminate news embarrassing to the Colonels' regime. These foreign broadcasts acquired a large listening audience in Greece as time went by. Their criticism of the government undoubtedly did much to discredit official propaganda.

The United States expressed an initial disapproval of the regime by cancelling scheduled deliveries of a few heavy weapons of war and by letting the post of ambassador remain vacant for almost a year. But when Russian armies invaded Czechoslovakia in 1968, American military planners were able to argue that wanton sacrifice of a potential ally was absurd, and arms shipments were resumed. A new ambassador arrived in 1969 and set about mending fences with the government. This policy reached a climax when Vice-President Spiro Agnew, himself of Greek descent, visited Athens in 1971, and made numerous remarks supportive of the Colonels' regime.

The really critical foreign policy question, however, was Cyprus. A few weeks after the Colonels took power, a new clash between Greeks and Turks induced the government in Ankara to prepare an expeditionary force for dispatch to that troubled island. This was headed off, largely by American and British diplomacy, but only on condition that the Greek government recall most of the army officers Papandreou had sent to Cyprus three years earlier. This humiliating withdrawal rankled; but when Papadopoulos attempted to solve the Cyprus issue by arranging a summit meeting with the prime minister of Turkey, he discovered that summitry was as futile as the nuances of lower-level diplomacy.

Advantages in Cyprus lay increasingly with Ankara. The Turkish community of the island, being a small minority, was compelled to act in concert with the Turkish government. Only so could its survival be assured. The Greeks of the island, on the other hand, were divided more and more sharply between those who continued to agitate for union with Greece and those who found sovereign independence to have charms of its own superior to anything union with Greece could offer.

This division among the Greeks of Cyprus was enormously exacerbated by tensions between Communist and anti-Communist ideologies. Since the 1930s a fairly powerful and well-organized Communist party had existed in Cyprus, enjoying legal toleration under British rule. Between 1955 and 1960, when the struggle for union with Greece had become an armed guerrilla war against the British, the Communists had been compelled to take a back seat to fiery Greek nationalists. It was hard for the Cyprus Communists to oppose a national uprising against British imperialists; but it was even harder to welcome union with Greece, where the Communist party was illegal and where anti-Communist feeling remained high. Independence, which came in 1960, opened a freer field of action to the Cypriot Communists, since Archbishop Makarios, the elected president of the Republic of Cyprus, sought to buttress his authority by cultivating their support. He simultaneously flirted with Moscow in the hope of finding there a counterweight to Ankara's patronage of the Turkish Cypriots.

Such a policy, however, offended the anti-Communist convictions that inspired Colonel Papadopoulos and his fellows. Here was treason to Hellenism staring them in the face, all the more insidious because it wore the garb of the church. Moreover, Makarios tolerated the use of Cyprus as a base by Greek exiles who were seeking to overthrow the military regime in Athens. Tit for tat, the government in Athens decided to support those elements in Cyprus opposed to Makarios. Before Athens had time to organize its sympathizers in Cyprus, the archbishop was easily reelected as president in 1968. The Greek government thereupon set out to revive the armed organization that had so successfully opposed the British, in the hope of thereby changing the balance of opinion within Cyprus by first altering the balance of armed force within the island. Consequently, Greek army officers who had been assigned the task of training the Cypriot National Guard started to patronize a variety of political extremists. In the name of union with Greece, some of them were ready for desperate measures, up to and including attempts against Makarios' life.

Difficulties and disappointments abroad soon made the Colonels' regime less secure at home. The acquiescence that they had been able to command, though widespread at first, was intrinsically fragile. Obedience to orders barked out by a self-appointed master, who, in the name of getting things done, carried over the manners of the drill field into the offices of government, could only be sustained by a compelling sense of emergency. By emphasizing the heroic and Orthodox aspects of Greek tradition, that normally take only a marginal place in everyday life, the regime set out to maintain crisis behavior indefinitely. But when the demand for unity and obedience failed to secure tangible results in the form of victory in Cyprus, such appeals swiftly lost persuasiveness.

Mounting disillusionment intensified a sense of emergency among the self-appointed masters of Greece. Though they felt power slipping from their hands, how to react became increasingly problematic. A policy of concession to civilian attitudes and penchants was one logical alternative. Stronger and more emphatic resort to the manners of the barracks was the other obvious possibility. Advocates of both paths could be found in the inner circles of government; but who stood for what is not clear.

Disagreements among the leaders of the coup had probably existed from the start, but they only became visible in 1971, when almost all of the original circle of conspirators were dismissed from governmental positions in Athens and took up relatively modest military posts in the provinces instead. These moves brought a single man, George Papadopoulos, to supreme authority. This may have reduced infighting and bickering around the seats of power, but it did nothing to solve the long-range difficulties the regime was facing. Eventually, Papadopoulos decided that he would have to broaden the base of his authority by establishing constitutional forms that would legitimate his personal exercise of power.

Efforts in this direction were not new. As early as September 1968, when the regime was still comparatively fresh, the government had promulgated a new constitution for Greece and arranged a plebiscite to approve it. Police pressure achieved a 92 percent affirmative vote, with 22 percent of the voters abstaining. Then, after all the fanfare, key provisions of the new constitution were suspended indefinitely, including those provisions prescribing a civilian administration and guaranteeing civil rights. By 1973, however, Papadopoulos concluded that he ought to dust off the new constitution and put it into operation, after suitable modifications had been contrived to give him a permanent veto authority over the future government of the country. This involved the abolition of the monarchy and the substitution of a president for the king as head of state. Presidential powers were defined in a generous way, tailoring the post to fit Papadopoulos himself. Accordingly, a second referendum in July 1973 made Greece a republic; and in the next month Papadopoulos was sworn in as president. Soon thereafter he appointed a civilian government, headed by none other than Spyros Markezinis, the clever politician of the radical right and one-time idea-man for Field Marshal Papagos.

Disaster swiftly followed. It began when students at the Polytechnic Institute in Athens barricaded themselves inside the school building and defied the government. Improvised radio broadcasts from the Polytechnic roused an electric response throughout Athens, so that within hours a massive crowd of sympathizers appeared in the streets around the school. Police were overwhelmed. Markezinis eventually called on units of the army to batter down the barred gates. Several people were killed and a great many others were bloodied before the soldiers succeeded in dispersing the angry, excited crowds. Altogether, the affair lasted from November 14 to November 17, 1973. By the time it was over, Papadopoulos' claim to popular support was utterly discredited. The Greeks of Athens had again manifested the national capacity for sudden reversal of behavior. Instead of passive submission, as in earlier years, suppressed irritations had suddenly achieved a massive, brief, and passionate, though not very coherent, expression.

Papadopoulos had tried the policy of relaxing military control. The Athenian response showed how dangerous that could be to the regime's most cherished principles. Subversive political ideas obviously had as strong an appeal as ever; bad Greeks still abounded, at least in Athens. Army officers promoted to the top commands by the regime itself concluded that Papadopoulos would have to go. They let the new president know their will, and when he did not hasten to abdicate the field commanders prepared to move their troops towards Athens. As soon as it became clear that his critics did indeed control the main strength of the Greek army, Papadopoulos' hold on the army in Athens crumbled away. Accordingly, on November 25, exactly a week after the Polytechnic demonstration had been suppressed, an armed column surrounded his house and put the erstwhile president under arrest. The generals promptly installed a new, fictitious set of governmental authorities; but real power continued to be exercised from behind the scenes by the field commanders of the Greek armies.

Precedence among the new rulers of Greece was never clearly defined. The most energetic and ruthless advocate of military high-handedness was a hitherto inconspicuous commander of the Greek military police, Brigadier General Dimitrios Ioannides. But Ioannides was only one among a coterie of generals, each of whom kept his own base of power in the form of command over a body of troops stationed, for the most part, in northern Greece. Being a particularly bullheaded person, headquartered in Athens, General Ioannides tended to dominate the scene, but he never controlled the other generals any more than they controlled him. Nevertheless, in most matters, and particularly in foreign affairs, Ioannides was, or seemed to be, the man who mattered most. He used the military police in an unscrupulous way to terrorize opposition and suspected opposition.

As a policeman, Ioannides apparently thought that force or the threat of force was a sovereign remedy for all disagreement. What Greece needed, therefore, was a little more policing, to keep everyone in line. Though this recipe might have worked at home, foreign affairs did not permit any such simple remedy. In all probability, before taking power the new rulers of Greece had thought very little about how to deal with the thorny problem of Cyprus. However, results were what mattered; and to get results, force and faits accomplis seemed obviously superior to endless talk and futile diplomacy. Cyprus was already near the boiling point, as the rival Greek factions conspired vigorously against one another. The new activism—and greater stupidity— that prevailed in Athens after Papadopoulos' overthrow probably acted as a catalyst in this situation, although exactly who precipitated the attempted coup d'etat against Makarios on July 15, 1974, has never been made clear. Athens almost surely had a hand in it, although Cypriot firebrands may have acted without waiting for instructions, or even in defiance of instructions, from the Greek capital.

For a brief while the coup seemed successful. Makarios was not captured, but he had to go into hiding while a new president took power in Nicosia. Then on July 20, just five days after the coup and before the new government of Cyprus got around to proclaiming union with Greece, the situation was abruptly transformed by the landing of a Turkish expeditionary force which had been marshalled on the coast opposite Cyprus. The Greeks of Cyprus were completely unprepared to resist the invading Turks. Athens was equally unready, and could not possibly improvise a suitably powerful expeditionary force capable of crossing the intervening distance and coming to the aid of the Greek Cypriots. What could be done was to order general mobilization against Turkey; and this was undertaken at once.

The prospect of an all-out conflict between Greece and Turkey called American and British diplomats into action; but their efforts to cool tempers and forestall open war between the supposed NATO allies was not really decisive. What happened instead was that generals in command of the Greek armies along the frontier refused to obey orders from Athens to attack the Turks by crossing the Evros river in Thrace. Like generals everywhere they undoubtedly felt that their forces were not quite ready; perhaps, too, some or all of them doubted the feasibility of a march on Constantinople, which General Ioannides in Athens thought was the only appropriate riposte to the Turkish invasion of Cyprus.

Once the generals in the field refused to obey orders from Athens, the morale and cohesion of the Athenian government cracked wide open. With a revulsion of feeling that swiftly became all but universal, the demoralized remnant of the military regime decided that the only thing to do was to call on Constantine Karamanlis for help. Only he, with the lingering prestige of his long tenure in office, seemed likely to be able to negotiate a settlement with the Turks and thereby extricate the Greeks from their cruel dilemma. Hour by hour the Turkish troops were advancing in Cyprus, driving Greeks ahead of them and slaughtering others who fell into their hands. A fait accompli of a totally different character from any that General Ioannides and his fellows had contemplated was occurring before their eyes; and there was nothing the Greeks in Greece or the Greeks in Cyprus could do to prevent it.

For a few short hours, the Athens government, in hope of assuring a formal military veto over civilian authority, tried to dictate terms to Karamanlis. But the ex–prime minister was completely unwilling to bargain, and the Greek military leaders soon lost the will to resist. Consequently, on July 24, 1974, Karamanlis returned from his exile in France and became prime minister at once. He was received as a savior, and announced his intention of restoring legal, democratic government to the country as swiftly as possible. In the meantime, the crisis in Cyprus had been temporarily relieved when a cease-fire halted the Turkish advance on July 22. By that time, however, the Turks had already won control of a substantial part of the island, and had brought most, though not all, of the Moslem Cypriots within their lines. This, in all probability, was all that the Turkish government had planned to accomplish when it decided to send the expeditionary force to Cyprus.

Three weeks later, August 14–15, the Turks briefly resumed active operations. This appears to have been aimed at rescuing some remaining Turkish enclaves from harassment by the angry and vengeful Greek Cypriots. When fighting ended, the Turks held about 40 percent of the island. They had partitioned Cyprus despite the will of the Greek majority and had done so in a way that favored their fellow Moslems disproportionately. Constituting about 18 percent of the island's population, the Turks of Cyprus now controlled nearly half—and the richer, better-developed half—of the whole island. Makarios returned to office, but now governed only a part of his former domain.

Anger and chagrin reigned in Greece, and it became fashionable to blame the United States for what had happened. The

American government, Greeks believed, had favored the Turks. Whatever role the Greek government may have had in precipitating the crisis in Cyprus was hushed up and soon forgotten. After all, Karamanlis' regime had no responsibility for the events of mid-July, 1974; whereas the influence of the United States in the eastern Mediterranean was an ongoing reality—before, during, and after the disaster that had come to Greek hopes and expectations in Cyprus.

Blaming the Americans was all the more necessary because it was clearly suicidal for Greeks to blame one another for what had occurred. Karamanlis could not lead a purge against collaborators without endangering his own supporters, who, in varying degrees, had made deals with the military regime in order to retain their wealth and power. Moreover, it seemed needful to restrain civil disagreement in order to present a common front to the Turks. Recrimination over events of the dictatorship was therefore kept to a minimum. Only the most prominent leaders were punished. Greek army officers, no matter how sympathetic they had been to the Colonels' regime, were urgently needed to man the nation's defenses against the Turkish danger. Political inquisition and purges of the army were therefore postponed; and when they came, in the course of 1975 and 1976, dismissals from active service were mingled with normal promotions and retirements in such a way as to avoid head-on challenge of the will and collective morale of the officer corps. Army officers and civilian authorities agreed, in effect, that it was best to let bygones be bygones so as to get on with urgent current tasks.

The first item of public business, once active hostilities in Cyprus ended, was to arrange for elections. The climate of opinion reacted strongly against the way the Colonels had tried to enforce unanimity. Karamanlis went along by legalizing the Communist party for the first time since 1947, and allowing a new socialist movement, headed by Andreas Papandreou, to organize itself unhindered. This policy was probably facilitated by the fact that the Greek Communist party had split into mutually hostile halves back in 1968. One faction—Communists of the Exterior—remained loyal to the ideals of international Communism as defined in Moscow; their rivals—Communists of the Interior—repudiated foreign connections and emphasized the more radical, libertarian, and anarchic aspects of Marxism.

Obviously a fragmented left and a center deprived of its radical wing improved Karamanlis' own chances of electoral success; and so in fact it turned out. When the election took place in November 1974, Karamanlis' party won 54 percent of the popular vote and 70 percent of the seats in Parliament. A succession party to the Center Union, led by George Mavros (George Papandreou had died in 1968, and his funeral constituted the first public manifestation of the fragility of the Colonels' popularity in Athens), came in second, with 20 percent of the vote and 20 percent of the seats. Andreas Papandreou's socialists were third with 14 percent of the vote and 6 percent of the seats; and the two Communist factions divided the remaining 12 percent of the vote, but won only 4 percent of the seats. The elections were conducted without the sort of police pressure that had created such resentment in 1961. Karamanlis thus attained a hold on power far more secure and unquestioned than he had enjoyed at any previous time.

Another important change also strengthened Karamanlis, to wit, the disappearance of the Palace as a rival center of power. Despite King Constantine's record of opposition to the Colonels, there was no effective move to bring him back. A plebiscite overwhelmingly endorsed the republican form of government, and a new constitution reduced the powers of the president to merely ceremonial proportions.

As a result, in 1975 and 1976 Greece attained a comparatively stable political life. To be sure, acute friction with Turkey continued. The Greeks could not forget Cyprus and resisted any ratification of the de facto division of the island. Active negotiation, however, was entrusted to the Cypriots themselves, even though everyone realized that a lasting settlement could only be achieved if both Athens and Ankara also concurred.

Months of immobility in Cyprus did not permit tempers to cool very noticeably, for a second Greek-Turkish conflict blew up in the Aegean. The issue was how rights to the seabed should be defined. Greece claimed possession of the entire Aegean on the strength of the way Greek islands were scattered throughout that sea; the Turks asserted that since the Aegean was an international waterway, they had the right to explore the seabed for oil and other valuables.

The dispute was far from academic because, in 1974, oil had in fact been discovered in the Aegean off the island of Thassos.

Since both Greece and Turkey had to import oil, the possibility of finding a source of this valuable fuel close at hand and within their own jurisdictions was a matter of real importance to both countries. Neither was ready, given the inflamed state of feeling already existing between them, to concede anything to the other. Yet there was an element of pretense in these confrontations. Each government was playing to the gallery at home; and both clearly recognized that an all-out war, using modern means of destruction that NATO planners had so lavishly provided for each of them, would be mutually disastrous.

Karamanlis did what he could to mend his fences with the Americans and with western European governments as well. The agreement for associating Greece with the European Economic Community, suspended under the Colonels, was renewed in 1976; and in the same year the Greek government concluded a new agreement with the United States for American use of military bases in Crete and Rhodes. Previous arrangements had been cancelled in 1974 in the white heat of public resentment against the American role in Cyprus; and the terms Karamanlis offered in 1976 were notably less generous to the Americans. Nevertheless, the negotiation demonstrated a willingness to forgive and forget past bitterness.

Domestically, the new Greek regime made no very significant changes. The Colonels had allowed private enterprise—both Greek and foreign—relatively free scope; and this accorded exactly with Karamanlis' own predilections. The political upheaval of 1974 had hurt the Greek economy, for tourists stayed away exactly at a time when a world depression of unusual intensity settled in. By 1976, however, this setback to the economic growth of Greece seemed to have come to an end. A record tourist influx was certain to help the ever-precarious balance of payments; and the possibility of resuming the galloping process of urbanization, which had carried Greece so far away from its peasant roots within a single generation, seemed open once more.

As of the summer of 1976, obstacles to the further economic development of Greece seemed less than at any other time since World War II. Obviously, sudden disaster may intervene if war should come; and in the Balkans, the Greek-Turkish friction is not the sole conceivable trigger for war. Time will tell what happens next; and only a foolish man would venture prediction, given the numerous surprises of the past and the Greek capacity for sudden changes of collective behavior in response to novel circumstances. Yet one can be sure of this: whatever the twists and turns of Greek public life in the years ahead, it will continue to be conditioned, as in the past, by the subtle force of inherited tradition and attitudes. The village past may be dying, but much survives. A sampling of that life and how it has changed in the past generation constitutes the theme of the next chapter.

Four

Village Experiences

Each of the two-thousand odd villages of Greece has a character and local history of its own, and the various regions of the country, as defined by geography and history, also differ markedly one from another. This means that any small sample of Greek village experience since 1945, such as that I am able to provide here, will be defective from a statistical point of view. It so happens, for example, that none of the six villages I have observed sent substantial numbers off to Germany in the 1960s, even though other communities only a few miles away almost emptied out during those same years. Hence the six villages described in this chapter cannot be treated as symptomatic of all that has happened in rural Greece since 1945. Each community faced changing conditions in its own way; and the differences are perhaps more striking than the uniformities. Yet all six have what can properly be called a success story behind them, at least when measured by the dismal prospects and seemingly insoluble difficulties of 1947. That basic success in resolving human needs, shared with all the other villages of Greece to some degree, is what sustained the comparative calm of the public life of Greece since World War II as against the far more difficult years that followed the conclusion of World War I.

The initial selection of these villages for study was largely accidental. Early in 1947, the Twentieth Century Fund sent a team of three persons to Greece in the hope of providing the

American public with background for the expected debate over aid to Greece.[1] At that time the guerrilla movement was expanding rapidly through the mountainous regions of Greece. A central purpose of the Twentieth Century Fund team, of which I was a member, was to hear both sides: and this involved finding ways to penetrate hill villages where the guerrilla power was based. Kerasia and Kotta came within my ken as a result of this effort and, indeed, I first came to understand the role of food-deficit villages in providing manpower for the guerrilla bands of Greece as a result of these visits.

Access to villages of the plains was far easier; and here personal connections through American institutions led me to visit Old Corinth and New Eleftherohori (now renamed Methone) in 1947. Later, in 1956, when I returned to Greece with the intention of writing a book on what American aid programs had accomplished in their first ten years of operation,[2] I returned to these same four villages; and, having now achieved a grasp of the political and economic axis of traditional Greek society as between regions of food surplus and food deficit, I sought to balance a hill village against a plains village within each of the three contrasting regions where the first four villages were located. Accordingly, in 1956, I visited Kardamili and Lofiscos for the first time. I entered both communities cold, without any prior personal connection or confidence-inspiring introduction. The result, naturally, was that the inner workings of these two communities remained hidden from me; and even after subsequent visits in 1966 and 1976, it remains true that the villages I first visited in 1947, when strangers were rare and times were very hard, remained far more open in answering what must often have seemed silly or impertinent questions from a stranger than was true in either Kardamili or Lofiscos.

Nevertheless, to have the same observer able to look back on thirty years of change within four villages and twenty years of change in two others is sufficiently uncommon to make it seem worthwhile to record here what impressed me during my visits.

Moreover, village life changed fundamentally during these

1. The team findings were published as Frank Smothers et al., *Report on the Greeks* (New York: Twentieth Century Fund, 1947).

2. Published as William H. McNeill, *Greece: American Aid in Action, 1947–56* (New York: Twentieth Century Fund, 1957).

years. Local isolation broke down and old-fashioned peasant patterns of behavior altered in response to new urban-based national and international ideas. This gives such observations additional significance, if, as seems likely, this process is a one-way street. Assuredly, communities once having entered into more intimate contacts with the wide world and having begun to harbor ideas and aspirations propagated through national and international mass media cannot revert easily and automatically to older localism and autonomy. Even if the new network of communication were to fail and local survival became necessary once again, so many of the older peasant ways have been eroded in these postwar decades, that a new and presumably different structure would probably emerge, and only at severe human cost of impoverishment and personal frustration.

The Guerrilla War and Its Aftermath, 1947–50

In normal times, villages of the plains exported food. A fortiori, such communities usually produced enough grain and other foodstuffs to sustain the village population itself, though inequities in landholdings and the desire to sell as much as possible in order to command other goods and services sometimes meant that not everyone in such villages actually had enough to eat. In the early months of 1947, however, times were far from normal in Greece. The market system of the country had almost broken down. Fertilizers and spare parts had been unavailable for years; wheeled vehicles had all but disappeared, and draught animals had become scarce. Forcible or semiforcible requisitioning from plains villages had occurred throughout the years of Axis occupation, often erratically and inequitably as between different households. Political violence was widespread, and fear of such violence cast a shadow that reached much further than actual beatings, murders, or acts of spoliation.

Consequently, village life and productivity were at a very low ebb. Even in the plains food resources were dubiously adequate to feed the local population. Only by hiding what one had, and hoping that no one from outside would find and seize it, could a family expect to escape hunger from harvest to harvest. Merely having enough to eat excited anxiety. At any time a tattling neighbor might provoke a visit from hungry, armed, and impatient men, ready and eager to seize by force whatever was not proffered willingly.

New Eleftherohori in Macedonia suffered all these problems in the winter of 1947 when I first visited it. The village stands in a fertile, rolling landscape at the foot of Mount Olympos, facing directly on the Thermaic Gulf across from the port of Salonika, some fifty miles distant as the crow flies. The name of the village means "New Free Village," and was a reminder of the community's past. (It has since been officially renamed Methone, for the village is near the site of an ancient settlement of that name.) Before 1912, the village lands were owned and cultivated by Turks. When the Greek army came north in the course of the First Balkan War, the inhabitants fled and the land fell vacant, only to be occupied by Greek woodcutters and itinerant carpenters who had previously lived high on the slopes of Mount Olympos in two villages called Eleftherohori ("Free Village") and Katopygi ("Lower Spring").

The newcomers never occupied all the cultivable land of New Eleftherohori. Manpower was short, since the newly liberated Greeks of Macedonia had to pay for their freedom by being conscripted into the ranks of the Greek army. The land was malarial as well; and woodcutters from the mountains must have found it difficult to accumulate the necessary capital— plows, draught animals, seed—to keep the previously cultivated area under crops. There was more than enough land for all comers, and each family took what it could use, without formal title or exact survey.

When peace returned to Greece in 1923, the country faced the question of how to accommodate more than a million refugees from Asia Minor. With help from the League of Nations, the government set out to settle as many of them as possible on lands vacated by the Turks. As far as New Eleftherohori was concerned, this meant that in 1927 surveyors arrived and divided the village land into allotments of 27 stremmata (6.6 acres). This was the amount of land officially estimated to be sufficient to sustain a single family; and a family was defined as a man and wife together with any children they might have.

By the time government agents got around to assigning the

lands of New Eleftherohori the Greek squatters had been in possession for fifteen years. It was therefore decided that they should be given allotments too, so only land left over could be assigned to refugees. As a result, when the ground rules for distribution of allotments had been made clear, all boys of marriageable age in the community hastily found wives so as to qualify for an allotment. By doing so, most families attained legal possession of about as much land as they had previously been able to cultivate. With the tools available, 27 stremmata was in fact about all that a single man could farm by himself. Hence, the old settlers from Mount Olympos did not feel any particular resentment at seeing about half the village lands assigned to refugees from Pontus in Asia Minor. The refugees received identical allotments, but erected their houses at a slight remove from the cluster of old settlers' dwellings. The Greeks from Pontus seemed wild and uncouth to the old settlers, and for a generation the two groups kept their distance within the village, though the uniformity of their economic status and shared vicissitudes of life made this fissure unimportant, except when it came to such things as intermarriage between the two groups.

On an allotment of only 6.6 acres, it was in fact possible for a family to raise enough wheat to feed itself and have enough for next year's seed. But in most seasons there was little left over once these essentials had been attended to. In other words, the land settlement of 1927 practically compelled the inhabitants of New Eleftherohori to become subsistence farmers, and this is what happened in the 1930s, though the village always exported some food to pay for clothes and tools, and for various small embellishments of life, so far as they could be afforded. But bare survival in the 1930s had a time-bomb built into it. Youthful married couples began to have children, and in such numbers that the total population of the village almost doubled in twenty years, rising from approximately 450 in 1927 to 812 in 1947.

As the children grew older, the question of how they would make a living became more and more pressing. Division of the family plot among several children was plainly suicidal: no one could live on half or some other fraction of the amount of land that had been assigned to each family in 1927. The dowry system meant that a young man who could expect to inherit half an allotment could marry and live as well as his parents only as long as his wife brought with her an equal share of land. But, in effect, if a family had more than two children, something else had to be done. Alternative careers, outside the village, would have to be found. Otherwise the level of life prevailing in the village could not be sustained; loss of status and perpetual hunger, or even the risk of actual starvation, would clearly ensue.

Children born in the 1920s grew up during World War II. In most families, they were the eldest of a long line of siblings, and knew, as well as their parents, that either they or their younger siblings would have to leave home if living standards were to be maintained. But jobs in town were unattainable in a time of economic disorganization. For such young people, the brightest spark of hope was that offered by EAM/ELAS, with its promises of a better life after the war. As a result, about twenty young men left New Eleftherohori to serve in ELAS ranks. Only three returned to the village after 1945, for in truth they had nothing to come back to. During the war, opinion within the village was about evenly divided between families that sympathized with EAM and others who distrusted the leftists.

The changes on the national scene, referred to in Chapter 3, were registered in New Eleftherohori by abrupt reversals between EAM dominance, 1944–45, and dominance by the right, 1945–47. Only a few villagers ever committed themselves irrevocably to one side or the other, by carrying arms or acting in some public leadership position either for or against EAM. The majority remained passive, hoping to avoid being singled out as an enemy by one party or the other, and thereby incurring the risk of crippling confiscation of whatever precious store of food and other property had been husbanded through the hard war years.

When first I arrived in the village, no one was sure of his neighbor. Food was scant. Even an ordinary meal had become a furtive occasion. A knock at the door meant a scurry to put bread and cheese out of sight lest a stranger see what the family had to eat. An exaggerated report of abundance, after all, was likely to lead to demands for contributions to either or both of the armed camps then disputing control of Greece. To be sure, the right was somewhat precariously in command. Armed men patrolled the village at night, keeping a wary eye on known or suspected leftists. The gendarme post, located at one edge of the village, was nervously alert, for only a few days before our arrival, guerrillas had plundered an UNRRA storehouse that had been set up in the village. The raiders made off with only a few mule-loads of food; the rest of what had been in the warehouse was pillaged and carefully hidden by the villagers while the gendarmes went chasing after the guerrillas. Some fifteen persons from the village were arrested in the aftermath of this raid, on suspicion of having helped the guerrillas reach their goal; one of them was executed.

Cold darkness enveloped the village at night; fear was close at hand all the time. Hopelessness about the future daunted almost every spirit. No escape from the trap created by too many children for the available fertile land seemed possible. I remember how bitterly a man, introduced to me as the best farmer of the village, explained how he had tried fertilizer before the war and found that it did indeed increase wheat yields on his land; but when he sold what he could spare from his crop at the support price that was then maintained by the Greek government (even though it was above world levels), the interest on the debt he had incurred for the fertilizer cancelled out everything he had gained, and made him, in fact, a little worse off than he would have been without having incurred the debt in the first place. Only if weather were good, he explained, did fertilizer increase the yield enough to pay back the loan plus interest, and leave something over. In a middling or bad year, the borrower hurt himself. Since that was too great a risk for a poor man to run, he had given up using fertilizer, even though he knew very well how it could increase the production of his land.

Such experience meant that intensification of agricultural production seemed as hopeless as finding jobs in town. There was no escape: the ancient brutality of famine, pestilence, and war seemed the only way of adjusting population to available resources, and this no one could welcome. Yet in the early months of 1947, the village seemed on the verge of being engulfed in exactly that kind of disaster.

The guerrillas subsequently returned once or twice to New Eleftherohori, but the band that had formed on Mount Olympos was soon compelled to withdraw to a region nearer the frontier, and New Eleftherohori was therefore not evacuated. Instead its young men (except for a handful who joined the guerrillas) were drafted into the Greek National Army. This relieved them, for the time being, of having to face the problem of what to do at home. Gradually, the acute uncertainty that reigned in the early months of 1947 subsided, so that, when the guerrilla war ended in 1949, sentiment within the village was sufficiently relaxed to allow speedy reconciliation between rival political factions. The critical act came in 1950 when the president of the village, a committed man of the right, asked the gendarmes to release two village boys who had been arrested after returning from serving with the guerrillas. He did so despite the fact that his own son had been killed in the war; and when the gendarmes decided to release the two suspects this sealed the political reconciliation within the village effectively and lastingly.

By 1950, the worst was over; few had been killed; and though the old dilemma of how to find a decent living for extra children was as pressing as ever, new possibilities had begun to dawn, however faintly. Where bleak hopelessness had formerly prevailed, there now seemed to be some chance of escape, given enough hard work and self-denial. Easier credit terms offered by the Agricultural Bank made use of fertilizer practicable, and the farmers of the village already knew what this could accomplish for them. In addition, a bus service made it possible to send village boys to a secondary school located in Katerini, a nearby small town; and since tuition was free, the other costs of education—bus fares, books, paper—came within the range of every family in the village, even if such costs might require skimping on other expenditures.

Secondary education led to a job behind a desk. Of course, no one could be sure that such jobs would be available after the years of schooling had been completed. But one could always hope, and hope made life worthwhile and provided each family with a practicable strategy for maintaining existing standards of living, even when there were five or six children to provide for. As a result, by 1956 when I next visited New Eleftherohori, no fewer than thirty-six boys from the village were attending the gymnasium (classical secondary school) and a few had graduated already. Of the graduates, not all had found suitable work in town; but some had made it, and those three or four who were

still looking for white-collar jobs on the strength of their school
certificates expected to find something eventually. Life was still
hard and precarious: only the clever and lucky could count on
success. But things were no longer hopeless. Every boy in the
village who could qualify for secondary schooling had embraced
the newly glimpsed opportunity with the energy of desperation.

The second plains village I visited in 1947 was Old Corinth.
As the name implies, this village is located on the site of the
ancient city of Corinth, immediately adjacent to the towering
mass of Acrocorinth, with its extraordinary Venetian fortifications. After the opening of a canal across the Isthmus of Corinth
in 1893, the commercial functions for which the ancient city was
famed shifted to New Corinth, located about five miles away,
alongside the gulf and adjacent to one end of the new canal. Old
Corinth therefore remained, as it had been in Turkish times, no
more than a village, although it was almost twice the size of New
Eleftherohori, having a population of about 1,530 in 1947.

Unlike in New Eleftherohori, no governmental action had intervened to change the way inheritance and marriages across
unnumbered generations distributed property among the inhabitants of Old Corinth. The result was a far more complex
socioeconomic pattern than anything in the north, where every
family faced essentially the same situation, the only variable
being the number of children who had to be somehow freed from
dependence on the land. Old Corinth, on the other hand, was
dominated by a class of substantial farmers. The largest landowner possessed 200 stremmata (49.4 acres); but this was
exceptional. Others with as little as 25 stremmata (6.1 acres)
were counted as substantial property owners. About one-fifth of
the families owned between 25 and 10 stremmata (6.1 to 2.47
acres) and another fifth owned less than 10 stremmata. One
hundred families were without any land at all, and lived as wage
earners working for the substantial farmers, or as laborers for an
American-managed archaeological excavation that had been in
progress at Old Corinth for many years before the war but
which had not yet resumed work in 1947.

It may seem strange to count the owner of a mere 6 acres as a
substantial farmer; but in Old Corinth this was not unrealistic.
Currants constituted, as they had since the seventeenth century,
the major cash crop. Currants are made from a special kind of

grape, and require intensive labor so that more than two or three acres planted with currant vines could not easily be tended by a single family. Anyone with 25 stremmata in currants had to hire extra labor at critical times of the year when the vines needed cultivation, spraying, or harvesting. The landless or nearly landless of the village were accustomed from time immemorial to provide that labor on terms negotiated personally between employer and employee each time such help was needed. Moreover, once the currants had been harvested and turned over to one of the two cooperatives that processed and sold currants, there was further wage work to be done. The fruit first had to be turned on drying racks until the sun had evaporated natural juices. After that, the dried currants had to be stripped from their stems, graded, and packaged for shipment abroad.

Through 1943 a more or less satisfactory market for Old Corinth's currants continued to exist, since the German army was glad to take possession of such a concentrated and portable food. Thereafter, sale at a satisfactory price ceased, since delivery to distant markets became impossible. However, land planted to vines could not easily be shifted to grain, even when currants had ceased to bring in their accustomed returns. Rather than uproot the vines, therefore, the farmers held on in hope that the market would soon revive. The two cooperatives went bankrupt. This was serious, for the co-ops had performed vital marketing functions, bringing into the village the poisonous Paris green required for spraying, and shipping the packaged currants out. As supplies of Paris green ran out, currant production sagged; and marketing descended to the barter level. Individual families set out to exchange currants for such vital commodities as grain or olive oil, both of which Old Corinth was accustomed to import. Wage contracts, too, were often made in terms of commodities rather than money. The economic structure of the village survived, therefore; but as production diminished and the awkwardness of contractual exchanges increased, everyone was worse off. Uncertainty as to the future and worry about where next month's or next year's food would come from correspondingly increased.

This kind of economic dislocation stoked the fires of political antagonism within the community. Not surprisingly, during the war EAM commanded wide support among those who worked for wages. Correspondingly, the class which traditionally dominated village life, the substantial farmers, being employers of labor, gravitated to the right. Because class interests clashed in Old Corinth, political polarity within the village had a bitterness that was entirely absent in New Eleftherohori.

During the last months of 1944 and early 1945, an EAM committee controlled the village, and thoroughly frightened the village property-holders even though the committee made no effort to redistribute land ownership. What EAM did challenge was the traditional way in which labor contracts were arranged through secretive private negotiation. Instead, anyone wishing to hire help was supposed to employ the next man listed on a public roll of job-seekers, whoever he might be and whatever the personal relations existing between the employer and his prospective employee. This deeply offended employers; and since there was little work to be done anyway, the system did not really help the poor. Other aspects of EAM's management of affairs, for instance, the collection of oil and other food from those judged able to part with such precious possessions, also contributed to fueling a fierce reaction when events in Athens led to EAM's overthrow in Old Corinth. Several wartime deaths among the villagers, some inflicted by Germans, some by ELAS, exacerbated political tensions. But it was impossible to get a clear picture of what had happened within the village because the rival versions as told by supporters of the different factions were wildly discrepant.

Yet in spite of the potential class war in Old Corinth, the situation of the village was in other respects less critical than that of New Eleftherohori. First of all, Old Corinth was situated far away from any area where guerrilla bands were operating in 1947. Consequently, political fears and hopes were hypothetical, aimed less at existing circumstances than at what might happen if Communists should come to power. Moreover, bruised hopelessness, so prevalent in New Eleftherohori, was absent from Old Corinth. The landowners of the village, after all, needed only to retain what they already possessed to be able to look forward to a satisfactory existence along traditional lines; and the landless class was at least free of the fear of losing status—a fear which haunted the allotment holders of New Eleftherohori all the time. In other words, a very old, deep-rooted social hierarchy prevailed in Old Corinth. Individuals and families might rise and fall, but the village could always be expected to accommodate rich and poor, the fortunate and the unfortunate. No structural crisis seemed to confront the community as a whole, even if life for the poorest in the village was becoming nearly desperate.

Everyone grumbled, to be sure. The rich blamed the poor for being lazy and unwilling to work, and the poor blamed the rich for selfishness and being unwilling to pay a proper wage. Yet hostility was modulated by the constant readiness of both sides to conclude short-term personal contracts, buying and selling labor as the needs of the moment might require. This meant that however strongly a spokesman might denounce the other class, he was always ready to make an exception of those persons with whom he might hope to make a deal sometime soon. Class war could not assume real fervor under such circumstances. Personal links between employers and employees were just too manifold and intimate.

Finally, everyone in Old Corinth knew of ways in which the productivity of village agriculture could be increased. Thirty irrigation wells had been sunk before the war, but spare parts for the pumps were lacking in 1947 and fuel for those pumps that were still in working order was seldom available. Hence irrigation had almost stopped, but the possibility of using artificial water supplies to raise fruits and vegetables for the Athens market (a mere seventy miles away) was universally recognized. Spokesmen for both left and right agreed that a proper solution to village problems depended on irrigation. Other possibilities— use of fertilizers and tractor cultivation, for instance—were also familiar, though no one thought that these would do as much for the village as irrigation.

The difference in social structure between Old Corinth and New Eleftherohori was typical of a general difference between "Old Greece," that is, that part of the country that had been liberated from the Turks early in the nineteenth century, and "New Greece," acquired for the most part in the period from 1912 to 1918. Thessaly, acquired in 1881, belongs with New Greece in the sense that large-scale governmental intervention in the twentieth century reassigned land ownership on egalitarian principles so that the village social hierarchy flattened out almost completely.

Nothing of the kind happened in northern hill villages, however, where Greeks had lived immemorially. There, as in Old Corinth, rules of marriage and inheritance governed the distribution of property rights. The result was to establish a closely graded hierarchy of wealth. The difference was that in the hills almost all the inhabitants of a village were in the labor-selling class. Lacking sufficient local employment, they had to look for work outside the village, with the fateful consequences for Greek society as a whole that I have already explored.

The two hill villages I visited in 1947 conformed to this pattern. The more southerly of them, Kerasia, is located on Mount Pelion, about six air miles from the port of Volos. It lies on the northern slope of the mountain where exposure to the cold winds of winter makes it impossible to raise olives such as adorn the protected southern slopes of Mount Pelion, where a cluster of relatively prosperous villages exists. The north slope, by contrast, can scarcely be farmed at all. Shallow patches of soil erode rapidly if put under crops. The villagers of Kerasia had once been shepherds. As such they looked down upon the plowing peasants, whose back-breaking toil and subservience (until 1881) to Turkish masters compared unfavorably with the freedom of the mountain heights and the leisure of the shepherd's life.

In wintertime the shepherd community of Kerasia occupied a spot at the edge of the Thessalian plain at a place where a stream debouches from a ravine and provides a convenient water supply. Kerasia's sheep pastured in winter on land belonging to a plains village named Kanalia. Relations between the two communities were normally strained, because the sheep, expected to graze only on wasteland and fallow fields, were constantly tempted to invade the winter wheat where even a brief period of unrestrained nibbling could wreak lasting damage upon the harvest. Kerasia did have some lowland of its own. In particular a small area of cultivable ground formed by the stream's delta lay within the bounds assigned to Kerasia; but the shepherds of the mountain cared little for such land. Three village families took legal title to all of it in 1905, without provoking any special protest. Free men did not yearn to work in the fields; and when some of the villagers began to cultivate the delta land, the others pitied rather than envied them.

By 1947 the social structure of the village had been pressed into new shapes by a series of collisions with ecological limits. First of all, between the wars shepherding proved inadequate. Population grew and pasture shrank because in the plains the Kanalia villagers began to abandon the practice of fallowing their fields every second year. With improved cultivation they could keep more land under wheat, and thus increase their crops. But in doing so they deprived Kerasia of the best of its customary winter pasture. This seriously hurt the interests of the shepherds of Kerasia, but resort to force was effectually fore-closed by the fact that the law was clearly on the side of the plains villagers. The armed authority of the Greek government, in case of need, stood ready to back up the plainsmen's property rights in their land.

The scale of sheep-herding, therefore, had to be cut back to fit the amount of winter pasture still available. Casual labor on public works and the like took up some of the slack; tillage of what cultivable soil there was within the village bounds of Kerasia was intensified, making the three families that had taken possession of the delta land the wealthiest in the village. But the most promising alternative to shepherding was woodcutting and charcoal burning. This took little capital—axe, shovel, and donkey to carry the charcoal to market in Volos was all anyone needed. Moreover, charcoal commanded a ready sale in town, where it was used both for cooking and for space heating in winter. Nevertheless, reliance on woodcutting was ecologically destructive. Trees grow slowly on the north slope of Mount Pelion at best; and once the mountainside had been cleared of wood, destructive erosion set in. By the end of the 1930s, therefore, the villagers found themselves trapped once more. There was not enough wood remaining for them to live as woodcutters and charcoal burners much longer.

The war years were very hard in Kerasia; and the villagers, for the most part, sympathized with EAM. I could not find out how many of their young men had served in ELAS; but a good many undoubtedly did. The major disaster of the war, however, was the destruction of Upper Kerasia by the Germans in 1943, in retaliation for some act of violence against the Occupation regime. Upper Kerasia had been the villagers' real home, where they spent the summer months, breathed the mountain air, pastured their sheep on the heights, and enjoyed the freedom Greek mountaineers cherished. The village I visited in 1947 was merely a place of winter refuge, where a demeaning dependence on the masters of the plains was the inescapable condition of life. To have their mountain homes rendered uninhabitable was therefore a great blow, materially and psychologically. After the war, the Greek government stepped in to forbid the reconstruction of Upper Kerasia, and, in the early months of 1947, army and police authorities issued an order to the effect that no one would be allowed to go up to the heights in the coming spring, despite the fact that this was where the village pasturelands and woodlands were situated.

There was, to be sure, a reason for the government's policy. Late in 1946 three veterans of ELAS, native to Kerasia, appeared on Mount Pelion, having returned from Yugoslavia. They summoned the villagers to renew the armed struggle, and had little difficulty in attracting some forty boys and young men from Kerasia and a few similarly situated communities. The ruins of the upper village became the guerrilla encampment. Thereafter, the lower village found itself in the interesting position of falling by day within the jurisdiction of a Greek army detachment stationed at Kanalia, some three or four miles out into the plain; whereas at night the guerrillas came down from the heights above and took control of the community. Not surprisingly, the risks inherent in such a situation had begun to destroy village solidarity. A few weeks before the plebiscite of September 1946 a band of rightist bullyboys came to Kerasia, searched out EAM sympathizers, beat them up, and burnt a few houses. Shortly thereafter the new guerrilla band formed in the upper village, and this emboldened leftists within the village to take revenge by burning a few houses belonging to rightists.

At the time we first visited Kerasia, March 1947, everyone actively known to sympathize with the right had departed from the village, taking refuge either in Volos or with the army encampment in Kanalia down the road. Consequently the dominant tone of the village had become leftist, though in fact only a few bolder spirits really chose to commit themselves openly in conversation with strangers, and the majority certainly cared nothing at all for political ideologies. Even the professed and vocal leftists of the village freely admitted that they had voted for the return of the king in September 1946 (after the rightist raid), just to keep out of trouble. What made the situation intolerable was the fact that the presence of rival armed establishments so close by made the pursuit of ordinary occupations quite impossible. If a man went to the hills to cut wood, the soldiers beat him for consorting with the guerrillas, as, in fact, he would have to do to be able to come and go. But unless the villagers were free to use what scanty property they had at their disposal up the mountain, how could they survive at all?

Caught thus between the upper and the nether millstone, life in Kerasia was truly desperate. The impasse did not, in fact, long continue. A few weeks after our visit, the Greek army ordered Kerasia evacuated. The villagers were sent to a refugee camp on the outskirts of Volos where they spent the rest of the war years. This deprived the guerrilla band of an important source of supply, for when we visited Kerasia the band was getting some of its daily food from the lower village, where a covert but effective committee structure existed to assess and gather contributions from individual families for the band's support.

As long as this system of requisitioning prevailed, the effect within the village was to compel everyone to help support the sons of those who had taken arms and joined the guerrillas on the mountain. Obviously, any family that was hard pressed to find food for a grown son could solve the difficulty by encouraging or permitting him to join up. Richer neighbors and families with whom for one reason or another relations were strained, could thus be forced to contribute to the support of a family that had a son under arms among the guerrillas. This kind of calculation, building upon the romance associated with outlaw life, made recruitment into guerrilla ranks from Kerasia relatively easy.

Nevertheless, not all the members of the band camped in Upper Kerasia were from the village itself. The commander, who went by the nom de guerre of Captain Dimitrov (a provocatively Bulgarianized form of his given name, Dimitrios) had come down from Mount Olympos with a few followers late in 1946. Only after his arrival had the local band on Mount Pelion attained regular organization and been folded into the larger command structure of the guerrilla army. The Communist party also had its representative in Upper Kerasia. He was a strikingly handsome young man from Volos. Being a secondary school graduate and an articulate Marxist, he took his duties as propagandist and ideologist seriously. Very few rank-and-file members of the band hailed from villages far away; the overwhelming majority were from Kerasia itself and villages similarly situated within no more than a day's walk.

Exactly how extensive the network of supply that sustained the band on Mount Pelion may have been was of course kept hidden from casual visitors. Rations arrived punctually enough, one meal at a time, during the twenty-four hours we spent with the guerrilla band. The supply network that made this possible probably extended a good deal beyond Kerasia. Villages out in the plains were where real food surpluses could be found; and the covert committee structure that operated within Kerasia probably also existed within some of the agricultural villages of the flatlands, perhaps even under the very noses of the Greek army detachment stationed in Kanalia. If so, Kerasia was serving as a point of concentration for supplies gathered from the plains villages; and insofar as contributions from those villages were in fact available for the support of sons of some of Kerasia's families who had joined the guerrilla band, the burden of their support had been shifted from poverty-stricken Kerasia to the wealthier villages of the plains.

Other young men from Kerasia were serving with the Greek National Army. They, too, relieved their families of the burden of feeding them, though in that case, the food they ate came mostly from the United States rather than from plains villages of Greece itself. Almost half as many young men from Kerasia served in the national army as joined the guerrillas. Accidents of call-up and timing probably decided who served in which forces as much or more than ideological conviction. But once committed, one way or the other, a man found it difficult to change sides safely. Hence the two-to-one ratio in favor of the guerrillas registered fairly accurately the way political polarization divided the village as a whole.

In March 1947 when we visited Kerasia, the local balance of power was a precarious deadlock. The army detachment in Kanalia was three or four times as numerous as the guerrilla band on Mount Pelion, yet it could not attack, much less destroy, the band, primarily because the soldiers in the ranks. had no wish to shoot other Greeks. When ordered to climb the mountain in pursuit of the guerrillas, they contrived to give such warning of their coming that the band could easily get away. The guerrillas proudly told us of several such brushes, when an exchange of gunfire at extreme range was all that occurred, with no casualties whatever. Neither side was eager to kill. A shot fired at a distant running figure, not aimed too carefully, was all the situation called for; or so a great many Greek soldiers on both sides believed. Such attitudes went a long way to blunt the clash of incompatible political ideologies. Committed ideologues of either side were conscious of finding themselves in a relatively exposed position. Everyone knew that any obvious shift in the balance of forces could soon result in the melting away of the mass of followers from either side.

The fact that the Greek army found itself in a position to break up the guerrilla supply system by removing inhabitants of villages like Kerasia to refugee camps was, in this situation, a decisive advantage. Soon after the population of Kerasia and other similarly situated villages had been relocated, the guerrilla band on Mount Pelion withdrew northward, presumably because its food supplies had been effectively cut off. When that happened, the young men who had joined the band disappeared from the ken of the villagers. By 1956, ten had returned to the village, thirteen had written letters or in some other way renewed contact with their families from behind the Iron Curtain, and forty were missing. The missing and absent taken together just about sufficed to counteract the natural increase of the village. To be sure, official statistics were unusually imperfect because of confusion surrounding the evacuation of 1947–50. But on the basis of records available in 1956 it appeared that during the preceeding decade births exceeded recorded deaths by about forty-five.

However effective the evacuation of Kerasia may have been as a way of checking the expansion of guerrilla power, the costs of removal were high. Apart from the direct expense of feeding idle people for two entire years in the outskirts of Volos, the experience of the refugee camps was disruptive and demoralizing. The people of Kerasia remembered the camp with distaste in 1956. Yet they envied the handful of their number who, by hook or by crook, had managed to find some sort of job in town and thus were able to evade the official orders that came in 1950 to return to the houses they had been forced to abandon two years before.

When the guerrilla war ended, therefore, Kerasia comprised a bruised and disorganized population, politically divided against itself, but uniformly resentful of the officialdom that had first driven them away and then compelled them to return to lower Kerasia. The economic cul-de-sac that had closed in on them before the war confronted them again in 1950, almost unaffected by all that had happened since 1940. Sullen hostility to constituted authority was the natural response. Official programs for improving use of resources met with subtle (and not so subtle) sabotage. Kerasia therefore remained an angry and potentially rebellious community long after the war had come to a close.

The other hill village I visited for the first time in 1947 had a totally different war experience. Named Kotta, it is located on the upwaters of the Aliakmon River, not more than fifteen miles from the point at which the Greek, Albanian, and Yugoslav borders come together. In Turkish times, the community was called Roula. The inhabitants spoke Macedonian Slavic, but being Orthodox Christians could count themselves Greek. As it happened, a famous guerrilla chieftain named Kotta lived in Roula. During the struggles of 1905–6 between Greek and Bulgarian bands for dominion over western Macedonia, he opted for the Greek cause. Consequently, soon after the Greeks took over sovereignty of the region in 1912, they officially renamed the village in honor of the guerrilla leader, who had been hanged by the Turks a few years previously.

Early in the twentieth century, a few individuals from Kotta established themselves in Toronto and Sydney, and began to bring relatives across the oceans to join them. As a result, by 1947 about 2,000 Kottans were living in Australia and Canada. Those remaining behind considered everyone overseas to be still members of the village, even though they might be children or grandchildren of the actual emigrants. There were telling reasons for taking such a view, for the village became heavily dependent on remittances from the two overseas communities. Kotta's land supplied enough food for about four months of the year; all the rest had to come from outside if the 630 persons living in the village in 1947 were not to starve. Before 1940, this shortfall had been made good with the help of money orders coming from Toronto and Sydney. To supplement this income, men of the village sometimes found work as construction laborers. In the late 1930s they had helped with large-scale draining of the Strymon Valley near Serres, for example, even though this involved walking to work clear across Macedonia, from extreme west to extreme east, about two hundred miles.

Remittances of course were cut off during the war. I never found out how the village managed to survive this disaster. Perhaps the villagers worked for the Bulgarians, who occupied Greek Thrace and part of eastern Macedonia during the war. The government in Sofia put a major effort into building houses and making other improvements intended to facilitate permanent Bulgarian settlement in the disputed territories. Since the Bulgarians counted Slav Macedonians as fellow nationals, even a village as distant as Kotta might have benefitted from Bulgarian favor in the form of differential access to construction jobs. But by the time we arrived in Kotta, early in 1947, it was impolitic to talk of wartime relationships with the Bulgars, if any such had in fact existed. The village lay well within the zone firmly controlled by the Greek guerrilla army, and the Slavic claim to sovereignty over Greek Macedonia was a theme peculiarly painful to the Greek Communists. Hence we heard nothing of how the village had adjusted to the wartime interruption of overseas remittances.

Yet somehow the population did survive. Soon after the German retreat, in 1944, money orders began to arrive again from relatives overseas, supplemented in 1946 by UNRRA food deliveries. But by November 1946 these freshets of outside aid were again cut off, since Kotta, being close to the Yugoslav and Albanian borders, was one of the very first parts of Greece to come permanently under control of the new Greek guerrilla army. Since the guerrillas were hard-pressed to supply themselves in such a barren land, by the time we reached the village starvation had begun to set in. Some of the children had bloated bellies; many suffered from running sores; all were painfully thin. All too obviously physical survival was soon going to be in question for everyone in the village. Local food resources simply could not keep the resident population alive throughout the coming year.

Nonetheless, Kotta was responsible for feeding a garrison of fifteen guerrilla soldiers. Only two armed men were actually in the village when we arrived, and they were mere boys, not fully grown. They were, however, of Greek speech, strangers to the village, and not altogether popular, since the burden of feeding even a single additional mouth was hard to bear with equanimity when starvation was already staring everyone in the face. As in Kerasia, some of the village young men were serving in the Greek National Army—about fifteen of them; and a slightly smaller number were said to be with the guerrillas.

Sentiment in the village was far more united than in Kerasia: no one was rich, everyone faced imminent starvation. Hope for the future focused unambiguously on the possibility of reopening contact with relatives overseas, who, everyone was confident, would come to the rescue if permitted to do so. Since neither Greek nationalism nor Communist revolution offered any sort of practical solution to their difficulties, political ideology in the village was at a low ebb. The two guerrilla soldiers were apolitical and illiterate, less interested in abstract causes than in posing for a photograph, glaring at the camera fiercely amidst an array of bandoliers and guns.

A few weeks after our visit to Kotta, Communist authorities acted to relieve the acute food crisis. What they did was to remove from the village all children between the ages of two and fourteen and take them off northward where they were distributed among various east European countries. This meant a reduction in local population of about 50 percent and allowed the village children to survive the war in such remote places as Tashkent and Warsaw. The children were taken by force, and at the time no one knew what the authorities were going to do with them. The result was a profound anguish and resentment among parents who saw their children marched off to an unknown fate. Memories of how the Turks had seized children from the mountain villages of the western Balkans to serve as slaves in the

Sultan's household did nothing to reconcile the parents to the loss of their offspring. Long afterwards this act was remembered in Kotta as by far the worst thing the Communists had done, and this despite the possibility that it may have been inspired by humanitarian sentiment and a desire to save the younger generation from the starvation that clearly impended in Kotta, and in similarly situated hill villages under guerrilla control.

Certainly the Communists were quite unable to issue rations to the adult and infant population that remained behind, as the Greek government was able to do for the population of Kerasia. The remaining inhabitants simply had to take their chances of survival. Somewhat more than half of them succeeded, so that when I went back in 1956, 188 persons were living in Kotta, or almost exactly one-third of the number who had been there in 1947.

It will be remembered that village lands could supply food for only four months of the year for a population of 630 in 1947. For 188 persons, however, local resources could be stretched to sustain them all year round; and this, undoubtedly, was why the number of survivors was what it was. Between 1947 and 1950 disease and hunger, together with armed violence, had cut down the village population in a harsh and thoroughly traditional way. Not surprisingly, the survivors remained far more firmly rooted to old-time folkways and village values than was true for any of the other places I visited in 1956.

Yet the war did make some differences. For instance, in 1956, instead of speaking Slavic, the men of the village preferred Greek. The language shift was a necessary protection against discrimination, which had been almost as sharply anti-Slavic among the guerrillas as in the ranks of the Greek National Army. The women of the village, on the other hand, having had little or no occasion to deal with outsiders, continued to speak Slavic by preference, and wore their traditional peasant dress as before.

Despite the harshness of the experience through which the survivors had passed, remarkably little else had altered in Kotta. Loss of their children was the memory that rankled most. The pangs they had themselves experienced from hunger, death, and disease were all but forgotten. To have survived was obviously a gift of God, not attributable to merely human action; and when,

marvelously, after 1950 there was enough food for all once
more, it would have been an impious soul who did not feel
grateful and glad to be alive. A remarkable cheerfulness therefore pervaded the village when I saw it in 1956, in striking
contrast to the sullen resentment so evident in Kerasia.

How the Rural Balance
Tipped, 1950–66

When I returned to Greece in 1956, the situation of each of these
four villages had altered for the better, as I have already
suggested. Yet the fundamental dilemmas and difficulties each
had faced in 1947 remained recognizably present. Changes that
might eventually be capable of solving the problem of population pressure on the land had begun to show; but none of the
villages had yet been able to carry such innovations far enough
to assure everyone against a recurrence of the desperate poverty
that had been so widespread in 1947.

Travel was much easier in 1956 than it had been in 1947; and
since I now had a clear idea of the critical role food-surplus and
food-deficit villages played in Greek public affairs, it seemed
best to give a better balance to my enterprise by adding a plains
village in Thessaly and a food-deficit village from the Peloponnese to the list of villages to be studied. In this way, Old Corinth
could be compared with a hill village of Old Greece; Kerasia
could be compared with a village of the Thessalian plain; and the
pairing of Kotta with New Eleftherohori in Macedonia would
not stand alone.

Since the critical factor after 1950 was whether, how, and to
what extent peaceful exchanges between food-deficit and food-
surplus communities could operate in Greece, it seems best to
look at each such pair successively, starting in the south, where
the impress of the guerrilla war was weaker than in the north.

Old Greece

Old Corinth had begun to prosper by 1956 as never before. For
one thing, tourism had revived. The new roads built during and
after the guerrilla war made it easy for busloads of tourists to
come from Athens and stop for awhile at the ancient site of

Corinth before hastening on to Mycenae and Epidauros and returning to Athens at the end of the day. As a result of such tour arrangements, some seventy-two thousand foreigners passed through the village in 1955. Many of them left at least a little small change behind, making purchases in the cafés or from village shops which sprang up to cater to the tourist trade. Only a few village families benefitted directly from such income, to be sure; and the agricultural portion of the population seemed, in fact, remarkably little affected by the sight of so many oddly-garbed strangers trouping through the village square.

What mattered for them was that no fewer than 163 irrigation wells had come into operation. The water thus newly available made possible an entirely new range of crops on land that had previously been suitable only for wheat. The president of the village, a man of remarkable wisdom and openness, estimated that the value of crops produced in Old Corinth had multiplied ten times since before the war. Yet this extraordinary expansion of income had not involved any shift away from the production of currants. On the contrary, the currant crop in 1956 promised to be as large as it had been in 1955, which was a bumper year; and even more important, the price of currants was higher than ever, thanks to shortage of labor in the currant fields of Australia. The two cooperatives that handled the processing and sale of Old Corinth's currants had been reorganized in 1952, with the help of a loan from the Agricultural Bank; and each of them had expanded its functions by purchasing a tractor and grain-harvesting machine on credit. These were rented out for a fixed fee to anyone who wished to use mechanical help in cultivating or harvesting his fields. Returns were so spectacular that two-thirds of the cost of the tractors had been paid off after a single year's operations.

All this was good news for Old Corinth; but what really commanded the farmers' attention in 1956 was the all but fabulous reward to be had from raising tomatoes. The boom began in 1953 when a landless villager got hold of a ramshackle truck and started to haul tomatoes from Old Corinth to Athens each day. Prices were such that the villagers reaped a bonanza. Consequently, ground planted with tomatoes expanded rapidly in the two succeeding years, so that by 1956 half a dozen trucks were busily engaged in carrying the fruit to market. Prices fluctuated each day, but though less glittering than in earlier years, they remained high enough to bring cheer to every Old Corinth farmer.

The situation was further improved by the fact that use of fertilizer and a better kind of seed, first introduced in 1953, tripled wheat yields. This meant that the same amount of wheat could be raised on one-third as much land. Acreage thus freed from the task of feeding the village could, with irrigation, be devoted to highly profitable and labor intensive crops like tomatoes. Tobacco, apricots, and garden vegetables competed with tomatoes for new acreage. But in 1956 the boom was in tomatoes: and the main problem farmers faced was how to make the best possible deal with pickers and with the truckers who carried the tomatoes to Athens. Making such deals had always been part of the currant business, so the farmers of Old Corinth were prepared to manage these negotiations shrewdly. Similarly, the landless laborers and small holders who worked for wages in the fields were accustomed from time immemorial to negotiating labor contracts with other village families, and could rejoice in the abundance of work that the intensification of agriculture had brought in its train.

Life, in short, had resumed its accustomed patterns, with bells on. Simultaneously, the unexpected and unimagined new wealth flooding into the village diminished the political tensions that had been so troubling in 1947. The new wealth brought changes, of course: a spanking new church decorated one end of the village, built entirely from the community's own resources. Hookup with the national power grid occurred only a few weeks before my visit, and the improvement of life this permitted was the liveliest topic of conversation while I was there. Light at night and electric pumps for irrigation were the first, and in 1956, the only new benefits electricity brought into Old Corinth; but men's minds were already dwelling on refrigerators and a host of other modern improvements that they could now confidently look forward to.

The newfound prosperity of Old Corinth affected neighboring villages too. When no one in Old Corinth wanted the tractors or harvesters, they could be (and often were) rented for use outside the village. More important, as new demands for labor multiplied, a definite pattern of in-migration from poorer villages located in the hills nearby manifested itself. The population of

Old Corinth had grown from about 1,530 in 1947 to 1,732, enumerated by the census of 1961. Natural increase accounted for part of this growth. Between 1947 and 1961, 506 children had been born in the village; 187 persons had died. Natural increase in those years thus amounted to a total of 319 persons; but this was offset by emigration of about 180 persons from the village. Emigrants left for Athens, New Corinth, Australia, Canada, and the United States. All such figures must be taken as inexact. Village registers lagged behind actual facts, sometimes by years; and even though the village president knew the community very well and corrected official figures from his personal acquaintance with the facts, oversights were bound to occur.

Nevertheless, the beginning of a pattern of migration that promised to relieve pressures in the poor villages of the hills had clearly set in. Between sixty and seventy persons had moved into Old Corinth between 1951 and 1961, and found work. Farmers were complaining in 1956 that it was difficult to get enough people to work in the fields at peak times of the year; but no one had yet begun systematically recruiting extra help from distant villages. News that wage work might be had down in the plain was enough to attract a sufficient number of willing hands during most of the year; and since everyone was still unsure how long the boom might last, it seemed best not to advertise the village's new wealth too blatantly, lest some ill luck ensue.

Memories of EAM levies were still fresh among the propertied class. Indeed all Greek peasants have a deep folk wisdom about the bad habits of tax collectors and the ways in which they were accustomed to demand a share in any newfound prosperity that left visible traces. Poverty was safer; and an outward semblance of poverty, even after new wealth poured in, had a double advantage. It warded off dangerous outside curiosity about just how much a family owned and simultaneously allowed a more rapid accumulation of capital, whether in the form of hoarded gold coins or the purchase of land. Buying and selling land was, of course, the supreme test of individual bargaining skills. Negotiations were conducted in the same private, secretive way that labor contracts were made; but since the deal was vastly more important for both parties than any other they could enter upon, agreement usually came only after prolonged haggling and repeated offers and counteroffers had been made.

Overall, the new wealth had not altered established attitudes and values in Old Corinth very noticeably in 1956. The village was more cheerful than before; but outward expression of satisfaction was carefully restrained. Probably most of the villagers felt that the way things had been going was too good to last. In fact, the bottom fell out of the tomato business soon after my visit in 1956. Competition from Crete and elsewhere lowered tomato prices to a point at which other crops became more remunerative to the farmers of Old Corinth. Yet even after the tomato boom collapsed, fruit trees, (requiring a greater capital investment and therefore less exposed to competition from elsewhere,) proved able to sustain a prosperity among the farmers of Old Corinth that, with minor ups and downs, continued uninterruptedly for twenty years.

To get a look at the type of village that supplied Old Corinth with extra hands for work in the fields, I travelled to the opposite corner of the Peloponnese, visiting a community called Kardamili.[3] Kardamili is located in a district known as Outer Mani, where the western side of Mount Taygetos plunges into the Gulf of Messenia. Like Old Corinth, Kardamili claims a classical past, and with good reason; it is referred to in Homer, and ancient carved stones have been recovered from an acropolis located about a mile from the center of the existing village.

Kardamili, however, always remained small and insignificant by comparison with the former importance of Corinth. Yet on its own miniscule scale, the place served as a metropolis for about a dozen villages sprawled higher up the slopes of Mount Taygetos. Thanks to the existence of a small island offshore, ships can find a safe anchorage at Kardamili just opposite a precipitous inland track that follows the valley of a winter torrent. No better anchorage exists all the way between Cape Matapan, at the tip of Mani, and Kalamata, some thirty miles to the west at the head of the gulf. Hence as long as all important

3. Professor Fred Gearing, an anthropologist, studied Kardamili in the early 1960s, and has kept in close touch since by spending summer vacations in the village. He very kindly allowed me to see his manuscript entitled "Kardamili: Work and Honor in a Greek Village." From this manuscript and from conversation with him in 1976 I gathered much information and improved my understanding of the village; but he should not be held responsible for what I say here, and indeed, probably disagrees with some of my judgments.

movement of goods was by sea, Kardamili acted as a local port and transshipment point. For a short time at the end of the eighteenth century, ships based in Kardamili visited Odessa and other Russian ports; but this ended with the War of Independence, when the village reverted to a merely local importance.

In the 1930s an olive press and soap factory were built in Kardamili. These, together with work in the port, provided employment for some of the poor families of the community. Population in 1940 was about 750; but the war disrupted the manufacture of soap, and a few months after guerrilla bands appeared again on Mount Taygetos in 1946, the villagers were evacuated to Kalamata. In 1949 the government ordered them back and gave some help towards repairing the dilapidation that two years' abandonment had caused. The most important thing the government did, however, was to offer employment for work on a new road, connecting Kardamili with Kalamata to the west and with the Mani peninsula to the south. This road, completed in 1950, brought two sharp and unwelcome changes to the community. On the one hand, when trucks began to move back and forth easily, the former importance of coastal shipping abruptly ended, so that Kardamili lost its role as a port. In the second place, the wage income from work on the road ceased; and nothing took its place. This spelled real crisis for the poor of the village. Wage work sufficient to keep them from starving was simply not available within the confines of the village itself.

The village lands extended up a bare and rocky mountainside, except where, just north of the village, a small delta of thicker soil had been deposited by the winter torrent. Here wheat could be raised; but, as in Kotta, the harvest only sufficed to feed the population of the village for about four months of the year. Food for the other months had to come from sale of olive oil, for olive trees did well on the rocky slopes of Mount Taygetos. Every available crevice and pocket of soil was, accordingly, adorned with an olive tree; and property rights in individual trees were carefully apportioned among the village families, as inheritance, dowry, and occasional buying and selling had chanced to define them.

There were great inequalities among property holdings, but exact information could not be obtained. The richest man of the village was said to own about 1,200 trees; but this may have been deliberately exaggerated, or a wild guess. Villagers kept such information from one another insofar as possible, and often preferred to mislead a stranger even when they may have known a correct answer to his questions. Mutual suspicion was, in fact, a leading characteristic of village life. Kardamili seemed to be composed of disaggregated nuclear families, each regarding all the others as rivals, and responding to the hard times that had descended upon the community with a surly, intensified secretiveness.

Hard times had already persuaded a good many persons to leave. The population of the village was about five hundred in 1956, one-third smaller than before the war, and this despite the fact that sixty-nine births had been recorded in the village as against only forty deaths since 1946. But such signs of natural increase were far overbalanced by emigration. Exact numbers were unobtainable, since long after a person had left the village his name was kept on the official register, and even those who had been absent for years commonly kept title to their inherited property, entrusting the cultivation of their olive trees to a relative, or else arranging a sharecropping deal with some other family in the village.

Still, word of mouth estimate was that about two hundred persons had left Kardamili, some going to Athens, others to Kalamata. A large exodus had occurred a few weeks before my arrival when work in newly established rice fields near Kalamata had become available. Some thirty families from the village took advantage of this opportunity to earn regular wages. At the time of my visit in 1956 they were camping out in tents near the rice fields, and were expected to return to Kardamili in time for the olive harvest, when local demand for labor was at its peak. Some may have returned; but in the course of the next few years nearly all of the rice workers moved away permanently by finding winter quarters in Kalamata, where better work opportunities existed. An overseas exodus affected only a few Kardamili families in 1956. A total of about thirty persons had emigrated since the end of the war, dividing about evenly between Australia and the United States.

Nevertheless, unemployed and underemployed persons remained abundant in the village. The rhythms of olive culture required idleness most of the year, for when harvesttime came, in October or November, each tree had to be picked by hand; and if the fruit were left too long, wind and rain would knock the olives to the ground, causing bruises that permitted the precious oil to seep away. The only insurance against losses from wind and storm therefore was to have an abundant labor force at hand when the time for harvest arrived; and if there was nothing for such persons to do during the rest of the year, as was the case, well, it had always been that way. Somehow or other people had always survived. Yet for those who depended largely or entirely on wages, survival under such a regimen was difficult at best. Dissatisfaction found expression in the form of a small leftist vote (about fifteen persons) who stood in conscious and deliberate defiance of the royalist majority, amounting to about 180.

All the same, political polarization was not acute. Class war was checked in Kardamili in 1956, as it had been in Old Corinth in 1947, by the fact that buyers and sellers of labor had to get together at every harvesttime. Consequently ideological venom could never be carried so far as to endanger one's chances of making a deal with someone from the other class.

In many ways the most serious problem the village faced was the deficient supply of water. Women had to walk about a mile to fill their water jars at a spring; but in the summer the flow dwindled and sometimes dried up. When that happened, water had to be brought in from Kalamata by truck. Under such circumstances every glass of water was precious, and women's work became burdensome in unusual degree, since water jars are heavy and the walk was both long and precipitous. Government engineers had devised a scheme for bringing water down the mountain in pipes, and work had begun. But financial and technical questions were still unresolved and construction was proceeding at a pace that left everyone dissatisfied, even though the villagers' unwillingness to agree to extra taxes as a guarantee of repayment for a loan was the principal obstacle to the completion of the project.

Overall, therefore, Kardamili was still suffering from ills inherited from before the war, and changes that had come since 1949 tended rather to accentuate than to relieve the difficulties the community faced. Emigration was the main response to the hardships faced by the poor of the community; but sons and daughters of the propertied class were also keen to leave home if the alternative was Athens and its bright lights. By drawing off the young people, emigration was clearly endangering the long-term continuance of village life. The elderly were already disproportionately in evidence; the pace of life moved slowly at best; and in summer, when I was there, with no work on the olive trees to be done, and no work in the grain fields, which had already been harvested, the men of the village simply drowsed in the shade, while the olives swelled on the trees and the women walked wearily after water.

The bustle and prosperity of Old Corinth and the readiness of its inhabitants to talk openly with an interested outsider stood in sharp contrast to the clannish secretiveness of the people of Kardamili. Old ways were not working very well for them. They knew it, yet were unable and unwilling to think of anything else. Traditional peasant distrust of indebtedness still hampered efforts by agents of the Agricultural Bank to persuade the farmers of Kardamili to buy fertilizer for their trees. Indeed, I heard a man explain that even though the amount of oil was increased by using fertilizer, the quality of the oil diminished, so that the apparent improvement was illusory. Such statements were devoid of truth but rationalized his refusal to go into debt for fertilizer, and affirmed a traditional distrust of outsiders giving advice, especially about how to grow olives—an art in which the farmers of Kardamili believed, with some reason, that they were past masters.

By 1966, when I returned to these two communities once more, Old Corinth's prosperity had lost its first hectic bloom. On the plus side, export of fresh fruit all the way to Germany in refrigerated trucks had added a new dimension to the village economy, providing a counterbalance to the ups and downs of the Athens market. In addition, a small factory making plastic packing boxes for fruit had begun operations within the village boundary, although its location near the shore associated it rather with the southernmost fringes of the industrial district of New Corinth than with the village of Old Corinth, located about two miles away. Yet the establishment of such newfangled industrial establishments enlarged employment opportunities for wage workers. About twenty village girls were now employed in the factory or in adjacent plants in New Corinth.

On the negative side, limitations of water supply had begun to loom as a really serious problem. The irrigation wells that had brought such prosperity to the village had the effect of lowering the water table. By 1966, some of the shallower wells no longer could provide all the water their owners had become accustomed to using. On top of this, too much pumping from deeper wells ran the risk of salination; for the Gulf of Corinth fronted on the village lands. Plans for solving the difficulty by running an aqueduct from a distant mountain lake had been proposed; but the costs were vast and any such undertaking would depend on the central government. In the meantime a more careful use of irrigation water had become mandatory; and some fields had to be put back into wheat.

Another negative aspect of the village economy was the decreased profitability of the old staple, currants. Australian production had picked up, and Great Britain, which from the seventeenth century, had been the principal market for Greek currants, offered a preferential tariff to the Australian product. As a result, both of Old Corinth's cooperatives were again in financial difficulty by 1966; currant production was on the decrease, but equally valuable crops that did not require irrigation were hard to find. Tourism, on the other hand, was booming as never before, with as many as a thousand persons a day passing through the village square at the height of the summer season, and, as before, leaving behind small sums of money that became cumulatively important.

The biggest change in Old Corinth, however, was that consumption patterns had begun to creep up on the enhanced incomes farmers had been enjoying for more than a decade. Instead of laying aside gold coins, the villagers had begun to buy refrigerators and to install bathrooms with flush toilets in their houses. An earthquake in 1957 had damaged many of the village structures. Thereafter, funds made available by the government at low rates of interest persuaded many families to rebuild their houses on a much grander scale. Private purchase of tractors had supplanted renting from the co-ops; indeed the village boasted more than a hundred "traktorakia," little tractors well suited to the tasks of Old Corinth's kind of cultivation. This was far more than were needed to cultivate the fields; but possession of such a machine had become a status symbol. Ownership meant that one no longer depended on someone else for the essential routines of farm work. Each tractor-owning nuclear family, in other words, gained or regained its autonomy as an independent work unit; and this autonomy was much prized. Having to bargain with someone else for use of a tractor was felt to be both disadvantageous and demeaning.

The abundance of tractors and of special attachments for them that could be used for specialized work like spraying altered the nature of field work. Farmers' wives no longer had to help in the fields at peak times, as had once been the case; and in general farmers needed less labor to achieve the same results. Hence the pattern of in-migration from hill villages that had begun to show itself in the 1950s failed to gain additional momentum. A trickle continued, often taking the form of a marriage alliance between someone native to a poorer hill village and the son or daughter of a resident of Old Corinth. The village president estimated that between ten and fifteen new families had moved into the village in the ten years since 1956; but this in-migration was almost exactly offset by emigration. Births in the village exceeded deaths by a total of 123 during the same decade; and village population grew accordingly to about 1,800 in 1966 from the enumerated figure of 1,732 registered by the census of 1961.

New ideas had also begun to make their mark in Old Corinth. The agriculturalists still kept themselves insulated from the tourists. Language barriers made communication difficult, and the foreigners' folly in allowing themselves to be charged unreasonably high prices excited a general contempt among the local people anyway. On the other hand, movies were shown twice a week in the village square, and this brought a new and glittering world of megalopolitan values to the attention of the young.

The political storms of Athens, which had reached an acute phase in the summer of 1966, were felt, though only faintly, in Old Corinth. The elections of 1964 had brought Papandreou's Center party to power in the village, with the result that a new village president took over. But I was assured that the new village officers got along well with their predecessors. No very noticeable change in local affairs had occurred or was expected. The landless class of the village was less dependent than formerly on employment offered by village farmers. New jobs

connected with the factories in New Corinth, with trucking, and
with servicing the tourists as they milled around in the village
square, not to mention the resumption of American archaeological work, all made for a greater range of choice for persons who
worked for wages.

Hence the fact that farmers needed to hire less labor, thanks to
their new machines, had not exacerbated class relations within
the village. The simple polarity of 1947 and 1956 was much
modified; and the political differences within the village were, if
anything, less deeply felt than they had been ten years earlier. It
was not in communities like Old Corinth that Papandreou
roused such strong emotional response: the locus of political
passion had clearly transferred itself to the cities.

Kardamili, too, offered no sounding board for political
protest and change in 1966. Emigration had continued, and
population accordingly dropped to about 380 from the 500 who
had lived in the village ten years before; but by counting an
outlying settlement as part of the community the total could be
raised to 480 or so. Local pride, fearing further decay, preferred
this larger figure. Deaths within the village almost exactly
equalled births between 1956 and 1966 so that natural increase
no longer could counteract emigration. By 1976 the population
of Kardamili had therefore decayed still further to about 250,
though almost twice that number remained officially registered
as residents of the village. As a matter of fact, the president of
the village council of Kardamili refused to give me information
about births, marriages, and deaths since 1966, so that I lack
exact figures for the most recent demographic history of the
community. Nevertheless, an all but total absence of small
children—indeed I saw only two persons under five years of age
in the village—made it obvious that a still more precipitous
demographic crisis lies ahead.

The central reason for Kardamili's difficulty is not so much
economic as psychological. Use of fertilizers and tractors for
cultivation of olive groves has increased yields and incomes for
all who own trees. Tourism offers another potentially significant
source of income for villagers. But what makes marriage and
birth rates catastrophically low is the rebellion of the young
women of the village (and of neighboring villages) against the
patterns of life their mothers submitted to. In Mani, blood feud

lasted until the 1930s; and the men of the peninsula, idle most of the time because tending olives requires only a few weeks' work each year, cultivated a truculent pride that disdained the female sex to a degree unusual even in Greece, where the traditional status of women was low to begin with.

Since World War II female rebellion against these attitudes seems unmistakable, though I met no spokeswoman who expressed her views to me. Instead, the young women voted with their feet, by leaving the community en masse. In Kardamili, where as recently as 1962 women had to carry water from a distant spring on their heads in heavy water jars, young girls apparently resolved on escape from the hardships they saw their mothers enduring. The depth and force of this resolve is such that young men of the village, heirs to hundreds and even to thousands of olive trees, who stand at the very top of the traditional village hierarchy, cannot find wives who will bring them the accustomed and appropriate dowry. For it was precisely the daughters of the propertied class who most passionately rejected their mothers' roles and who found it easiest to leave for Athens or Kalamata.

This put the young men of Kardamili in a dilemma. Family custom has long accepted the idea that the most capable of a family's sons should leave home and try to make a career in the city. Hence those selected to remain behind and look after the olive trees already suffered from a sense of personal deficiency. In reaction, they were tempted to assert their masculine prerogatives all the more emphatically. A man in such a position could certainly marry a poor girl from some village up the mountain, since his wealth of olive trees would still prevail over any other consideration. But such a marriage was unacceptable because it meant marrying beneath one's station. Marriage alliances were traditionally the way the standing of families and individuals within the community were assessed. The exact size of dowry and its match-up with the husband's prospective inheritance was a matter of delicate negotiation. Like any other market transaction, it established a price defining the personal and pecuniary value attached to bride and groom by their families and by the community. Hence to marry anyone who did not bring with her a handsome dowry was particularly painful for a young man who was the heir to an extensive olive grove but nevertheless felt personally insecure because of invidious decisions made within the bosom of his parental family.

Under the circumstances, therefore, such young men naturally decided to wait until the right girl with the right dowry showed up. Consequently, the propertied class of Kardamili had begun by 1976 to commit a strange sort of genocide upon itself. The village president, for example, a man in his forties, and possessor of comparatively enormous wealth, was still looking for a suitable bride. Yet given his personality, his attitudes, and his expectations, it is unlikely that any such bride will ever appear. To be sure, traditional family patterns allowed for very late male marriages. In former times a son had to wait for his father to die or retire from management of the family olive trees before he could expect a well-dowered wife to accept him in wedlock. Girls, on the contrary, by custom had to be married off in their early twenties if the family was to retain the respect of the community. This often meant as much as a twenty-year difference in age between man and wife. Hence the postponement of marriage that had attained such striking proportions in Kardamili between 1966 and 1976 did not seem altogether anomalous to the villagers themselves, and it is possible that the proud possessors of Kardamili's olive groves will yet find themselves wives—somehow.

As a matter of fact, in 1976 one of Kardamili's eligible bachelors had recourse to an Athenian marriage broker who put him in touch with a young woman who was teaching secondary school and whose only dowry would be her capacity to earn a salary. The negotiation had not been concluded when I was on the spot. It is not altogether fanciful to suppose that Kardamili's future may depend on how the negotiation turns out. Certainly standards of household comforts equivalent to those familiar to middle-income families in Athens are now available to the richest families of Kardamili. What was lacking was a familial and psychological pattern of relationships acceptable to "modern-minded" young women.

Another and more immediate difficulty in Kardamili's traditional way of life had become apparent by 1966. Labor for the olive harvest was no longer available within the community. All persons of working age without trees of their own to hold them to the spot had departed. In 1965, a government-managed scheme brought laborers from Thessaly and Macedonia to help pick the ripe fruit. But the olive-owners of Kardamili were highly critical of the result, for the northerners knew nothing of how to treat an olive tree and received higher wages than their employers felt were justified. The plan therefore collapsed, no doubt in part because the poor mountain villages of the north were simultaneously emptying out as thousands streamed north to Germany where work conditions were far more attractive, even for the unskilled, than anything Kardamili could offer.

By happy chance, a regular and liberal application of fertilizer to olive trees not only increases the yield but also toughens the stem of the ripe fruit. It therefore became less vital to pick the olives quickly, before wind and storm could shake too many of them onto the ground. Use of fertilizer became normal, indeed universal, by the early 1960s; and a longer harvest period became acceptable as a result. Cruder, less laborious methods of harvesting trees also came into use. Instead of picking the fruit by hand, one at a time, as aforetime, now the villagers shook the ripe fruit onto a plastic sheet spread under the trees, and then gleaned the few remaining olives by hand.

Yet by 1976 even these solutions were beginning to wear themselves out. Labor for olive harvesting came mostly from hill villages above Kardamili; but these villages, too, were emptying. The work force available for harvesting olives consisted in large part of women who had stayed behind when their husbands went off to work in town; or who, as widows, were eking out the last years of their lives in familiar, poverty-stricken environments. But year by year such workers diminished in number, and younger age-groups were unavailable to replenish their ranks. A new labor crunch clearly lay ahead. In 1976 it already had visible manifestations, for some olive groves were not properly tilled, and Kardamili's grain fields, which had never been very fertile, were abandoned—unused even as pasture. Unless some new outside source of labor can be attracted to the village in the near future, productivity is certain to decrease sharply, and the demographic crisis, already apparent, will begin to manifest itself in a corresponding retreat of cultivation.

A compensatory growth point in Kardamili's horizon was tourism. The first foreigners to select Kardamili's rocky, sun-swept shores for their summer vacation arrived in 1958. They camped in tents by the water's edge and immediately shocked the village by exposing far more skin than the local inhabitants thought decent. Campers remained few until 1962, when the number of foreign visitors rose to forty-seven, only to double the next year to ninety-five and double once again by 1965, when a total of 205 strangers spent at least a night—or as much as a month—by Kardamili's shore.

Stimulated and financed by agents of the Ministry of Tourism, the village council went so far as to build a small hotel to accommodate those foreigners who did not insist on camping out. But indignation at the near nudity that the tourists so often displayed ran very deep in the village. Eagerness to exploit their readiness to pay high prices was counterbalanced by a clannish desire to keep such people at arm's length. Hence even those storekeepers and restaurant owners who benefitted directly from tourist expenditures, did not try to make their establishments attractive to the foreigners. For several years after its construction the hotel was not even open, because no one could be found to manage it. Clearly, those who remained in the village had opted for traditional ways of life. The tourists threatened to upset those familiar ways, and were treated accordingly.

Yet by another irony that may well dominate Kardamili's future, the unwillingness of the local inhabitants to cater consciously to tourists means that Kardamili remains "unspoiled." As a result, in Athens, Germany, and Scandinavia, small circles of sophisticated urbanites pride themselves on knowing about Kardamili as a place to go for vacations. Attitudes intended to keep strangers at a distance may therefore prove to have an opposite effect from what the villagers of Kardamili intended. If so, the pressure upon the old ways, already severely strained, will certainly increase in the very near future.

Politically, Kardamili preserved old antagonisms as painstakingly as it preserved other aspects of local tradition. In faithful memory of their EAM days, a group of about a dozen leftists continued to vote for the most extreme party available to them on the ballot at each election. But by 1976 the little band of dissidents within the village had grown old. They flaunted political heterodoxy as a sort of game—a way of passing time in the coffeehouse—with absolutely no expectation that their phrases would ever be acted on or even taken seriously. All the vitality of the village had departed for Athens, Kalamata, or more distant cities overseas. By 1966, it was in these places that political tensions found their expression, not in sunbaked, slow-paced Kardamili.

Thus in Kardamili, as in all the other food-deficit villages of Old Greece, the problems once faced by peasants who owned too little land to support themselves locally had been solved in the most direct and simple way, by exporting population from the village to distant cities. The result was to allow the remnant to cling close to age-old patterns of life, even when the departure of young adults in general, and the rebellion of young women in particular, deprived established family patterns and social hierarchies of nearly all their meaning.

Just how severe the social and community cost will be remains unclear. How much those who left the village may have actually improved their incomes or increased the satisfactions of their lives cannot be discerned; but the emptiness of the old village is an obvious depressant upon those who remain. The negative selection that went into family choices about whom to leave behind and whom to educate for entry into the urban world, means that the average talent and energy of the remaining population of Kardamili has probably declined. Under these circumstances, really successful responses to the crises ahead remain problematical; although the return of one young man from Australia to look after the family olive groves, and the in-migration of a retired air force officer who had no prior connections with Kardamili whatever and became manager for the hotel, demonstrated that a countermovement into the village was not beyond the bounds of possibility.

In Old Greece, therefore, where village ways were deeply rooted, both Old Corinth and Kardamili managed to solve the problems that in 1947 had threatened to tear the two communities apart. Class war was headed off; and in both villages the general pattern of traditional routines was still very much in evidence, even though customary behavior and time-honored family roles did not any longer automatically command the assent of the young. Generational change will therefore create new problems, especially in Kardamili; but for the time being, thirty years after the dark time of 1947, both communities could take comfort from the success with which, in contrasting ways,

they had managed to solve the pressing problems of the generation now passing from the scene. No wonder, then, that political
calm prevailed. Everyone with real grievance against things-as-
they-are had departed.

Thessaly

The rural life of Thessaly did not change as much, nor were old
antagonisms as thoroughly overcome, to judge from the two
villages I observed there. In Kerasia, the wounds of the guerrilla
war were deep and healed very slowly. Poverty continued to
haunt the village for many years, and material improvements,
when they came, continued to fall far short of those that other,
nearby communities took for granted. A sense of alienation and
of being cheated could therefore flourish even in face of a rising
standard of living. By contrast, in Lofiscos, a village out in the
Thessalian plain, some fifteen air miles from Kerasia, prosperity
was an old story. Consequently, the economic bonanza of the
postwar years had remarkably little impact on village ways until
after 1967.

In 1956, when I first stopped at Lofiscos, the outward
appearance of the village was most unprepossessing. It lay about
a quarter of a mile to the east of the main road between Volos
and Larissa. The approach consisted of an unimproved track
which had become a spreading morass of mudholes as vehicles,
seeking to avoid one quagmire, created new ones by their
detours across the soft, rich loam. The village lands, located on a
dried-out lake bottom, were very fertile. Immediately to the east
of Lofiscos lay a shallow remnant of what was formerly a much
more extensive body of water, known as Lake Karla. Its margins
moved back and forth across an almost flat terrain each season,
exposing lush grasslands in summer as the waters receded, and
then swelling each spring to the verge of the village wheat fields,
or even inundating them in unusually wet seasons.

As one approached Lofiscos, the irregularly scattered mud-
brick houses and sheds looked shabby and run down. Being
small, one-story structures, they blended inconspicuously into
the muddy landscape. Not a tree relieved the starkness of the
scene, but in the center of the village towered a stout, two-story
mud-brick structure, dominating all the rest. It had once been

the home, storehouse, and castle of a Turkish pasha who farmed
the lands of Lofiscos before 1881, when this part of Thessaly
passed under Greek sovereignty. The Turk thereupon sold his
land to a Greek in Larissa who became an absentee landowner.
In 1920 a land law passed several years before by the Greek
Parliament was applied to Lofiscos, with the result that the
landowner was compelled to sell most of his estate to the Greek
government, which transferred possession to the families that
had been tilling the land as hired hands.

What this meant in practice was that allotments of 137
stremmata (33.9 acres) each were distributed to thirty-three
eligible families. In addition, shepherds who had been accustomed to feeding their animals on the summer pastureland
exposed by the shrinkage of the lake received allotments of 15
stremmata (3.9 acres). As later in New Eleftherohori, because
only heads of families received these allotments, every young
man of marriageable age hastened to find himself a wife in order
to qualify. In many cases, families founded in 1920 were still in
possession in 1956.

If one remembers that in New Eleftherohori, seven years later,
a mere 27 stremmata of less fertile land was judged sufficient for
the support of a family, some idea of the comparative affluence
of the inhabitants of Lofiscos in the interwar years becomes
apparent. Before 1881, their forefathers had been miserable,
malaria-ridden, servile laborers at the mercy of their Turkish
master. Between 1881 and 1920, their fathers had been scarcely
any better off, under the thumb of a Greek absentee landlord.
Suddenly, in 1920, the income formerly siphoned into the hands
of the landowners came into the villagers' own possession, for
they continued as before to raise wheat for market.

Yet their changed circumstances did not lead the villagers to
alter their outward manner of life in any very noticeable way.
They had inherited from their time of subjection to landlord
domination a lively distrust of urban dwellers in particular and
outsiders in general. Folk wisdom taught them that to exhibit
any outward sign of wealth was dangerous folly. Sooner or later
visible wealth would attract some powerful stranger who would
start collecting money or goods from the community as aforetime. Consequently, the people of Lofiscos continued to live in
the squalid mud-brick houses their fathers and grandfathers had

lived in before them. Public improvements were eschewed for the same reason. The villagers had achieved their hearts' desire by throwing off the landlord's control over their lives. The best way to keep what they had won, they all believed, was to remain utterly inconspicuous.

Such a strategy proved its worth during the German occupation, which made remarkably little difference to Lofiscos. Wheat was easy to sell in time of food shortage, and Lofiscos continued to produce a surplus of wheat. No one from the village was killed; and if there were political differences among the villagers, I was not told of them. The village had inherited a radical bent from the days of struggle against the Greek landlord; and EAM's line, accusing the rich of collaboration, probably struck a sympathetic chord in the minds of most villagers. But political commitment was tepid, one way or the other, and the restoration of Athens' authority in the spring of 1945 created no particular problems either. When the guerrilla band started up on Mount Pelion in 1946, Lofiscos remained unaffected. The guerrilla supply system was never able to extend far enough from its mountain base to affect the village. Thus the war and its hardships passed Lofiscos by, leaving remarkably little residue in anyone's memory at the time I first began asking questions of the inhabitants. Somehow the fields had been tilled, wheat planted, and harvests brought in throughout the war years; and there had never been the slightest difficulty in disposing of surplus wheat on relatively advantageous terms.

After the war, the big change in village life at Lofiscos was the work of the public health experts of UNRRA, who in 1945–46 sprayed Greece with DDT on such a scale as almost to annihilate the anopheles mosquito. As a result, malaria disappeared from the entire country. This made life in Old Corinth, New Eleftherohori, and in most plains villages of Greece far more comfortable. In Lofiscos it made an enormous difference, since before the war malaria had been universal in that community and recurrent bouts of fever often interfered with field work. Yet bodies wracked by malaria for decades did not recover normal vigor all at once; and the apathy apparent in the manner of the inhabitants when first I visited Lofiscos—an apathy quite uncharacteristic of Greeks—was almost certainly a carry-over from the time when everyone suffered from malaria throughout the summer and could not function at full physical efficiency. By 1976 all trace of that apathy had disappeared; but by then a new generation of farmers was in charge of the village. Malaria had become only a memory.

Until 1952, cultivation remained completely traditional. The fact was that Lofiscos inherited a technically efficient, export agriculture. Thessaly was by nature the granary of Greece, and for at least 2,500 years the cities of the Aegean had constituted a good market for grain surpluses. The first postwar change in Lofiscos, resort to fertilizer, was initiated in 1952. This, followed by improved seed, had the effect of multiplying harvests two-fold. Then in 1955 an agent from the Agricultural Bank persuaded one farmer of the community to put in an irrigation well and plant cotton instead of the usual wheat. This proved a good investment, for the farmer in question tripled his cash income from the irrigated field; and in 1956 others were planning to dig wells and buy pumps next year, even though it involved going into debt.

Yet this "takeoff" did not change life in Lofiscos nearly as much as similar technical advances changed Old Corinth. This was because the farmers of Lofiscos soon backed away from the new possibilities of irrigation farming, finding an enhanced cash income not worth the risks entailed. Cotton prices fluctuated, whereas the price of wheat was fixed by the government. Since they were located on excellent wheat land, the support price necessary to keep marginal lands in wheat meant a guaranteed fortune for Lofiscos. Loss from a hail storm was about the only risk the farmers faced; and that was not serious. By comparison, if they had ever gone in extensively for irrigated crops—cotton or something else—as Old Corinth did, prices would have been uncertain, and the need to hire outside labor would have interfered with the "low profile" that the people of Lofiscos preferred. The farmers of Lofiscos knew that they were extraordinarily well-off by Greek standards, and did not think it wise to bring in villagers from places like Kerasia to work their fields for them. They remembered, after all, how their fathers had displaced one landlord. To become landlords themselves, hirers of labor, was a change of role for which they were not ready. Far better to stick with wheat which required no outside labor, since even before the war the plains of Thessaly were reaped by combine.

Consequently, when I returned in 1966 the effect of irrigation, though visible, was not spectacular. Fields showing bright green amidst the brown of the wheat stubble were few and far between. The outward appearance of the village was almost unchanged: only a bright red combine and a machine shed of corrugated sheet metal near the main road seemed new. All this conservatism altered abruptly in 1967, when the inhabitants agreed to redesign the layout of their village by putting in a new grid of gravelled roadways, and improving the access road from the highway so that wheeled vehicles could come and go at any time of year without danger of getting stuck in the soft, rich mud. To run a rectangular grid of roads through the village required most households to change outbuildings or relocate living quarters. One change led swiftly to another, and the net result was that almost every family decided to build an entirely new house.

By 1976, the transformation was complete. Where shabby, tumbledown mud-brick had previously been the sole form of architecture, now plastered and decoratively painted exteriors made the village look like a small, tidy suburban town. Trees had grown up since 1956, giving both fruit and shade; and the village was dominated by the facade of a fine new church, much taller than the former Turkish pasha's house, which however still stood despite its tumbledown state. (It was used as a storehouse by the absentee landowner, who retained title to some 1,000 stremmata of land in the village.) The church had been built between 1974 and 1976, and was paid for by contributions from the families of Lofiscos. Donors' names were displayed throughout the interior, attached to icons and other objects individual gifts had made possible. Among the contributors to the church was an old shoemaker who lived in a small town in Indiana. In his youth, probably before the distribution of allotments in 1920, he had emigrated to America, but remained in touch with relatives, and obviously regarded himself as still a member of the village where he had been born. Other adjacent villages also had built new churches. Rivalry to see whose church would be largest and most magnificent obviously played a part in persuading the villagers to contribute as lavishly as they had to the construction of their new church.

The result was an urban level of comfort in Lofiscos. The new houses all had modern plumbing, TV, radio, electric refrigerators, washing machines, and similar household appliances. Once the fear of any form of conspicuous consumption (or investment) had been overcome, the village wealth, instead of reposing in the form of secret hoards of gold coins, as formerly, had found new and far more obvious embodiment.

With this change, former inhibitions against looking beyond the village itself for standards of dress, behavior, and career aspiration also abruptly crumbled. Until 1967 no child from Lofiscos had gone away to secondary school. There was enough land in the village to make it quite unnecessary to look abroad for livelihood; and even though many of the allotments of 1920 had been subdivided to accommodate a new generation, as long as living standards remained hobbled by a desire to be inconspicuous in the eyes of potential tax collectors, the diminution of family income inherent in possessing smaller quantities of land did not make much outward difference.

Yet there were obvious limits to such a policy. To head off the need to subdivide holdings, in 1967–68 a few young persons prepared to leave the village by going off to Larissa to attend secondary school. By 1976 the fashion had become all but universal. Secondary schooling opened the way to a career in town; and the glitter of the city had begun to dazzle all the young people of Lofiscos, who by 1976 unanimously clamored for the right to a secondary education. This created consternation among their fathers, whose rich farmland, however attractive to the older generation, looked only like dirt to the young. Complaints about the bad manners of the rising generation—how schoolboys demanded money to spend frivolously instead of studying hard, and how they no longer deferred to their elders—were strong and heartfelt among the farmers of Lofiscos in 1976. Fathers of families obviously felt that the value and meaning of their way of life was suddenly being called into question by the behavior of their children. They were both puzzled and resentful.

For the time being the withdrawal of youth from village routines made little difference. Available farm machinery— tractors, combines, multiple gang plows and the like—allowed cultivation of the flat loam of Lofiscos by far fewer hands than remained in the village. What was in danger was the psychological autonomy and self-sufficiency that up to this time had governed local life. Smug satisfaction with the knowledge of how well-off they were by comparison with other Greek peasants had sustained the people of Lofiscos since the 1920s. Marriages had been carefully arranged so as to exclude outsiders, with the result that all the villagers were related to one another by blood or by marriage. A few marriages brought brides from immediately adjacent villages, occupying the same lake-bottom land and enjoying very similar allotments. But a wife from these outside communities was unusual. Careful parents, negotiating a suitable marriage, preferred someone within the village where the exact quality of land offered as dowry and inheritance could be assessed accurately and the personal qualities of prospective bride and groom could be weighed with precision. All the more shocking, therefore, was their children's breakaway from a style of life that had been so tightly and deliberately self-contained.

Yet dismay at their children's behavior did not prevent the farmers of Lofiscos from vigorously affirming the values inherent in their own way of life. This found expression in 1976 in their struggle to add additional acres to the land they already owned. A government-financed engineering project had just completed the drainage of Lake Karla. This had been talked of before the war, and actual work had begun in the 1950s. Twenty years later, in 1976, it had finally come true. The former lake bottom was dry, but government officials had not decided how to apportion the land that had thus become available. The villagers of Lofiscos claimed that their rights extended to the furthest limit that had ever been exposed by the natural shrinkage of the lake in summertime; and in fact they had always been free to make what use they could of such land in the weeks or months when it was exposed. By choosing the lowest point the lake had attained in living memory, the villagers of Lofiscos, and of thirteen other villages with lands fronting on the former lake margins, could make good their right to almost the whole of the reclaimed area.

Official decision was not forthcoming, so the villagers determined to take matters into their own hands. By plowing and harvesting the disputed land, they figured that they would reinforce their claim in the most direct of all possible ways. Accordingly, in the spring of 1976, the men of fourteen villages whose lands fronted on the old lakeshore fixed on a day when all together they "marched" their tractors—one thousand strong, I was told, with what must have been considerable exaggeration—onto the new land and began to cultivate it. At the time I visited Lofiscos, a law suit in Athens was pending to explore the legal consequences of the act. The villagers were awaiting the ripening of the wheat—some two weeks in the future—with lively interest. They had committed substantial sums of money to the purchase of seed for the new lands, not to mention the costs of cultivation, and realized that once they had brought in a harvest, it would become more difficult for government authorities to refuse their claim to full possession.

The flavor of life was vastly improved for the farmers of Lofiscos by this collective struggle against bureaucratic authority. It refreshed old memories of the time before 1920 when a similar contest over title to land had dominated village affairs. Moreover, if the villagers were successful they would double or more than double the lands at their disposal, and be able to utilize their machinery far more effectively than otherwise.

The alternative before government authorities was to transport poor, marginal farmers onto the new fertile land from the mountain villages that surround the Thessalian plain. As we shall soon see, some steps had been taken in that direction as early as 1964, when families from Kerasia had been allowed to rent newly drained plots of land from Lake Karla's former flood plain. Social justice might seem to require a policy of equalizing agricultural wealth as between villages like Lofiscos and Kerasia. On the other hand, efficient production required larger farms and more machinery—exactly what Lofiscos already possessed. What the decision would be was still unclear in 1976. But the issue gave spice to life in Lofiscos and provided the people of Kerasia with another grievance against the government. The income gap between the two communities, enormous in 1947, may have been narrowed in 1976, but not by much; and the psychological differences between the two villages, despite their geographical propinquity, remained as great as ever.

Kerasia, so roughly handled by official authorities during the guerrilla war, received much assistance afterwards from government funds and agents; yet most of the population remained alienated and ungrateful. The reason was not far to seek. Even

after government funds had permitted repair of the village
houses, had constructed a new road, brought a good water
supply down from the mountain above, and carried through
several other less important public improvements, the villagers
still had no adequate way of earning a living. Efforts to improve
land-use by planting vines and olive trees met with sullen
suspicion, and soon proved vain. Olive trees, planted in the
early 1950s, were killed by a severe winter in 1957, and vines
fared little better. Age-old ecological boundaries which made the
north slope of Mount Pelion inhospitable to Mediterranean
crops could not be transgressed as easily as government
agronomists had hoped.

The situation in 1956, when I returned to Kerasia, was this:
wage work for road building and the other capital improvements
had terminated; within the village everything that could be
rebuilt had been rebuilt. About fifty men were employed on the
drainage project for Lake Karla, and rumors about what might
happen when that had been finished circulated freely. But since
the drainage had been talked of for many years, skepticism was
more prevalent than hope.

Confidence in the benevolence of official authority was at a
low ebb in Kerasia. On top of the harsh experiences of the
wartime removal to Volos, shortly after the villagers had been
forcibly returned to Kerasia part of the slope of Mount Pelion
from which they had been accustomed to cut wood to make into
charcoal had been reserved for reforestation. From the villagers'
viewpoint, therefore, while the government handed out various
plums in the way of wage work for this or that project, perhaps
worthwhile, perhaps not, it simultaneously was taking away
their basic livelihood. Since the late 1930s, the sale of charcoal in
Volos had become for most village families the only source of
income they could control themselves, and thus the only reliable
supplement to whatever could be gained from local cultivation
and sheep-herding. At best, wage work involved humiliating
subservience to a boss; and, as experienced in Kerasia, it was an
undependable source of income, liable to be cut off each time a
particular construction project ended.

Under the circumstances, it is not surprising that the villagers
decided to continue woodcutting in the prohibited areas, in spite
of all the government could do. They proceeded as against a

hostile force, with scouts to discern the whereabouts of the
rangers who were supposed to guard the forest, diversionary
actions to draw the rangers off to a spot remote from the
intended area of woodcutting, and routes of retreat carefully
planned in case something went wrong with the battle plan. In
effect, guerrilla action continued, but in a modified form. The
spirit of defiance that such expeditions nurtured and reflected
dominated the community in 1956, despite all the money the
government had put into the village.

Ten years later the situation in Kerasia had begun to improve
in two ways. In-migration to Volos opened up a bit, and some
ninety persons had been officially transferred from the village to
that nearby city. This merely ratified accomplished facts; but the
lowering of obstacles to free transfer of legal residence, which
had been one of the ways the government had sought to force
refugees back to their original homes, eased emigration signifi-
cantly. Volos, however, had few jobs to offer. The city was
economically depressed. Since the days of Achilles (who sailed
thence to Troy) Volos had served as Thessaly's port. But after
World War II, improved roads made it cheaper to ship goods to
Athens or Germany by truck, thus saving the costs of transshipment in Volos. Alternative economic roles for the port city were
hard to find. As far as Kerasia was concerned, this meant that
migration into Volos offered no effective escape from the dead
end into which the village was heading through ecologically
destructive exploitation of the mountainside.

Yet there was another and more promising possibility on the
horizon. The drainage of Lake Karla, so important to Lofiscos in
1976, had already made some progress in 1964. Lowering of the
lake level had exposed new, fertile land; and the government
officials in charge assigned some of it to the poverty-stricken
inhabitants of Kerasia. To forestall a rash of early marriages of
the kind that had occurred in Lofiscos and New Eleftherohori,
the basis of assignment was per caput: each family head was
allocated the right to rent 5 stremmata (1.2 acres) of land for
every family member. Thus a man and wife with three children
would receive 25 stremmata; a single man would get only 5.

This effort at social justice was countered, in the eyes of the
community, by the fact that title to the new land was not
transferred to the villagers. Instead they were invited to sign an

annual lease with the Agricultural Bank. Simultaneously, credit
terms for seed, fertilizer, and costs of cultivation were agreed
upon. Each year leases were renegotiated and any change in
family situation—births, deaths, or departures—dictated adjustments in the quantity of land leased to the particular family for
the new year. At the end of each year the account with the bank
had to be settled before any new lease could be signed. In this
way the Agricultural Bank exercised a close control over the use
to which the villagers put the land, and family finances remained
subject to external, bureaucratic supervision.

All this was intensely distasteful to the proud people of
Kerasia. Satisfaction in at last having the means to feed themselves throughout the year from the produce of their own labor
was diminished by the terms upon which this release from
unbearable poverty had been achieved. The men of Kerasia had
been compelled to give up their ancient freedom and personal
independence for a mess of pottage offered them by unsympa-
thetic government bureaucrats. The shepherd's life had become
impossible; but was enslavement to other men's wills and to the
laboriousness of agricultural routines an acceptable substitute?
For most of the village the answer was a sullen negative.

All the same, after 1964, for the first time in a generation, the
population of the village did have a secure food supply. The
rental and credit terms offered by the Agricultural Bank assured
the leaseholders of enough wheat to feed themselves, with some
left over to sell to the government at the support price. From this
the loans for fertilizer could be paid back, and a little spare cash
would remain for other family purposes. It was a viable, if
dependent and therefore undignified, mode of life. The desperate
spirit so evident in 1947 and 1956 had accordingly disappeared.
Charcoal burning continued; but within limits defined by official
regulation. The village now lived fully within the law for the
first time since 1940.

Memories of past conflict remained vivid, nonetheless, so that
political hatreds had by no means disappeared from the community. Indeed supporters of the rival extremes refused to talk
freely in each others' presence, and obviously looked upon one
another as enemies still, even if active hostilities had been
suspended. Ten years later, in 1976, this situation still prevailed,
although with the passage of time the old debates had perhaps

begun to lose their ferocity. At any rate, no one any longer expected fundamental change of the balance of power within the village in any near future; and everyone admitted, by the very fact of remaining in situ, that life had become tolerable in Kerasia, even if it was not as rich or attractive as in other, more favored communities.

Two other changes were apparent by 1976. First of all, newly established factories on the outskirts of Volos employed some twenty to thirty men from the village. They went off to work each morning by bus. A few women from Kerasia also worked in town as cleaning women, and commuted by bus. Second, no fewer than thirty-three youngsters from Kerasia were attending secondary school, commuting in the opposite direction to the nearby village of Kanalia each day. Ten years before, going to secondary school had been much more costly, since a student then had to leave home and take up residence in Volos. Now a broad highway to white-collar status opened up to village families that could not have afforded to support a child living away from home. Accordingly, a prospect of escape from the depressed condition from which Kerasia had suffered for at least fifty years began to dawn, with consequences which it will take another decade to reveal.

For the time being, however, the fact that the villagers of Kerasia encountered urban life as factory hands and as cleaning women meant that older patterns of political alienation from the establishment did not change very much among those who took these low-status jobs. A previously proletarianized village was supplying recruits to an urban proletariat. Hence, the enhanced income regular employment provided did little to affect old and well-established political and psychological attitudes.

For some reason, the people of Kerasia never resorted to large-scale emigration. Perhaps the marginal life experienced by those who removed to Volos during the guerrilla war discredited this response to their economic problems. At any rate, the village population hovered at just about five hundred throughout the period. War losses nearly balanced natural increase in the decade before 1956. Thereafter, emigration to Athens, Larissa, and Volos did much the same. The total number of inhabitants was reported to me as 430 in 1940, 505 in 1956, 510 in 1966, and 487 in 1976. This last figure represented an increase from 1971, when the census recorded only 411 persons living in Kerasia. At the time of that census, emigration to Germany, begun in 1965, had removed a few persons from the village, and emigration to Volos and other Greek cities was at or near its maximum. What had happened between 1971 and 1976 to restore village population was that several families working in Volos discovered that it was both pleasanter and cheaper to live in their own houses rent-free and pay the cost of bus transportation into town each day instead of having to rent living quarters in the city. Hence, as a result of an improved bus service, which in 1976 ran into Volos four times each day, a substantial reverse movement back to the village had occurred.

By 1976, in fact, activity once critical to village life had become marginal. Charcoal burning was unimportant. The market in Volos had almost entirely disappeared, because other fuels supplanted charcoal for cooking and space heating. Only twenty-eight families still kept sheep or goats—and the total number of animals was only about a quarter of what had been kept before the war, when herding was still a major economic support for the community. The upper village remained uninhabited and the old values of the shepherd past were fast fading away. But though everybody had enough to eat, thanks to the allotments in the drained lake bottom, the compromise of personal independence that exploitation of the allotments required and the no less awkward compromise of liberty involved in accepting wage work in town, meant that the old heroic moral code had been betrayed. The price of survival turned out to be surrender of the old, proud shepherds' style of life. The residual anger of the people of Kerasia registered their indignation at having had to pay such a price in order to have enough to eat.

Macedonia

Oddly enough, in Macedonia, where the impact of the guerrilla war affected plains villages as well as hill villages, recovery came faster; and, by 1976, the result was a good deal more satisfactory than in Thessaly, both to the villagers concerned and to Greek governmental authorities. Through higher education of its youth, New Eleftherohori discovered a way to enter urban life at a level far more satisfactory than anything available to the people of Kerasia; and Kotta, by paying the full price of war, unassisted by governmental bureaucratic intervention, emerged with its traditional life style intact, so that new prosperity, when it came, involved none of the psychological costs that the people of Kerasia paid so reluctantly.

To be sure, to achieve this comparatively happy result, the people of New Eleftherohori had to pass through a difficult transition time, when the success of the strategy of sending their sons to secondary school was still in doubt. In 1956, for instance, the situation of the village remained precarious. To be sure, use of fertilizer, made available through loans from the Agricultural Bank, had the effect of more than doubling wheat yields. Families hard-pressed to make out on their allotments of 27 stremmata thus secured a small margin between production and what they needed for sheer survival. With this, after paying off the bank loan, they could finance education, accumulate a dowry, or replace a draught animal more easily than before. But the crunch was this: those sons and daughters who stayed back on the farm with the prospect of some day inheriting a full half of the family allotment had to postpone marriage until such time as the older generation was ready to retire, or died. Different family situations worked out differently, but the principle whereby each sister had first to be suitably dowered and wedded before the brothers could marry was generally recognized in the village. This made for many years of rigorous saving; yet to give land in dowry was to condemn the rest of the family to a reduced standard of living and made suitable marriages for other siblings more difficult. The result was that young women in their late twenties and early thirties remained at home unmarried, waiting to accumulate a dowry, while their brothers waited too, often impatiently, for the day when they might look forward to marriage themselves. The sense of being trapped remained intense. Envy of the easier life of townspeople was acute.

By 1966 the village had found a fairly promising solution to the problem. Income had been expanded in three ways: by new, labor-intensive cropping; by tourism; and by emigration. Marriages still waited upon finding a suitable livelihood for the new couple; but the enhanced cash flow coming into the village made this easier than before and took the edge off the tense, prolonged waiting of 1956. Let me say a bit about each of the new possibilities that opened before the villagers in the decade between 1956 and 1966.

The Greek government regulated tobacco growing closely, aiming to keep prices up and to avoid disrupting the economy of old-established tobacco villages by prohibiting competition from fresh land. Before 1954, consequently, official regulation forbade planting tobacco in the part of Macedonia where New Eleftherohori was situated. In that year the prohibition was lifted—partly, perhaps, because many of the most intensive tobacco-growing villages of Greece were located in western Thrace and inhabited by Turks. As relations between the two governments worsened, the willingness of the Greek government to protect Turkish tobacco growers from Greek competition disappeared. Whatever the reason, from 1954 the farmers of New Eleftherohori were permitted to raise tobacco, and swiftly moved into the new business, since a field planted with tobacco brought in 3.5 times as much money as the same field planted with wheat. From 480 stremmata (119 acres) in 1954 the land under tobacco increased to 898 stremmata (234 acres) in 1956 and crested ten years later at 1,207 stremmata (296 acres), which was about as much as the labor-power of the village could handle.

Tobacco, as traditionally raised in Greece, required transplantation of seedlings by hand from seedbeds, hand-watering of the transplants till they rooted themselves successfully, hoeing to keep down weeds, and then hand-picking the ripe leaves every morning until the end of the growing season. Harvested leaves had to be strung and hung up to dry before being ready for sale. All this required long hours of work in which men, women, and children could take part, thus mobilizing the labor of all the family throughout a considerable part of the year. The people of the village sweated hard to earn the extra income tobacco brought—no doubt of that; but the crop also made possible effective use of the village's labor force as never before, since wheat, except in the brief harvest period, requires no particular attention.

Obviously, with the new cash tobacco brought in, life on less land became feasible; and the old inhibitions against subdividing allotments among several children were lessened. The result was considerable departure from the former rigid equality of circumstance among all the villagers. Some small holdings of half an allotment or even less came into existence; in a few cases, an heir of an intact allotment married a girl who also brought with her an entire allotment, thus doubling the land possessed by the new family. Various labor contracts between those with much and those with little land began to proliferate.

In 1966, therefore, New Eleftherohori seemed to be well on its way to becoming a stratified rural community more or less like Old Corinth. Plans for irrigation wells and other improvements were also under discussion; but rainfall in New Eleftherohori is a good deal more abundant than it is further south in Greece and the rewards of irrigation were correspondingly less dramatic. For this, and perhaps for other reasons, irrigation wells were never sunk. Some other improvements, such as the plantation of 900 stremmata (222 acres) with olive trees, proved to be a mistake when, after a promising start, the trees all froze during a hard winter early in the 1960s.

What cut short the intensification of cropping and the differentiation of holdings in the village was the success the community started to have in two other directions. The village lands fronted on the sea, and a narrow sand beach made the stretch of waterfront particularly attractive to tourists. The first rather ramshackle tourist accommodations were built shortly before 1966. By 1976 a mini-community had grown up along the shore, separated from the village by half a mile or more. There businessmen from Salonika occupied summer cottages, or speculated in real estate by buying a few stremmata from the farmers of the village, erecting an apartment building, and renting it to summer visitors. Some of the villagers began to play the game on their own behalf, making a deal with a building contractor for part rights in a finished apartment building in return for contributing the land upon which to build. Open-air restaurants sprang up along the shore, specializing in fish delivered fresh from the sea. This meant new employment possibilities, and brought a substantial flow of ready cash into the community. Here, then, were new and sometimes very lucrative sources of income. By selling off a few waterfront stremmata, a family could finance an education, arrange for a dowry, or achieve some other major goal in the twinkling of an eye; and those who kept their waterfront property and went into partnerships in its development did even better for themselves. Income of this kind came far easier than money earned by raising and curing tobacco. Not surprisingly, in proportion as this sort of easy cash became available, the villagers began to give up on tobacco.

But what made reversion to wheat cultivation so widespread in 1976 was the scale of in-migration to town. Salonika began to boom in the 1960s, partly as a by-product of industrial investment, particularly the Esso-Pappas complex of new plants, and partly as a result of the opening up of the Bulgarian as well as the Yugoslav frontiers to the movement of goods. As jobs in Salonika multiplied, the educated young men of New Eleftherohori stood ready and eager to occupy available white-collar posts. Moreover, successful jobholders sent part of their salaries home to help siblings get an education and qualify for urban white-collar work. They also stood ready to help their relatives find employment in town when their schooling was completed.

The result, by 1976, was remarkable. About half the families of the village lived most of the time in Salonika and commuted to New Eleftherohori on weekends, where all the tasks of wheatfarming could easily be accomplished on a part-time, weekend basis. To facilitate weekend farming, the village boasted no fewer than forty tractors, although the village president opined that three would suffice to cultivate all the fields if used at full capacity. But Sunday farmers who were due at their desks next day in Salonika could not wait their turn to use a tractor. Hence their extravagant investment in machinery, which the Agricultural Bank had vainly tried to head off by refusing credit to the villagers once a suitable number of tractors had entered the community. Credit extended by tractor sellers got around this form of bureaucratic wisdom, even if the credit terms offered were more onerous than those the Agricultural Bank customarily extended.

Obviously, tobacco cultivation was incompatible with part-time farming. Only the half of the village that had not made lodgment in town continued to find intensive labor in tobacco fields worthwhile. Acreage in tobacco had therefore dropped sharply from a peak of 1,207 stremmata in 1966 to 704 stremmata in 1975 and 541 stremmata in 1976.

Population statistics as officially maintained in New Eleftherohori had lost much of their former significance by 1976, thanks to the interpenetration of town and village that had occurred. Thus, for example, most babies were born in hospitals in Salonika or in Katerini, the nearest town where hospital accommodations existed. Even if the mother returned at once to New Eleftherohori with her baby, such births, since they occurred elsewhere, were not entered in village records. Hence an apparently catastrophic drop in birthrate was largely illusory, but exactitude became unobtainable.

The village seems to have attained an almost stable population. That, at any rate, is what its president asserted, offering a thousand persons as his own estimate of the village population in 1976. This was exactly the same figure I was given in 1966, and may be compared with the figures of 814 for 1947 and 875 for 1956. Statistics of school attendance—thirty-five children from the village were attending secondary school in 1976— prove that the community has not lost all of its young people. What was new in 1976 was that girls as well as boys were attending secondary school. They, too, now looked forward to careers in town, where an income-producing job was as good as a dowry when it came to getting married and settled in life.

Some families—about fifty persons in all—had pulled up roots entirely and sold their land; but such departures were balanced by newcomers to the village who had moved in to provide services connected with the tourist trade by the shore. This, together with a substantially reduced birthrate, resulted in approximate stability in village numbers. Former differences between the Pontic refugees and the "squatters" from Mount Olympos had almost disappeared. Intermarriage across this social barrier had become common. Villagers' pride and self-satisfaction at how cleverly they had cashed in on education to qualify for a soft job in town sustained a collective consciousness of local superiority that quite eclipsed the older fissure between refugees and natives.

A further important change in the life of New Eleftherohori was the establishment of a small clothing factory in 1975. In that year the village council made a deal with a businessman from Salonika whereby he rented an unused piece of land near the center of the village and put up a shed where thirty young women from the village were at work when I visited the place in 1976. Shed, sewing machines, material, and patterns were all supplied by the entrepreneur, and he paid piece rates identical with those prevailing in Salonika. What made the deal attractive to him was that by moving out into the country he escaped special excise taxes levied within the city.

From the villagers' point of view, urban wages in a home setting were much to be preferred to labor in the tobacco fields. Indeed, the village president said that a single woman working for a year in the clothing factory could earn as much as a family of five could gain by cultivating tobacco. A year or two of such employment, therefore, would permit a girl to earn a handsome dowry for herself; and this path to independence and a secure settlement in life seemed better to many in the village than the harder way of pursuing secondary education and qualifying for white-collar work. It meant, nevertheless, that some village girls were beginning to follow a proletarian as against the older white-collar route to personal independence. This may widen social differences within the village in time to come. But nothing of the sort had yet been felt in the community. Instead, what prevailed was satisfaction at the appearance of still another and comfortably convenient economic opportunity for the members of the community.

Moreover, a much larger and more ambitious plan was afoot for locating a cannery in New Eleftherohori. This involved a relatively large investment. If ever built, the plant would constitute a focus for truck gardening in a dozen or more villages scattered across the plain that separates Salonika from New Eleftherohori. With authentic booster spirit, the village president was sure the plan would be achieved since the village had offered a better location for the projected plant than any of the competing communities. But the funds required were not in hand; discussion of the possibility had begun at least a decade before; and this further step towards industrialization seemed more indicative of the enterprising spirit of the villagers than of imminent urbanization.

Yet New Eleftherohori clearly aspired to become a small town rather than remain a mere village. Local boosterism had entirely eclipsed older jealousy of townsmen's easier life. Indeed, the villagers were fully conscious of the charms of country living. Urban tourists and weekend visitors from Salonika regularly demonstrated the attractions of life in New Eleftherohori con-

vincingly enough. Household equipment was of an urban standard; TV, introduced into the village in 1969, allowed full-time
as well as part-time residents of the community to share in the
glittering world of Hollywood and Paris, Athens and Munich, in
a way that made the dark, cramped, and fear-ridden life of 1947
seem like a bad dream.

The village, in effect, had entered enthusiastically into an
urban world at a white-collar rather than a proletarian level.
The resulting self-satisfaction and personal as well as collective
sense of worth stood in remarkable contrast to the lingering
discontents of Kerasia, whose entry into urban life was less
remunerative and affected a smaller proportion of the village
population. Unlike Lofiscos, where richer land and larger allotments had made New Eleftherohori's strenuous efforts to escape
rural poverty unnecessary, the village had already made a
successful accommodation with urban ways and life-styles.
After hard years of self-denial, capital accumulation, and energetic acquisition of urban skills, the villagers had begun to reap
the rewards of their foresight and effort. Small wonder that they
were generally satisfied with the result, and harbored scant
traces of the political radicalism that had polarized the community thirty years before.

As for Kotta, nestling in the high plateau of western Macedonia, there, too, satisfaction reigned by 1976. For a long time
after the war ended, the survival of the village was in question,
since the removal in 1947 of all children between two and
fourteen created a formidable gap in the age pyramid. Moreover, in the immediate postwar years, when contacts with
Sydney and Toronto opened up again, many of the survivors
decided to emigrate to one or other of these cities, where
relatives were both willing and able to finance the cost of
passage.

In 1956, when I first returned to Kotta, emigration seemed to
threaten the survival of the village, even though the sheer delight
at having survived when so many had perished gave talk in the
village café a buoyant, cheerful tone that contrasted sharply
with the resentment the survivors from Kerasia exhibited. In
1966 I was unable to visit Kotta because Greek army authorities
refused to allow me to travel so close to the frontier. Nevertheless, by correspondence with the village priest, a man of unusual

intelligence and commanding presence, I was able to discover that 149 persons were still living in the village; that 39 people had departed for overseas destinations in the preceding ten years; and that 23 deaths exceeded the 18 births that had occurred during the same period.

Only thirteen children of school age were living in the village in 1956. The school had been closed, since this was fewer than the minimum prescribed by the Greek government. The children, accordingly, had to travel by bus to an adjacent community for their schooling. On the positive side, sale of a variety of bean that grows well in Kotta was bringing cash into the community; and a tractor, financed by remittances from abroad, had altered the character of farm work radically, lightening the tasks of cultivation and freeing land previously needed for raising fodder crops for draught animals. As a result, the village was self-sufficient for its food and even earned a little by selling beans. Quite a turnaround from the desperate situation of 1947 when only four months' food could be produced within the village bounds!

By 1976 population was down to a mere hundred, but there were eighteen children of school age, and the government had reopened the village school. What made this turnaround possible was the fact that several persons who had been carried off to Communist lands in 1947 had made their way back to Kotta, and, instead of emigrating overseas, decided to remain in their native place. Their experiences in eastern Europe had not been such as to dim the attraction of Kotta's sparse, familiar way of life. Indeed, the two men with whom I conversed who had come back and founded families in the village were emphatic in rejecting communism as they had experienced it in Poland and Rumania respectively. They appreciated the freedom from governmental (or any other alien) control that they enjoyed in Kotta; and the material standard of living they achieved, while modest enough by Greek standards, was equivalent or superior to anything they had met while living abroad.

In 1976, the circumstances of the village were, indeed, very comfortable. The old folks, who still constituted a majority of the population, depended mainly on remittances from their relatives overseas. The eight families in the village that were of childbearing age worked land totalling about 1,000 stremmata

(247 acres); and the village's single tractor made this a relatively
easy task. Enough wheat to feed everyone was produced and
ground into flour within the village. A simple three-year rotation, whereby beans (for market sale) and alfalfa (for cattle feed)
alternated with wheat, kept the fields fertile without resort to
fertilizer. Nitrogen fixation by bacteria that grow naturally on
the roots of alfalfa and beans acted as a very satisfactory
equivalent to expensive nitrogenous fertilizer. The alfalfa provided winter fodder for cattle that pasture on the rough slopes
near the village in summer, returning each evening to be milked
and leaving each morning under the charge of a village cowherd.
The cattle provided milk and meat for village consumption; and
by selling a calf from time to time a family could secure extra
cash income as might be needed. Sheep and goats, which once
were important in the life of Kotta (as in most Greek mountain
villages) had all but disappeared, not because pasture for these
animals did not exist within village territory, but because a
suitable shepherd was not available to accompany them into the
higher and more remote pastureland round about.

As a matter of fact, the higher slopes had been systematically
reforested. The one complaint the villagers made about collision
with bureaucracy was that a defect in their title to the high
mountain pastures that they had been accustomed to use in times
past meant that they received no recompense from officialdom
when these lands were taken over for afforestation; whereas
some neighboring villages, with better titles to their accustomed
pasturelands, had received such payments.

In general, a striking feature of life in Kotta was the way in
which the farmers had escaped the sort of control exercised in
other villages by agents of the Agricultural Bank. After the
cancellation of peasant debt by the military dictatorship in 1968,
the people of Kotta broke off relationship with the bank.
Remittances from abroad had paid for the tractor, and the
pattern of crop rotation meant that they did not need to contract
for fertilizer, as did every other village I visited. This fundamental fact kept the bank and its agents at a distance. The
villagers could and did adhere to the old principle of staying out
of the clutches of moneylenders, even where they appeared in
the form of salaried agents of a (presumably) friendly government. Freedom, that is, immunity from bureaucratic interven-

tion in daily routines of life, was thus a reality in Kotta as nowhere else I visited. The farmers of the village liked it that way, and deliberately sought to preserve a way of life handed down to them from time immemorial.

Independence from the Agricultural Bank did not mean, however, that the farmers of Kotta were not market-oriented. On the contrary, when it suited their interest they dealt with the bank, for example, when selling surplus wheat. The villagers of Kotta fully realized the advantages of prompt and automatic payment from the bank as against the promises of private dealers, who might offer more on paper but often failed to come through with hard cash at the time of the actual delivery. But only a small portion of Kotta's wheat was offered for sale. Most of the crop was consumed within the village. Nevertheless, a third of their cultivated land was devoted to a cash crop—beans; and the price of beans was a matter of lively satisfaction when I was in the village in 1976, since it had been rising.

Careful calculation as to which variety of beans was most advantageous for their fields was a matter of the greatest importance; and the villagers were doubly pleased by the fact that two years before they had shifted from one variety to another and seen the price of their new crop rise more than the price of the variety they had abandoned. Thus they had increased their cash income by shrewd (or lucky) anticipation of the way the market would go, and felt very proud of their own cleverness. The exact price level at which it would be best to move back to the other variety was on the tips of their tongues, for the new variety yielded a somewhat smaller weight of beans, even though it brought in more cash. Altogether, it seemed to me that market sense was just as highly developed among the farmers of Kotta as among any of the other villagers I visited.

What seemed different was a greater solidarity among the separate nuclear families of the community. Presumably, in the deeper past the villagers of Kotta had been subsistence farmers and shepherds, experiencing minimal contact with outsiders. Their Slavic dialect would have been a handicap in dealing with the world beyond their narrow valley; and had such relationships been important, Greek speech to match their Greek Orthodox religion might have been expected to spread among them, just as has in fact happened since 1945. A subsistence style of life puts greater premium upon mutual help across family lines than can exist in a market-oriented society. Surplus, on the rare occasions when it may have existed, could only be shared; and on the principle that one good turn deserves another, help (whether in the form of labor or commodities) given by one family to another, could command repayment later when family situations might alter. Such mutuality, in fact, was a form of insurance against sudden, crippling disaster, such as the early death of an adult male breadwinner. Further north, as already mentioned, Slavic peasants met these needs by the *zadruga*, a collectivity for work and consumption that extended across nuclear family lines, and might embrace up to about a hundred persons.

In Kotta no signs that the *zadruga* had ever existed came to my attention; but in 1976 cultivation was carried on by means of a single tractor, operated by the village president. He did not, apparently, use his monopolistic position to advantage himself unduly. At any rate the other farmers who gathered in the café to discuss village affairs with me showed absolutely no sign of distrusting or disliking the president. On the contrary, he was clearly admired and respected—a leader of the community in every sense of the word, entrusted with most of the village dealings with the external world, and both eager and able to assume such a role without abusing his position or taking private advantage from it. Most Greek peasants would not have trusted one of their number with such powers. And rightly so, for most Greeks, confronting the possibilities of self-enrichment that lay before the president of Kotta, would have seized the chance to advance their own family fortunes at the expense of their fellow-villagers' well-being.

Yet this residual difference between Kotta and other Greek villages does not mean that the villagers did not feel themselves to be Greek. The preferred language among the men of the village was Greek, and they explicitly remarked that conditions in Greece were better than in Yugoslavia, which lay immediately adjacent, just over the crest of the mountains. The village had inherited a Greek identity from the days of struggle against the Bulgarian Exarchate under the Turks, and village experience since 1947 strengthened that inherited identity. The women of the village continued to prefer Slavic speech; children grew up bilingual; but the sense of community identity, embracing all the families of the village in a single whole, was so strong as almost to eclipse any sort of national feeling.

This sense of the village as a unit was far more powerful than in the other Greek villages I studied. In particular, the trans-oceanic daughter communities in Toronto and Sydney were counted as part and parcel of village society, and new offshoots in Tashkent, Athens, and Salonika, though too small to have comparable importance, were by no means forgotten by those who remained at home. The village, more than the nuclear family, appeared to be the in-group with which the people of Kotta most strongly identified themselves.

The outward aspect of Kotta in 1976 suggested that urban standards had made little imprint on the community. The women were still wearing peasant-style clothing, for instance, and maintained ancient manners by staying out of eyeshot of strangers, even though a lively curiosity sometimes provoked them to peek around corners when they judged themselves inconspicuous. Tumbledown mud-brick houses and a coffee house thickly populated by flies sustained the impression that nothing had changed. But indoors, much had altered. Piped water came to Kotta in 1958, for instance; electric refrigerators proliferated from the time that electricity arrived in 1967; and in 1974 a new house, erected by a man who had spent thirty-seven years in Australia, brought all the urban amenities of flush toilet, hot and cold running water, propane gas stove, and a TV set into the village. Bad TV reception, owing to the way the village nestles in a narrow valley amidst higher hills, made his TV set inoperative, however. Kotta therefore, uniquely among the villages of Greece I visited, had not experienced the impact of TV, and remained unaffected by the strange new world that Athens TV programs opened up to so many Greek villagers.

In 1976 the house built by the man from Australia stood out like an exotic flower amidst Kotta's drab mud-brick. His home was finished in smooth plaster, brightly painted and spanking new. All the other structures of the village were desperately shabby by comparison, much as Lofiscos had been prior to 1967. What the effect such a model of elegance will have remains to be seen. Probably the rest of the inhabitants of Kotta could not begin to pay for similar improvements to their own dwellings;

but such a demonstration, within the village itself, of little-imagined levels of luxury may have an unsettling effect in time to come.

A remarkable contradiction pervaded the life of Kotta. Thanks to long-established communities in Toronto and Sydney, and to the diaspora throughout eastern Europe and Soviet central Asia that the seizure of their children in 1947 had brought about, Kotta possessed a faint but real tinge of cosmopolitanism, despite the fact that it was one of the poorest and geographically by far the most isolated of the villages I visited. Every summer, English-speaking relatives came from Canada and Australia to visit their ancestral village; others came from eastern Europe, though less frequently. Most of the villagers were bilingual and in wintertime spent a good deal of time listening to foreign radio broadcasts. As a result, a number of the men in the village understood spoken English quite well, and they all could follow most of what was said in any of Europe's Slavic languages (except, perhaps, Czech and Polish). Letters connected them regularly with Tashkent, where many of the village children had ended up, as well as with other communities in the Soviet Union and across eastern Europe. Sydney and Toronto were alternate homes for almost everyone in the village in the sense that anytime one of them decided to move, he or she needed only to ask an appropriate relative to make the necessary arrangements. In addition, a few from the village had established themselves in Salonika and Athens, though their number was much smaller than the number of those who had gone abroad. None of the other villages I observed in Greece had anything like so extensive a range of connections. It gave a special flavor to the community, whose members—the menfolk at least—remained in Kotta because of conscious, deliberate choice, and no longer through necessity.

Politics was a minor spectator sport, nothing more. News from Athens and news from Skopje was regularly compared with what British, German, and other foreign radio broadcasts had to say. Consequently, the villagers had become shrewd judges of the reliability of news as filtered through these multiple refractors. Distrust of authorities and skepticism of official claims was perhaps the dominant attitude; but skepticism was selective. On the day we visited Kotta, for example, a riot in Athens occured in which one person was killed and several were injured. The village cowherd, who relieved the tedium of the day by listening to a little portable transistor radio, heard the Athens radio report of this event. On his return he came into the café and told the others what he had heard. The reaction was to accept the report as accurate. "Imagine Athens admitting anything like that under the Colonels," was the village president's comment.

Their Slavic background perhaps gave the villagers of Kotta a certain detachment from the passions that wracked Greek public life over Cyprus. At any rate I was spared the usual questions about why the United States had betrayed Greece so ungratefully. Life under the military dictatorship had been good in Kotta. In particular, the abolition of rural indebtedness had given the community a fresh start. The burst of prosperity and mood of optimism within the community, apparent in 1976, dates from that time. But, as the village president said: "Freedom is good." Being one of those who had returned from eastern Europe, he perhaps knew better than less experienced persons could, just what he meant by that phrase.

Another of his remarks: "No one need be poor today if he is not lazy," defined the spirit of the active farmers of the community. When one thinks back to the cruel starvation which was Kotta's lot in 1947, that was a tremendous thing to be able to say. Yet, by the modest standards of the community it was an undeniable fact in 1976; and that fact, together with the survival in essentials of the cake of custom which had sustained Macedonian peasant life from time immemorial, made Kotta a remarkably happy place so far as a visitor could tell by listening to the flow of talk in the flyblown café—a conversation which custom rigorously confined to the adult males of the village.

Because continuities with 1947 were strong, the contrast of conditions was all the more valued. Reality in Kotta had actually outstripped expectations as far as most of the survivors from the bitter times of the guerrilla war were concerned. Not change, as in New Eleftherohori, but continuity; not their own hard work and intelligence but God's will and a gracious providence were how the people of Kotta explained their good fortune. Such differences do not diminish the fact that the last three decades constituted a remarkable success story for both communities.

Each of them started at a desperate level and emerged by the
1970s to heights that would have seemed unattainable thirty
years before. No wonder, then, that in Macedonia as much as in
Old Greece and more emphatically than in Thessaly, the revolutionary spirit had utterly evaporated from the hill villages.

Two general points emerge from these brief sketches of how six
Greek villages have managed their affairs since World War II.
First is the rapidity with which changes came. Greek peasants
required little stimulus to alter old methods of cultivation if a
clear demonstration of financial advantages could be offered to
them. As soon as the Agricultural Bank became able to make
loans on terms genuinely advantageous to farmers, use of
fertilizer and other, more expensive improvements came thick
and fast, limited not so much by peasant attitudes and aptitudes
as by the availability of credit and of marketing and storage
facilities. A shrewd eye for pecuniary advantage has been part of
Greek peasant behavior from time immemorial. In even the most
remote villages this made far-ranging agricultural advances
possible in remarkably short periods of time.
    A second general point is this: each village had a different
experience, partly because of diverse natural environments,
land-population ratios, and location with respect to markets,
transport, and the like. But often it is possible to trace key moves
back to the acts of individual persons who either pioneered a
new, profitable activity, acted to reconcile old hatreds, or in
some other way demonstrated by personal example a path that
proved beneficial to the community as a whole.
    Qualities of mind and personality, as well as physical strength
and muscular skill, are no doubt the ultimate basis of wealth in
all its forms; and in this respect the villages of Greece seem richly
endowed. Some of the village presidents and private citizens
with whom I conversed in these villages would be outstanding
human beings in any context. The successes that have come to
these villages attest the impact of their leaders' personalities, as
well as the high level of general competence and capacity for
work which Greek peasants have long been accustomed to
exercise, whenever circumstances offered them a chance to profit
from their own efforts. Circumstances have been propitious

since 1956 and especially since 1966. The result far surpasses probabilities perceptible thirty years ago, even to an optimistic observer.

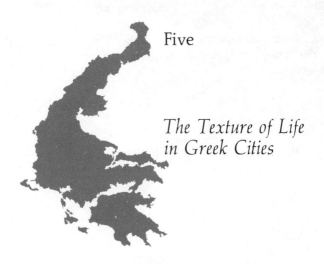

Five

The Texture of Life in Greek Cities

A really fundamental change came over Greek society in the 1960s. For more than two hundred years prior to 1965, food-deficit villages, tucked away among the mountain crevices of Greece, harbored a sufficiently large population to threaten the peace of the plains whenever economic opportunities in the lowlands, for whatever reason, shrank. Men from the hills, who could no longer secure enough to feed themselves and their families peaceably, took to arms, and tried to seize by force what they could no longer earn. Crises of this kind broke out irregularly at something like fifty-year intervals from the 1770s until the 1940s. Fighting was inspired by different ideals and triggered by widely differing political circumstances. These factors, as historians have always recognized, had a dynamic of their own, related both to Ottoman and to European develop-ments, and affected the outcome in fundamental ways.

Nevertheless, as long as the main local source of fighting manpower was the hill villages, and as long as insurgent bands supported themselves by seizing food and other resources from farmers in the plains, such movements had intrinsic limits and natural rhythms of their own. Without importation of food from abroad, as happened in the 1940s, prolonged violence provoked starvation and death, whereupon a sharply reduced local popula-tion made pacification relatively easy, whether the hillsmen won, as in the Greek War of Independence, 1821–30, or met defeat, as they did in 1770–71.

Kotta's experience in the 1940s was typical of that harsh traditional way of adjusting population to local resources. What made the guerrilla war of 1946–49 different was that, in most hill villages, government action created and then fed so many refugees that these traditional processes for cutting population back were blunted. Consequently, even when the fighting ended, so many people remained alive in villages like Kardamili and Kerasia that automatic resumption of old patterns of life could not occur.

In the 1960s, a different, more humane resolution of the crisis of too many mouths for local food resources became possible because the circumstances which had formerly driven Greeks to the hills in such extraordinary numbers no longer applied. DDT banished malaria, once rife in almost all parts of the Greek plains, after 1946; oppressive landlords and strong-arm tax collectors, who once had rivalled the anopheles mosquito in making life in the Greek plains miserable, disappeared after World War I. Life in free mountain villages, knowing no landlord and exempt from debilitating malaria, had once been preferable to anything available in the plains, despite the precarious poverty such life implied. After 1949 that was no longer the case. Hillsmen soon discovered the fact, and as job opportunities opened up for them, emigration assumed a scale that swiftly deprived the hill villages of their accustomed role in Greek society. It is hard to believe that the old life will ever revive. Communication has become too efficient, the villagers of Kotta, Kerasia, Kardamili, and hundreds of similar communities know too much about the conditions of life elsewhere in Greece and in the world to prefer their former hard, poor, proud, free style of life. Whatever the future may hold, it is not likely to involve another bout of old-style guerrilla war.

The Aegean islands, too, have lost population—in some cases drastically. This diminishes the nursery of sailors that for generations supplied the Greek merchant marine with man-power, just as the emptying out of hill villages diminishes the supply of muleteers who once kept the caravan trade going. Many of the Aegean islands are, in fact, mountain tops that

happen to rise above sea level; and it is not therefore surprising
that the islanders' traditional relation to the rest of Greek society
had many points in common with that of the hill communities.
Agriculture was as inadequate to support local population in the
islands as in the hills. Fishing supplemented farming as sheep-
herding did in the mountains of the mainland. Seafaring was
more important than the caravan trade ever was on the mainland; but in times of adversity, piracy played precisely the same
role as the klefts and guerrilla bands did on the mainland. It is,
therefore, not an accident that the recent depopulation of hills
and islands followed a parallel course. The difference is this:
accessibility of the islands by sea means that, at least for some of
them, a substantial tourist trade offers a new kind of income,
whereas mountain communities in Greece, (except for a few
places like Metsovo) have not been able to cash in on tourism,
being too inaccessible and too primitive to attract strangers.

Migration from remote hill villages and barren islands into
towns, both Greek and foreign, involved drastic changes in the
texture of everyday experience. Resultant psychological strains
naturally found expression in politics, especially in the tumult of
the early 1960s. Yet under the Colonels, and since the restoration
of parliamentary government in 1974, the breadth and emotional intensity of political protests has clearly waned. Massed
thousands of migrants concentrated in Athens and Salonika
somehow made out sufficiently well in their new environment
that they did not respond in really passionate ways to political—
or any other—causes. Why?

Two aspects of Greek rural life seem relevant. First, traditional peasant life was and remains market-oriented. Attitudes
and skills inculcated in Greek peasants by this basic circumstance presumably prepared them well for urban living where
market relations were even more critical than was true in the
village. Second, Greek rural society was and is organized into
tight-knit, nuclear family units, accustomed to looking upon all
outsiders as "them" rather than "us." Such families can move the
geographical base of their operation from village to city with
very little internal adjustment of family behavior. Thus the real,
human, everyday environment in which nearly all Greeks live
did not alter very much even when hundreds of thousands of

persons abandoned the islands and hill villages for Athens or Salonika.[1]

Those who migrated across linguistic and cultural lines to take up residence in German, American, Canadian, or Australian cities put greater strain on established family patterns. Abandoned wives and insubordinate children, disrespectful of their parents' broken German or English, occurred among Greek immigrant families as well as among other nationalities. There seems to be no reliable statistical basis for declaring that such difficulties were less prevalent among Greeks than among most comparable immigrant groups; yet I believe this to be so. Coherent Greek communities already existed in nearly all the cities of destination in Australia and North America; and these communities possessed an increasingly well-defined ethos and collective pride in their practical achievement, to which newcomers could readily assimilate.[2]

Newcomers usually chose places of destination where someone from their own part of Greece had already established himself. More often than not, relatives formed a sort of welcoming committee; and new arrivals commonly got their first jobs by hiring out to work for fellow countrymen in the new land. Terms of such employment were sometimes exploitative, taking advantage of the newcomers' inability to speak English and move independently in the alien society; but if so, the contract was certain to dissolve as soon as the immigrant learned his way around.

Human links of this sort obviously reduced the shock of acculturation. Before World War II, persons of Greek descent in English-speaking lands generally believed that success required them to shed all outward signs of Greekness, for example, by altering their names and systematically disguising their ethnic origin when dealing with persons not of Greek extraction. After 1945, this was no longer taken for granted: Greek restaurants, Greek music, even some Greek-American politicians became

1. Cf. Ernestine Friedl, "Kinship, Class and Selective Migration," in J. G. Peristiany, ed., *Mediterranean Family Structures* (Cambridge, 1976), pp. 363–87.
2. See, for instance, Evangelos C. Vlachos, *The Assimilation of Greeks in the United States* (Athens, 1968).

respectable. Greekness in general ceased to seem a handicap. Thus newcomers no longer had to suppress all signs of their ethnic past. Adaptation to the new environment became correspondingly easier.

In Germany, conditions were different. No preexisting Greek community stood ready to receive the newcomers of the 1960s. Instead, bureaucratic management regulated living conditions, jobs, and other aspects of the lives of the *Gastarbeiter*. It is not yet clear whether the Greeks of Germany will be able to duplicate the history of Greek immigrants into the English-speaking lands. It is even conceivable that the original official assumption that all such immigrants were temporary and would return home when no longer needed in Germany will actually come to pass. Many Greeks have in fact returned from Germany in recent years, when economic recession took away their jobs. After 1974 this reverse flow actually outstripped emigration.[3] On the other hand, Greek attitudes and aptitudes for clever exploitation of market opportunities have much the same potential scope in Germany as in English-speaking lands; and it is worth remembering that most of the Greeks who came to the United States before World War I arrived as single men and expected to return to their native land as soon as they had made their fortunes in the new world. Many did return; and it took about sixty years for the Greek-American community to achieve a sex and age balance—and a psychological assurance—that made possible the recent prominence Greeks have achieved in the United States. Official bureaucratic calculations notwithstanding, no one can yet say that the Greek residents in Germany will not eventually develop a Greek-German community similar to that which has recently emerged in English-speaking lands.

What I believe is this: the values and patterns of conduct inculcated by family life in Greek villages are readily transferable to urban contexts, whether within Greek-speaking towns and cities, or abroad. Individual lives, accordingly, suffer less disorientation, and signs of social disruption are fewer in Greece or among the new diasporas of the 1960s and 1970s, than would have been the case without the Greek village background. Other

3. *Greece: A Monthly Record* (Press and Information Office, Embassy of Greece, Washington, D.C.: March 1977), p. 2.

societies, with different traditional rural patterns, cannot be expected to make so smooth a transition to urbanism, nor are they likely to respond so swiftly to new opportunities, far or near.

A few statistics will make clear the scale of change within Greece itself. In 1951, 37.7 percent of the population lived in towns of ten thousand or more, and was classed as urban in the census of that year. In 1961, urban population rose to 43.3 percent; in 1971 to 53.2 percent. Only 35.1 percent remained rural according to the census of 1971, the other 11.7 percent being "semi-urban."[4] Such generalized statistics tend to obscure the fact that only Greater Athens and Salonika grew very much. The census of 1971 asked where each person had been living in 1965; and it thus became possible for the first time to calculate the scale and pattern of internal migration in Greece. During the six years in question, 764.5 thousand persons, or 8.7 percent of the entire population, had migrated across internal administrative boundaries. Where they went is indicated in table 5.1.

Table 5.1 — Internal Migration in Greece, 1965–71 (in thousands)

	In-migrants	Out-migrants	Net change
Greater Athens	256.1	65.2	+190.9
Greater Salonika	85.0	23.6	+61.4
Other urban	180.8	169.4	+11.4
Semiurban	93.8	113.4	–15.1
Rural	114.3	392.9	–248.6

SOURCE: Dimitrios Trichopoulos et al., *The Population of Greece: A Monograph for the World Population Year, 1974* (n.p., n.d.), table 4.8.

Official statistics do not record the destination of Greeks migrating abroad by city; hence it is not possible to find out exactly where those who leave the country go when searching for a new place to work. It is sure, however, that the sort of human chain that carried so many individuals from Kotta either to Sydney or to Toronto governs most Greek movement across national boundaries. Even in the 1960s, when large-scale migration to Germany was organized by officials at both ends, human chains played a very large role. In 1962, for instance, almost all

4. *Statistical Yearbook of Greece, 1975* (Athens, 1975), Table II:7.

of the four hundred Greek workers living in the little town of
Kürnbach, near Stuttgart, came from a single village in Macedonia, and managed to transplant something of their community
social structure with them.[5] Such a concentration was exceptional, but similar clustering of like with like occurred regularly,
and did something to counteract the anomie that *Gastarbeiter*
status in Germany might otherwise have created.

National boundaries are on the whole more confusing than
helpful in trying to understand the recent Greek movement from
village to city. Athens and Salonika, in effect, were competing
with Stuttgart and other German, French, and Belgian cities; and
European cities were competing with the attractions of still more
distant cities in the United States, Canada, and Australia as
alternative destinations for Greek emigrants. Since most migration statistics are collected at national frontiers, it is difficult to
get a comprehensive picture of Greek migration that embraces
internal as well as external movement.

One can say with assurance that migration across Greek
national boundaries assumed a new intensity during the 1960s.
The movement crested in 1965. In that year 117,167 persons
were officially recorded as emigrating permanently, and an
additional 59,241 left the country with the intention of finding
work elsewhere and returning within a calendar year. Thereafter,
the pace of emigration diminished, so that by 1974 a mere 22,448
persons were classified as permanent emigrants; but, on the
other hand, the number of temporary work-seekers had grown
to no less than 92,622.[6] In 1975 and 1976, when economic
slowdown took effect in all the countries to which Greeks were
accustomed to migrate, a significant reverse flow actually asserted itself, as table 5.2 indicates.

Table 5.2		External Migration from Greece	
	Emigrants	Returnees	Net Change
1975	15,989	27,137	+11,148
1976	15,126	26,226	+11,100
Source		*Greece: A Monthly Record*, March 1977, p. 2.	

5. Elie Dimitras, *Enquêtes Sociologiques sur les Emigrants Grecs: II,
Lors du Séjour en Europe Occidentale* (Athens, 1971), pp. 49, 127.

6. See tables in Appendix for the full array of official government
figures.

No similar record of migration into Athens and Salonika exists, because internal migration statistics are not collected annually. Exactness therefore remains unattainable; the human reality of Greek migration stubbornly escapes detection in the available records.

In most cases, movement was certainly from village to city, sometimes mediated by a period spent in some provincial town. In the census year 1971, for instance, 45 percent of those who had set up residence in Athens and Salonika since 1965 had come directly from a village; 35 percent had come from other urban centers in Greece, and 20 percent from semiurban locations. But this pattern of movement into cities is not the whole story. Almost one-fifth (18.9 percent) of all moves from one community to another that occurred in Greece between 1965 and 1971 involved a move from one village to another.[7] Sometimes this meant shifting down into the plains from a hill village, sometimes moving laterally from one community to another. This latter type of migration was often a by-product of a marriage across village boundaries. When accompanied by dowry exchange, as was normal, such transfers of domicile represented not a disruption of older rural patterns but their confirmation.

Within Greece itself the geographic effect of these movements has been to concentrate population in a belt running from Athens in the south to Salonika in the north, embracing the Boeotian, Thessalian and central Macedonian plains that lie between those two principal urban centers. A westward extension of the emerging population cluster extends along the shores of the Gulf of Corinth to the city of Patras in the northwestern Peloponnese, although this incipient third urban focus has hitherto shown only a very modest power to attract newcomers. The rest of the country is emptying out. The Aegean islands, the central and southern Peloponnese, the high mountains of Greece's western half, together with the regions adjacent to Yugoslavia and Bulgaria in the north, have lost population in the last twenty years on a scale that has excited considerable official alarm.[8]

7. Dimitrios Trichopoulos et al., *The Population of Greece: A Monograph for the World Population Year, 1974* (n.p., n.d.), p. 75.
8. The concept of an emergent loose urban conglomerate, extending

Plans for regional development in Crete, Thrace, western Greece, and the like have so far remained ineffectual. Despite much talk, official government policy had not, as of 1976, done much to alter, still less reverse, the recent patterns of population concentration. Anything effective would have somehow to make Athens less attractive; and since the seat of government is there, and high officials live there, a policy that would actively discriminate against the capital is almost inconceivable. On the contrary, the flow of government funds has the effect of building up the primacy of the capital. Only a radical decentralization of administrative authority could reverse this pattern: and no government is in the least likely to set out deliberately to reduce its own power by delegating real decision-making to the provinces. Indeed the more active government becomes in socioeconomic affairs, the greater the concentration of wealth, power, and population in the capital is likely to become.

Ecological limits do, of course, exist, and may be closer than Athenians commonly realize. Water supply and sewer systems are strained near their limits already, and it is hard to imagine where additional amounts of fresh water can come from without depriving other regions of Greece of a precious resource. Smog and traffic congestion are likewise troublesome.[9] But such unpleasantnesses do little to diminish the glamor of the capital for those living in the provinces; and as long as income levels in Athens remain substantially above those of the rest of the country, and jobs are to be had, the lure of bright lights can be expected to continue to attract swarms of newcomers.[10]

It is useful to think of recent migration patterns as a systolic counterpart to the diastolic ingathering of Greeks that domi-

---

between Athens and Salonika, was advanced by a French geographer, Bernard Kayser, *Géographie humaine de la Grèce* (Paris, 1964) and elaborated in Bernard Kayser, P.-Y. Péchoux, and M. Sivignon, *Exode rurale et attraction urbaine en Grèce* (Athens, 1971).

9. Cf. Evan Vlachos, "Urbanization and Development: The Case of Greece," *Rocky Mountain Social Science Journal* 6 (1969): 127–40.

10. Cf. Calliope Moustaka, *The Internal Migrant* (Athens, 1964). The author distributed questionnaires to emigrants from two remote regions of Greece living in Athens, and also asked opinions of those who had stayed behind. The result was overwhelming endorsement of migration to Athens, both among those who had made the venture and among those who remained in their villages.

nated the Hellenic experience between 1821 and about 1945. As
we saw in Chapter 2, the Greek diaspora that attained its apogee
in the eighteenth century and extended around the shores of the
Black Sea began to collapse after the emergence of the Greek
state. This meant elimination of urban Greeks from societies in
which the majority were of a different speech and religion. But
during the 120 years after 1821, the level of development within
the Greek state was such that urban occupations were hard to
find for refugees from the former dominions of the Ottoman,
Hapsburg, and Romanov empires.

Statistics are of course unobtainable. New diasporas arose in
the United States and elsewhere as the older ones disintegrated;
but there can be no doubt that those who established themselves
overseas before World War II were far fewer in number than the
Greeks whose urban roles were being eliminated from the Black
Sea and Aegean coastlands. Similarly, the growth of Athens and
of other cities within the Greek state prior to 1941 was not
numerically equivalent to the decay of Greek communities in
Constantinople and the scores of other cities in former Ottoman
lands. Hence if we try to imagine what was happening to the
entire Greek-speaking community between 1821 and 1941, it is
probably correct to conceive the experience as one of prolonged
impoverishment and an increase in the relative weight of rural
elements. Many urban dwellers escaped the pincers by taking on
a new, non-Greek nationality; those who clung fast to their
Greek identity suffered accordingly, and, when not killed or
expelled by force, faced hard times and a more and more
constricted life.

If this is the correct way to understand what happened to the
Hellenic world in the nineteenth and early twentieth centuries, it
seems clear that the process attained its height during World
War II, when the Occupation brought starvation to many and
hunger to almost everyone living in Greece. Since World War II,
however, the current of migration has run in the opposite
direction. Correspondingly, Greek society made a very rapid
shift from rural to urban preponderance. Within the boundaries
of the Greek state, the tip point came in 1967 when, for the first
time, 50 percent of the population became urban. If the urbanization effect of migration beyond Greek borders were taken into
account, the tip point between rural and urban preponderance

would be seen as having occurred a little earlier, and the swiftness of the movement from village to town would be more strikingly apparent than it is when one arbitrarily leaves the new diaspora out of account.[11]

Another significant point to bear in mind when considering the force of migration in recent Greek history is this: when they went abroad, most emigrants intended to return to Greece as soon as they had succeeded in saving enough money to buy a house, pay a dowry, or achieve whatever other family goal might have persuaded them to emigrate in the first place. Many acted on such plans. Net emigration was therefore substantially less than the total number who went abroad. One calculation holds that about 850,000 Greeks sought work in foreign lands between 1951 and 1971, a total that amounts to about a quarter of the entire active work force of the country. Of this number, about 450,000 went to western Europe and some 400,000 travelled overseas.[12] Net emigration, as officially recorded, was 666,355; and if one adds this figure to the in-migration into Athens and Salonika of almost 885,000 in the same twenty-year period,[13] the total number of migrants from village to city becomes 1.55 million. This seems the best available estimate of

11. I owe this perspective on recent Greek affairs very largely to Nicholas Vernikos, "L'Economie de la Grèce, 1950–70," (Thèse pour le Doctorat d'Etat des Sciences économiques, Paris, 1974) typescript, pp. 418 ff. Statistics he offers may suggest the magnitude of this alternation between ingathering and new diaspora.

Greek Movement across the Frontiers of Greece

Years	Thousands
1920–28	+855.2
1928–40	+ 91.9
1940–51	− 75.0 (a guess)
1951–61	−207.4
1961–71	−458.8

12. Ibid., pp. 591–92.
13. This figure is derived by assuming a rate of natural increase in Athens and Salonika equal to that of the country as a whole, and then calculating the gap between actual populations of those two centers in the census of 1971 and what they would have been by adding natural increase to the census figures for 1951. This is rough, needless to say, but cannot be more than a few thousand off.

the magnitude of urbanization in the last twenty years. It amounts to almost 17.7 percent of the total population of Greece as of 1971 (8.76 million), a ratio not far short of the proportion of the Greek people (commonly assumed to be about one-fifth of the entire nation) who used to live in food-deficit communities in the hills.

Obviously, this does not mean that in 1971 hill villages had all become empty shells, for an important number of migrants into town came from plains villages like New Eleftherohori. It does mean, though, that in a mere twenty years almost everyone who could not find a satisfactory living in his native village was able to shift into a city, whether in Greece or abroad, and make a new career there. The movement cannot continue far into the future. There are not enough people in Greece to sustain the recent growth rate of Athens and Salonika much longer; and unless foreigners come from more crowded lands to the east and south—a possibility that Greek national sensibility makes unlikely as long as the government can exercise effective control over the territory under its jurisdiction today[14]—the recent transformation will remain a one-time event: an abrupt metamorphosis of Greek society, consequent upon shifting from a mainly rural to a mainly urban base.

Migration into cities of course reflected the availability of jobs and the pull of urban standards of living that were much higher than anything attainable in remote villages. Statistics of gross national product as compiled by the Greek government reflect what happened. Between 1964 and 1975 the GNP grew at an annual average rate of 6.5 percent. Gross manufacturing product rose during the same eleven years at an annual average rate of no less than 10.2 percent.[15] Such growth rates, exceeded only by those of Japan, were attained in part with the help of foreign capital. Counting short-term commercial credit as well as longer-term investments of all kinds, Greek foreign indebtedness totalled about 2.2 billion dollars in 1976. Capital imports

14. A perceptible number of Arab and Pakistani immigrants resided illegally in Athens in 1976, working at menial tasks. Their number was not large, but their presence proved, if proof be needed, that official rules and regulations do not control human behavior totally, even in such an obvious matter as migration.

15. These and subsequent financial figures come from the *International Herald Tribune*, "Focus on Republic of Greece," March 29, 1976.

have regularly been required to meet the persistent deficit in the international balance of payments. This problem has haunted Greece uninterruptedly since 1831. How the resulting debts can ever be paid off remains problematical; but as long as new credits continue to become available, the precarious financial balance of the Greek national economy continues, like a breaking wave, to race forward, and at an ever mounting height.

All such statistics pale for ordinary people before the elementary fact that personal consumption spurted upwards in the past twenty to twenty-five years in truly spectacular fashion. Urbanization meant enrichment to hundreds of thousands: tangible, material enrichment, as well as the psychic income that may come from living where news is made and important things happen. The basic index of this change is to be seen in the income statistics I cited previously. Government figures show that average annual income per person rose from 4,775 drachmae ($157) in 1951 to 32,136 drachmae ($1,071) in 1972; whereas rural incomes rose from 3,036 ($101) to 16,395 drachmae ($546) per head in the same time.[16] The incentive for moving to town is apparent in these figures; and the extraordinary transformations of personal life that such increases in disposable cash reflect have

16. Vernicos, "L'Economie de la Grèce," p. 116. Drachmae were exchanged throughout this period at 30 to $1. Internal price levels rose less sharply than incomes, though reliable estimates are not available. The official index of consumer prices for 1972 offered an index figure of 126 when 1963 price levels were taken as base 100 (*Statistical Yearbook of Greece, 1975*, p. 454). Various errors (often deliberate) are built into this figure, for example, the unavailability of some goods at legally fixed prices which, if a bonus were offered, could nevertheless appear as by magic from shopkeepers' back rooms. Still, the official figure showing a 26 percent inflation across ten years was not totally out of touch with reality, since basic foodstuffs and other household supplies were always available in adequate amount at officially posted prices.

Another problem with any effort to calculate real income is that the assortment of goods ordinary Greek families purchased altered radically and expanded enormously during the twenty years in question. Any statistical artifact intended to discount inflation would therefore be misleading as a guide to real income. It seems necessary to abandon the effort at precision, recognizing merely that as cash incomes swelled so remarkably, most people did in fact consume more and better goods than ever before in their lives.

to be largely left to the imagination. But one final set of statistics may help.[17]

Percent of dwellings with	1961	1970
running water	39	80
electricity	50	90
flush toilets	14	46
baths	10	35

Private automobiles in Greece[18]

1962	56,893
1964	81,617
1966	122,479
1968	169,985
1970	226,893
1972	303,109
1974	380,234

Such figures disguise many inequities and inequalities. Not everyone prospered, and there is certainly a sense in which official Athens became a kind of collective exploiter of the entire country, taking revenues paid by all Greek consumers in the form of excise taxes, and disbursing them to salaried personnel living in the capital. Not only that: the prestige and appeal of Athenian living was such that many village girls used the savings their parental family accumulated through years of careful management to buy land or an apartment in Athens. Such real estate constituted an excellent base for an urban marriage to some young man who was perhaps, in his own way, also drawing upon the resources of a rural family that saved and pinched to give him the education that would permit entry into white-collar work in the city. Yet the remarkable concentration of Greek resources and population in Athens was experienced by the people involved as a process of liberation from older provinciality and poverty. To rise in the social pyramid and

17. Vernicos, "L'Economie de la Grèce," p. 218.
18. *Statistical Yearbook of Greece, 1975*, table XIV:12.

achieve success in one's own eyes and in those of one's con-
temporaries was a good in itself, and compensated parents and
siblings who willingly accepted a constricted life in some village
or provincial town in order to launch at least one of their family
into the higher plane of Athenian living.[19]

The ambiguity inherent in the relation between Athens and its
hinterland was also apparent in the relation between Greek
village communities and the foreign cities towards which Greeks
migrated. In this case, however, the Greek government also had
a stake in what happened. Consequently, since about 1967, most
Greek discussion of the pros and cons of emigration emphasized
the negative side of the balance.[20] By setting off the cost of
raising and educating a young person for twenty years or longer
against emigrant remittances, it can readily be demonstrated
that the mass departures of the 1960s cost Greece enormous
sums. By disregarding the welfare and preferences of the individuals involved, such a transaction can be seen as a case of the
rich exploiting the poor in the usual heartless, capitalistic way. A
parallel calculation of impending shortages of recruits for the
Greek army, if birthrates should continue to drop and emigrants
remain abroad, can lead to a different but no less dismal view of
the national price paid for allowing individuals to decide for
themselves where to live and how to maximize income and
personal satisfaction.

A more intellectually compelling argument, which does not
put presumed collective or state interests ahead of individual
rights and satisfactions, emphasizes the undoubted fact that
migrants often acted on the basis of imperfect information and
actually found themselves paying various costs implicit in
removal from familiar settings, of which they had no notion in
advance. Naive comparison of the wages to be had in a German
factory with those attainable in a Greek village may have led to
a decision to emigrate; but the emigrant may well have forgotten

19. For details of how this process worked for a single village see
Friedl, "Kinship, Class and Selective Migration," pp. 363–87. She
concluded that migrants retained their relative class status in Athens
despite an absolute escalation of standards of living.

20. See, for example, *Essays on Greek Migration*, Migration Series
no. 1 (Social Sciences Center, Athens, 1967). For an opposite view, see
C. P. Kindelberger, "Emigration and Economic Growth," *Banca
Nazionale del Lavoro Quarterly Review* 74 (September 1965): 3–22.

to count the heavier costs of housing, food, and transport to and from work in Germany as against their availability within the village, almost without financial expenditure.

On a different plane, excessive departures could certainly create very heavy community costs. Disruption and collapse of the sort that perhaps impended at Kardamili, for instance, may destroy the community and family structures which made it seem worth a man's while to emigrate for a few years in order to come back to the familiar setting of childhood as a man of property, higher up the social scale than otherwise would be possible. Some villages in northern Greece, where the pull of German wages was felt most strongly, clearly confronted just such a collapse in the 1960s. The long-term consequences of such events for those who emigrated, as well as for the lame, the halt, and the aged who remained behind, have yet to be faced.

Irremediable collapse was still relatively rare in 1976, how-ever, and if the pace of migration slows down in future, or even reverses itself, then such costs will not be as serious as some prophets of gloom, projecting the trends of the 1960s into the future, assumed. As we have already seen, limits of migration abroad manifested themselves in the mid-1970s, when Greeks began coming back home after losing jobs in Germany. Limits of migration into Athens are not so clearly apparent, though sooner or later the costs of concentrating so many people into the capital area will surely act as a brake on the process.

For the time being, however, limits on urbanization within Greece have barely begun to exert perceptible force. The joys of country living are only felt by those few sophisticates who never had to live in a village. For the majority, who have recent memories of the dour hardships of peasant existence, city life remains clearly superior to anything rusticity has to offer. The dominant attitude, indeed, is disdain for the idiocy of peasant existence and an eager desire to leave such a past as far behind as possible.

The only significant counterweight in Greek society to the attraction of Athenian living is to be found in the ethos of the lower ranks of the army. The great bulk of the Greek army is stationed in the north and, more recently, in Thrace and some of the Aegean islands close to Turkey. These are precisely the regions of the country that have been emptied out most pre-

cipitately by the emigration of the last twenty years; and the
costs and risks of such a process are therefore especially obvious
to military men. A series of small provincial towns have served
as headquarters for army units since 1949 or before; and in some
of these towns the military presence is by far the most important
economic, and the dominating social, reality in the entire
community.

For professional army officers, who spend most of their active
career in or near one of these garrison towns, the appeal of
Athens has all the quality of the Sirens' song which Homer sang
of: seductive but also corrupting. The defense of Hellenism and
the pursuit of the heroic ideal to which they are professionally
committed cannot be reconciled with the softness of urban living
as experienced in Athens. Yet, with an irony often to be
observed in human affairs, assignment to Athens and to one of
the headquarters services echeloned in the capital, is a goal
almost all army officers strive for; and on retirement a very large
proportion of them take up residence in a suburb of Athens close
beside the "Greek Pentagon" where a benevolent government
has made building lots available to officers at especially favorable prices. Hence the provinciality of army life, real though it is
for a majority of the active officers and men, has not blunted the
attraction of the capital, even though resistance to the charms of
Athenian urban living also finds open expression in the ranks of
the Greek army.

An interesting question which seems not to have been dis-
cussed or carefully observed is the effect of the peasant input
upon Greek urban life. In 1960 no less than 43.9 percent of the
population of Athens was made up of newcomers originating
elsewhere in Greece, and an additional 11.8 percent was constituted by immigrants coming for the most part from Turkey.[21]
This makes it certain that rural attitudes and outlooks are bound
to have a great influence on behavior in Athens. The same is true
of other cities which, with the partial exception of Salonika, so
often serve as way stations for migrants between villages of
origin and eventual lodgment in the capital or abroad.

This obvious point is very much obscured by the fact that

21. Eva E. Sandis, *Refugees and Economic Migrants in Greater
Athens* (Athens, 1973), p. 40.

those who made the move from the country did so with the idea of putting behind them all the things that made village life inferior to the life of Athens or Salonika. Deliberate efforts to adopt the standards of urbanity in all matters of outward behavior therefore tend to disguise carryover into town of distinctively peasant attitudes. Yet outward things, like the clothes one wears and the kind of house one lives in, may not tell the whole story. Indeed it is arguable that many of the features of recent Greek economic development (along with other non-economic dimensions of behavior) reflect values and capacities brought into town by peasant migrants and there given new (or at least distinctive) forms of expression.

An example of this is the extraordinary and by west European standards quite disproportionate emphasis on real estate. To own a piece of land and then build one's own house or apartment upon it is an overriding goal for almost all urban residents of Athens and Salonika. Newcomers will save rigorously for years to be able to make a start towards this kind of independence. They often get help from their families in the provinces for the initial outlays. Speculative builders make standard deals with impecunious owners of a piece of urban real estate whereby, in return for the land, he or she gets title to a share of the apartments to be erected on the site, while the builder, for his part, gets the right to sell off the remaining apartments to whomever he can find who will buy. Not unnaturally, land prices have escalated enormously under such a system; and investment in brick and mortar continues to bulk far larger in Greek national accounts than government planners wish. Renting is felt to be profoundly unsatisfactory. It puts the renter at the mercy of the owner; and no Greek family head wishes to be in such a dependent position if he can avoid it. To be an owner of property was, in village life, the sine qua non of full status in the community. It seems clear that this feeling, transferred to towns, has sufficed to distort the pattern of Greek economic development ever since the Athenian building boom began in the early 1950s.

A second instance of the way in which peasant patterns pervade modern Athenian and Salonikan life is the prevailing rhythm of work that often amazes or puzzles foreigners on first arrival in Greece. Salaried personnel and wage earners com-

monly spend only part of their time at a single job. Office hours
are short, sometimes starting as early as seven in the morning
and ending at one or two P.M., so that everyone can go home for
lunch, have a nap, and then arise refreshed, sometimes to return
to work, or sometimes to see what other income-producing
activity he or she can find for the rest of the day. By standards
familiar in the United States or western Europe, wages and
salaries remain quite low, and many offices are grossly over-
staffed. Work rhythms are correspondingly slack. Much overlap-
ping of function is built into shop and office routines so that one
person might check up on another and, in theory anyway,
prevent petty cheating. This makes for high administrative
costs, especially in such organizations as banks, big stores, and
government offices. On the other hand, it leaves lots of energy
for individual pursuit of gain in the afternoon and evening
hours.[22]

Such individual pursuit of gain takes the form of the sort of
short-term informal contracts between buyer and seller that
dominate village economic relations. When someone wants
something done, individuals, who might or might not hold
down a regular paid job, compete with one another in hope of
arranging a deal to perform the wanted service in return for
some share in the profit, for a flat fee, or for an hourly wage, as
the case might be. The proliferation of such arrangements is
enormous. Teachers and students, for example, regularly supplement formal classroom work by tutoring relationships. To
get high enough marks to win the much-coveted entrance to the
University of Athens is thought to require extra tutoring that
may extend across several years. Special cram schools exist to
prepare students for the exams; indeed, such extras often seem
more important to all concerned than the basic routine of
secondary school classwork.

Lawyers, engineers, businessmen all operate on similar principles. Even quite large-scale entrepreneurs do not like to build
up hierarchies of salaried personnel working within fixed routines under them. Instead they keep regular full-time employees

22. "The Capital of Greece," Ekistics, no. 140 (1967): 115–16, found
that the average working day for males in Athens was the longest of any
in a number of European countries surveyed. The reason was that so
many Athenians held more than one job.

to a minimum, and depend on subcontracting parts of a job to other independent entrepreneurs, to self-employed individuals, or to persons who seek out part-time work in order to supplement their wage or salary income. Tax regulations and social security legislation powerfully reinforce this penchant. Once a person gets onto a regular payroll, legal obstacles to his dismissal are very great. In many cases, separation payments amount to about a year's income; hence any employer hesitates to add anyone to his payroll, and often finds it better to rely on making a deal with an independent subcontractor.

Extensively ramified patterns of patronage and clientage thus surround and supplement bureaucratically organized corporate structures. Conversely, income generated by short-term, personal contracts constitutes a significant part of many, perhaps most, urban family incomes. Needless to say, such arrangements very often escape the tax collector's net. This is one of the reasons for the energy Greeks put into searching out and making such deals. The bargaining involved gives scope for individual enterprise and cleverness; and risk-sharing implies a chance for windfall profits that may eclipse anything to be gained from regular wages.

In addition, the struggle to get ahead is exciting. Making a deal offers each party a chance to outsmart the other and thus advance the wealth and prestige of one's own person and family. Such opportunities give a spice to life that many Greeks find preferable to the routine security of a regular salary or wage. Not everyone succeeds; many ventures turn out to be financial failures; fortunes can be lost as well as gained through moonlighting arrangements that involve outlay of capital. When one partner seeks to outsmart the other in some deal, quarrels and mutual recrimination easily ensue. Much wasted energy and vain attempts to ambush the small change of the community assuredly result. But Greeks have always known that fortune is fickle. A really clever man, defeated once, can always hope to come back a second time and prevail.

In this fashion, many wage earners and salaried personnel in Athens and Salonika are able to devote almost half the day to the sort of dealings that characterize village economic relations. In addition, a large number of persons live by such deals entirely, without benefit (and burden) of regular routines of daily employment. I think there can be no doubt whatever that the extraordinary prominence of such activity in contemporary Greek urban life is a direct consequence of the rural background in-migrants brought with them to the city.

There are, of course, costs to this kind of behavior. An employee may be tempted to scamp his regular job when work privately contracted for demands full attention. More important, when everyone is perpetually on the lookout for a deal that might be personally advantageous, it is hard to lend full loyalty to any common, corporate enterprise. Large-scale business and government organizations do not flourish under such conditions. Divided loyalties on the part of the staff are likely to produce mediocre results. Yet it should also be pointed out that foreign-managed firms operating in Greece in the 1970s were able to attract loyal and competent personnel by the simple device of paying salaries above the norm, and by making advancement in the corporate hierarchy clearly dependent on performance rather than on personal connection and favor.

Genuinely impersonal standards of management may, in other words, provoke much the same reaction among Greek employees as they commonly do in the United States or western Europe. But Greek owners and managers find such impersonal, formal, bureaucratic principles difficult to follow, even when, as is by no means always the case, they pay them lip service. Family and kinship obligations dictate a different kind of behavior; traditional relations of patronage and clientage require a man to make distinctions among persons, giving and withholding favors according to places in the network of power and personal acquaintanceship. To reject the obligations of kinship and friendship by treating each encounter as neutral, and giving everyone the same treatment according to the same rules, is rare; indeed it is immoral.

Consequently, formal legal and administrative channels in Greece are regularly supplemented (and sometimes contravened) by the giving and receiving of personal favors. Many humble persons, recently arrived from the countryside, assume that the only way to get something done is to know the right person who can act as intermediary with the powers that be. And, naturally, such powerful persons require a quid pro quo—whether cash, votes, deference, or some claim on future services.

The intricacies of governmental administration are such that this is a far from unreasonable point of view. Specialized professionals exist to get routine decisions from government officials, even for such simple things as clearing personal effects through customs, or mailing a parcel out of the country. These expeditors know the right persons and all the needful steps. They can get the task accomplished in a shorter time and with less confusion than would attend the effort of an uninstructed individual to accomplish the job for himself. Indeed officials and clerks often seem to obstruct efforts to do without the services of an expeditor. Conversely, the expeditors live by making things easier for the officials, whether by filling out forms more accurately, or by secretly splitting fees with them.

The official governmental hierarchy, itself overburdened with inspectors, and inspectors of inspectors, thus called into existence a mirror image of itself in the form of an unsalaried corps of experts who could get the administrative machinery to work in the way some third party—the man who employed the specialist—wanted it to work. This process runs throughout the government, and gives employment to an enormous number of Athenians.

Other bureaucracies function in similar fashion. To get a telephone installed in Athens, for example, a customer has to know somebody in the right position who will speak a word on his behalf. Otherwise he waits for months and years simply because so many other persons, knowing how to activate private channels of access to the good graces of the telephone company, get priority. Waiting one's turn routinely amounts to waiting forever. Admission to private schools, valued because their training is reputed to give graduates a better chance at passing the university entrance examinations, also provokes extraordinary and elaborate efforts to find the right person to open the gate. Institutional arrangements and administrative routines designed to assure equity by such devices as anonymously graded examinations are subject to continual probing as one family after another seeks to find a way to assure private advantage over others through some personal connection—whether open and legal, or underhanded and in contravention of formal regulation.

To abide by the rules and let officialdom work its will

unassisted seems to most Greeks a mark of stupidity or laziness. Things just do not get done that way, and everybody knows it. It is up to each man to make his mark by activating the network of friends and acquaintances he has been able to create, to get the services and permissions needed for whatever business he wishes to pursue. Anything else is simply self-defeating.

Such behavior, well enough attuned to a village or small town in which everybody knows everybody else, seems incommensurate with the massed millions of Athens. Yet the pervasive Greek network of patronage and clientage successfully survived Athens' tremendous growth and showed no signs of faltering in 1976. No one who has lived there for any length of time doubts that the most important transactions of everyday life occur at this personalized level, and are only registered and ratified by official, formal enactment afterwards.

Big business as well as small operates on this principle. Thus, for example, the $76.5 million investment that Standard Oil Company (New Jersey) made in Salonika—where it is known as Esso-Pappas—was negotiated by a Greek man of affairs, Tom Pappas. From a base in Boston, he pulled all the strings and touched all the bases necessary to get this enterprise going. Other foreign firms use other Greek expeditors to get their way cleared through the jungle of red tape that opposes anyone who is trying to do something new, whether on a big or little scale. Without such intermediaries, the government machinery simply will not move.

All societies work on this principle to some degree. Greeks merely carry it to a length undreamed of in the United States or west European countries. As long as merit and objective differences among large numbers of persons competing for a profitable contract are minimal—and this has long been true in Greece—personal connections are, in fact, likely to become decisive in affecting each individual's success. Only where the disproportion between sellers and buyers of services is less marked than has commonly been the case in Greece are impersonal, objective, and public criteria likely to prevail.

Greeks learn this fact of life in early childhood. Anyone excluded from the family in-group and its ramified external connections with patrons and clients is a potential rival. In such a system there is no space for the neutral person, entitled to the

same rights and services as everyone else. The notion of
evenhandedness to those one knows and to those one does not
know, regardless of personal and familial links or absence
thereof, is unacceptable. Hence, in spite of all the strains that
Athens' size puts on a strictly personalized system for getting
things done, that tradition remains clearly dominant. This, too,
is a village import, and must have been powerfully reinforced
and sustained by the recent, massive in-migration from the
countryside. It perpetuates in an urban setting an essential aspect
of intra- and extra-familial behavior that gave Greek village life
its flavor and distinctive character.[23]

An interesting sidelight shows how central these familial
attitudes are for Greek life. Kindergarten and first-grade children, when asked to draw a picture of whatever they like, nearly
always choose to draw family scenes; whereas children in the
same school but coming from an American background usually
prefer to draw animals or things. A related observation: small
Greek children maintain close physical intimacy—touching each
other, holding hands, sitting or standing near one another—
whereas American children establish a distinctly greater social
distance. And, long before starting school, Greek children learn
to treat persons of power (for example, teachers) deferentially,
whereas American children attending the same school are more
independent, defiant, and unruly.[24]

One of the reasons such a vast urban agglomeration as Athens
preserves so much behavior appropriate only to small, primary
communities is that the city does not have a single, articulated
social structure. Instead, Athens comprises a series of more or
less self-contained local communities only loosely encapsulated
within the larger urban whole. To be sure, there is also a more
modern aspect to the Athens complex. The heart of the city, into
which commuters stream in the morning and whence they
disperse at the end of the working day, much resembles the core

23. Cf. Adamantia Pollis, "Political Implications of the Modern
Greek Concept of Self," *British Journal of Sociology* 16 (1965): 29–47,
for instructive remarks on survival in urban contexts of familial rural
attitudes.

24. I owe these observations to Mrs. A. A. Evangelopoulos, who
heads a bicultural primary school near Athens, attended in approximately equal numbers by Greek-speaking and English-speaking
children.

of any other modern western city. There are also some newly built dormitory suburbs, where, just as in suburban America, upper- and middle-class wives and children watch the comings and goings of the breadwinner. But these westernized segments of Athens constitute only a thin net, recently superimposed upon the older structure of the city. That structure was defined in the 1920s when scores of thousands of refugees from Asia Minor swarmed towards Athens and squatted around the city, waiting in pain and squalor for something to be done on their behalf.

At first, the camps around Athens were staging areas, where refugees waited until land could be found for them in the north, as happened, for example, at New Eleftherohori in 1927, five years after the crisis in Asia Minor. Resettlement took a long time, and, in the end, land could only be found for about half of those who had fled. The rest remained in and around Athens, Salonika, and other Greek cities, not so much because anyone had planned it that way as because there was nowhere else for them to go. About 350,000 persons ended up in the squatters' settlements around Athens. Since the entire population of Athens had been registered as only 453,042 by the census of 1920, this sudden and unanticipated addition to the city's population utterly transformed the life of the capital.

Eventually, the refugees sorted themselves out into some two dozen relatively homogeneous communities. They clustered, insofar as they were able, according to the parts of Turkey they had come from, a fact attested by the names some of these settlements acquired—Nea Ionia, Nea Smyrni, Nea Philadel-phia, and so on. At first, everything was temporary: the newcomers were not expected to stay, and, to tell the truth, they were not altogether welcome either. Strange accents and strange ways, sometimes combined with superior airs of urban sophisti-cation and mournful tales of vanished wealth, did not sit well with the common people of Athens, who found that the refugees offered severe competition for jobs.

The newcomers were, therefore, thrown back very much on their own resources. Little by little they improved their camps by creating, insofar as means allowed, replicas of the architecture and urban layouts they had known in Asia Minor. Each of these communities therefore came to have a quality of its own, and, to begin with, a life pretty much of its own as well. Athens, as it had existed before 1922, simply had no need of, nor employment for, the newcomers. Survival required the refugees to find things to do within their own communities; and since many of them had been urban dwellers and possessed various artisan and commercial skills, this was not altogether impossible. Some had even preserved capital with which to start new businesses. League of Nations personnel and private relief agencies did something to ease the initial crises and helped individuals and groups to find a new basis for their lives, but in essentials the refugees had to fend for themselves.

Consequently, Athens' industrial proletariat as well as its most active capitalists emerged from the refugee communities between the wars;[25] but in spite of enormous ingenuity and effort, life remained impoverished for the great majority of those living in the shantytowns around Athens. Political attitudes among the refugees therefore remained or became antiestablishmentarian; and insofar as the refugees became proletarian, their dependent status as wage earners reinforced political alienation.

With the passage of time, the wounds of the initial implantation of the refugee communities around old Athens healed over, and the various communities began to fit more coherently into the mosaic pattern that greater Athens had become. After World War II in-migrants from the Greek countryside mingled with the Asia Minor refugees, for these suburbs were the natural ports of entry for any poor peasant seeking to establish himself in the city, being places where land and housing were cheaper, poverty near the surface, and casual labor a way of life for a substantial portion of the community. Yet such reinforcement did not disrupt the corporate consciousness of the various communities, nor erase their comparative autonomy within the larger context of the capital.

As recently as 1971, a study of Nea Ionia showed how strongly that particular community still preserved its special character. By that date, 52 percent of the inhabitants were newcomers, having moved into Nea Ionia since 1945 from diverse regions of Greece. All the same, 44 percent of the economically active population worked within the community

25. Cf. Alec P. Alexander, "Industrial Entrepreneurship in Contemporary Greece: Origins and Growth," *Explorations of Entrepreneurial History*, 2d series, 3 (1966): 106.

and only 35 percent held a job outside. The rest—21 percent—
had no fixed place of employment, but worked wherever a job
might be found, whether inside or beyond the community.[26]
Women, in particular, tended to work in the neighborhood
where they lived; and the job-seekers who most frequently
found work outside Nea Ionia were semiskilled construction
workers and white-collar employees. Exactly the same types
of workers had traditionally emigrated from Greek villages to
work at a distance; and there is much to be said for the
proposition that a community like Nea Ionia was merely an
overgrown village that happened to be located within the urban
mosaic of Greater Athens.

Consciousness of the distinctiveness of the community was
very high; no fewer than 37 percent of the persons interviewed
declared that all their relatives lived in Nea Ionia, and 66 percent
had some relatives in the community. Everybody ordinarily
shopped locally. Only for rare purchases—furniture, electrical
appliances, gifts—was it common to resort to the stores in
downtown Athens. Four-fifths of those interviewed declared
their intention of remaining where they were for the foreseeable
future, and of those who owned their own homes—half of the
total—practically all expected to remain. Exceptions arose only
when some impending family event—normally a marriage—
required rearrangement of existing living patterns, for example,
through gift of a house as dowry to a new couple.[27] Other

26. For Athens as a whole, *Ekistics*, no. 199 (June 1972): 495,
provides the following statistics of work locations:

> 31.9 percent in community of residence
> 36.3 percent in city center
> 31.8 percent in other parts of the city

In Detroit, by comparison, only 18 percent of the population lived and
worked in the same community (ibid., no. 152 [July 1968]: 138).
Distances travelled to work also provide an index of Athens' distinctive
layout. In 1963 Athenians were found to travel only as far to work as
did inhabitants of U.S. cities one-tenth the size of Athens (ibid.).

27. Sandis, *Refugees*, pp. 127–47 and passim. This work appears to
be the only urban neighborhood study that has ever been made in
Greece. Unfortunately the author made little effort to distinguish
between refugees from the 1920s and more recent arrivals. As a result,
her statistics probably obscure significant differences, and certainly
leave the life of Nea Ionia largely to the reader's imagination.

refugee communities were less self-contained than Nea Ionia, especially those located between Athens and the port of Piraeus; but data to allow exact comparisons do not seem to exist.

Salonika, the other urban center in Greece that has shown significant recent growth, was constructed on a quite different pattern. The structure of urban life that existed there before World War I was drastically transformed as a result of forced population exchanges with Bulgaria and Turkey between 1912 and 1926. In addition, a vast fire in 1917 destroyed the central part of the city, so that after 1923, when peace came, wholesale reconstruction had to be undertaken. City planners seized the opportunity to establish a new and spacious layout for the waterfront and adjacent central streets. In the process they found no obstacles to incorporating refugees from Asia Minor into the heart of the city. Hence, though the proportion of refugees in Salonika was almost exactly the same as in Athens— some 40 percent of the city's population according to the census of 1928—segregation in impoverished suburban communities, characteristic of Athens, never occurred.

Instead, between the wars the principal social demarcation ran between Salonika Greeks and a Jewish community—descendants of refugees from Spain who had fled to the Ottoman Empire after 1492. Then, between 1941 and 1944, the Nazis deported every Jew they could find to extermination camps in Poland. Only a few escaped, and some of the survivors preferred to emigrate to Israel rather than try to recover remnants of their property and begin life over again after the war. As a result, the old, territorially segregated Jewish community did not reconstitute itself on anything like its prewar scale, and the city of Salonika emerged from World War II as a relatively homogeneous social entity, far closer to patterns familiar in western Europe than was the case in Athens.

Post–World War II developments confirmed this character. In the 1950s, the establishment of a new industrial park outside the old city limits meant that relatively large numbers of workmen began to travel back and forth each day between home and work. Employment in the port, and in the railroad yards connecting the port with Bulgaria, Yugoslavia, and the world beyond, also reinforced spatial differentiation between living and working quarters.

The sort of community autonomy characteristic of Athens' refugee suburbs therefore remained quite impossible in Salonika. The city's modern growth, like that of Los Angeles, came only after bus and automobile made commuting across relatively long distances easy. Athens' suburbs, coming suddenly into existence in 1922, at a time when bus service was barely beginning, inevitably developed a local corporate consciousness and considerable local autonomy. Later improvements in transport fitted them more tightly into the general urban network without ever entirely erasing the mosaic of semiautonomous communities that had been quite inadvertently created after 1922.

Both cities, however, exhibit patterns of land use that seem anomalous to an American visitor. The reason is that so many Greeks pursue sideline occupations in their spare time. These have to be based within their places of residence, or, if the scale of operation grows, tends to locate in some adjacent yard or other open space. The result is to stud residential districts with small-scale repair shops, sales rooms, and artisan manufacturing establishments. Buzzer panels of fashionable high-rise apartments bristle with demure brass plates, indicating that some sort of income-producing activity is, at least sporadically, in progress within. Hence, even though some big factories, government offices, and commercial establishments are set apart from the rest of the city, the kind of separation between work and living space common in American cities is much modified, even in the newest, most westernized residential suburbs of Athens and Salonika.

This is indeed no more than a tangible indication of how work and family routines continue to operate along village lines in Greek cities. The small, sideline occupations with which so many Greeks piece out wage and salary income often employ all members of the family in one way or another—cleaning up, helping out, keeping store, or whatever. Because many of these small enterprises tap the labor of otherwise unemployed family members, they can and do survive with very low rates of return. Anything that brought in a few drachmae is judged worthwhile if it adds to family resources. Individuals will, as a matter of course, adjust their own activities as needed to keep the family enterprise going, without disputing too rigorously about how the proceeds should be portioned out. Common goals for the entire family take precedence over individual remuneration. If this means saving for a dowry or supporting a boy's education, any personal sacrifice involved is felt to be worthwhile because the family welfare as a whole will ultimately be advanced thereby. Not everyone adheres to such values of course. But a very large proportion of the inhabitants of Athens and Salonika do so, remaining in essentials true to the traditions handed down from their peasant ancestors.

Several consequences flow from these neighborhood patterns. For one thing, in almost every part of Athens or Salonika, at any given time during waking hours, a number of idle persons are to be found standing or sitting around, watching the world go by and hoping that some sort of profitable business transaction will turn up soon. Storekeepers and café patrons have lots of time to observe any unusual action occurring within eyeshot; and a vigorous network of gossip swiftly spreads reports of eccentric or extraordinary behavior. This means that neighborhood opinion exerts pervasive control over personal conduct—almost as strictly as in a village. To be sure, both Athens and Salonika have special districts where dissolute and morally reprehensible conduct is the norm. But most urban dwellers continue to be members of an effective primary community. Social discipline is correspondingly strong. The lost soul, so familiar in western cities, remains a rarity.

Another important result of urban family and neighborhood patterns in Greece is to diminish age segmentation. The economic and social standing of each nuclear family is a joint responsibility of every member. Thus, for example, schoolwork is considered a kind of capital investment expected to produce an enhanced earning power in the future. This puts enormous pressure on the young to use their time in school to the best of their abilities. Anything else is a betrayal of the family campaign to advance its status and wealth. Juvenile delinquency in such an atmosphere is almost unthinkable. Mimicry of the clothes and mannerisms of the young of the United States and western Europe does occur, and widely, thanks to the power of TV. But as of 1976 such mimicry was almost entirely confined to outwardnesses. Most Greeks were much too close to their

peasant past, when even getting enough to eat was an achievement, to reject the discipline and the focused economic aspiration that stand at the core of each nuclear family's behavior.

The strength of family discipline in urban contexts can be
quite surprising. Once, for example, I wanted the services of a
translator, and made arrangements through a school to hire a
young man, recently graduated, who spoke good English and
was unemployed. Next day when I drove to his house to pick
him up, the young man did not appear. I was informed that his
father, a factory hand who had gone off to work by the time I
arrived, refused permission on the ground that his son should
have consulted him before agreeing to accept any sort of outside
employment. Obviously, I had inadvertently infringed on the
principle whereby the head of the household conducts negotiations with outsiders on behalf of all members of the family. Both
the young man in question (who had been very eager for the job)
and I had to pay the penalty of insubordination, even though it
meant pecuniary sacrifice for both father and son.

The main aspect of behavior that seemed to be altering in
urban settings was the pattern of courtship and marriage. Village
custom dictated that marriage alliances should depend on prior
agreement in detail as to dowry and inheritance, so that the new
couple might start off with wealth as nearly as possible equivalent to what their parents had known. In 1976 arranged marriages still occurred in urban Greece, and professional marriage
brokers existed whose job was to match prospective brides and
grooms in the old-fashioned way. But western manners have so
intruded upon this pattern that most young people in Athens or
Salonika first agreed to marry, and only then worked out dowry
arrangements. Very often, as her share, the bride was expected
to provide an apartment or a house; but a young woman earning
a steady income could count that as her contribution to the
new household, matching her prospective husband's income-
producing capacity with her own.[28]

Another facet of traditional family life beginning to come

28. Constantina Safilios-Rothschild, "Dowry in Modern Greece: An
Institution at the Crossroads between Persistence and Decline," in
Constantina Safilios-Rothschild, ed., *Toward a Sociology of Women*
(Lexington, Mass., 1972), pp. 73–83.

under stress was treatment of the elderly. In villages, one son, often the youngest, inherited the parental house, and, when he married, his wife had to submit to the dominion of her mother-in-law. This was no light burden. Sometimes it amounted to tyranny until such time as the new wife gave birth to a son and. thus earned a secure status within her husband's family. In the city, young wives were often unwilling to live with a mother-in-law; and heightened standards of expectation with respect to privacy often made it difficult for two couples to live where a single family had dwelt before. An index of changing attitudes was the rather sudden development of private institutions to care for the aged, of which a score or more came into existence in Athens between 1965 and 1976. Such institutions clearly filled a need; yet many Greeks felt it shameful that anyone should ever allow his parents to spend their last days in such a place.

A third point of change in family patterns was the widespread resort to birth control. Commonly two or at most three children were all a couple wanted to have. The birthrate fell accordingly from the prewar level of 26.5 per thousand in 1935–39 to 15.9 per thousand in 1970–74.[29] Since death rates also declined with improved medical services and the elimination of malaria, natural increase remained at 7.4 per thousand, a little more than half the prewar figure of 13.4 per thousand that prevailed in 1930–34. But emigration reduced net population growth to a rate of only 4.3 per thousand in the five-year period, 1970–74.[30]

Long-range effects of smaller families, freer courtship, longer life-spans, and prolonged education will undoubtedly be important in time to come, and may make Greek family relationships

29. *Statistical Yearbook of Greece, 1975*, table II:22. A rather large number of abortions contributed to the drop in the birthrate, but since abortions were illegal in Greece exact figures do not exist. The number has, however, been estimated at 150,000 per annum, of which half were performed upon married women and half upon unmarried. This latter statistic, if reliable, indicates the erosion of what was formerly a very strict rule of Greek family life prohibiting premarital sex for respectable women. On abortion, cf. V. Valaoras, A. Polychronopoulou, and D. Trichopoulos, "Abortion in Greece," *Social Demography and Medical Responsibility*, Proceedings of the Sixth Conference of the International Planned Parenthood Federation, Europe and Near East Region (London, 1969), pp. 31–44.

30. *Statistical Yearbook of Greece, 1975*, tables II:3, II:22.

more like those familiar to the rest of the western world.[31] The compelling force of the nuclear family unit to govern personal conduct may weaken as urban life becomes more deeply rooted and the full force of modern communications begins to take effect.

Social workers in Athens, for example, who as recently as a decade ago were mainly concerned with problems of poverty, reported in 1976 that social dysfunction of the kind familiar in the United States was what principally required their attention. Child abuse and desolate old age had begun to make an appearance; yet such problems, real enough in particular instances, remained trifling in Greek society as a whole. The surprising thing to an outsider was the way in which the alteration of life experience inherent in the move from village to city left family structures and patterns almost unaffected. For nearly everyone the basic principle requiring all members of the family to band together in order to hold their own against an unfriendly outside world remained unquestioned; and with this, individuals found themselves living within a world of duties and reciprocal services which gave firm meaning to life and prevented the personal isolation that big cities in other countries often generated.

Social gains resulting from the adaptability of the Greek peasant family to urban settings were very real. The pangs of urbanization have surely been enormously reduced by this elemental fact—so far, anyway. By moving from village to city, families have nearly always improved their standards of consumption, which was the purpose behind making the move in the first place. They have done so without compromising the

31. This is the governing assumption made by Constantina Safilios-Rothschild in her several essays on Greek family life. See, for example, "A Comparison of Power Structure and Marital Satisfaction in Urban Greek and French Families," *Journal of Marriage and the Family* 29 (1967): 345–52, and her "Honour Crimes in Contemporary Greece," *British Journal of Sociology* 20 (1969): 205–18. The trouble with studies that depend on questionnaires is that Greeks will usually say what they think the inquirer wishes to hear. Hence it is easy to get impressive statistics that confirm one's hypotheses—but whether the responses are true or not is another question. The readiness of Greeks to mislead an outsider is hard to correct for—a fact that calls into question the value of much of the sociological survey work done in the early 1960s by the Social Sciences Center, Athens (EKKE).

scheme of life that made new wealth worth having. As long as memories of rural poverty remained vivid, the in-migrants therefore could take solid satisfaction from the way their lives had turned out. This was conducive to acquiescence in the existing distribution of political and economic power in Greek society—whether it was the parliamentary structure of 1950–67 (restored in 1974) or the dictatorial pattern of 1967–74.[32]

Of course satisfaction was not universal. As we saw in the case of Kerasia, villagers sometimes entered urban life at a proletarian level and in a frame of mind that predisposed them to expect the worst. By migrating to the city, large numbers of such angry and alienated people could come together and give organized expression to their discontent through labor unions and political parties. This was evident in the 1960s, when Andreas Papandreou's rhetoric stirred up a shadow of class war in Greece. Yet it was more a shadow than a reality that provoked the Colonel's coup; and after their overthrow, little residue remained, even if the possibility of a fresh flare-up of radical discontent continued to be a possibility.

The fact was that class solidarity on the one hand and class hostility on the other were both systematically muted by the entrepreneurial aspirations that infected rich and poor alike. In Old Corinth, it took no special acumen to see how hostility between buyers and sellers of labor was restrained by the fact that both parties looked forward to making deals in the future, and so could not afford to antagonize each other too deeply. Similarly, in Athens and Salonika it was obvious that neither labor unions nor the Socialist and Communist parties have ever been able to command unambiguous loyalty, even among the worst-paid factory hands. The hope of breaking away from the demeaning dependency implicit in wage-earning status was too widespread for Marxism to be really attractive. Class solidarity collided head-on with the conviction that the way to escape poverty was to be just a little cleverer than the next fellow, and then finding oneself in the right place to exercise that cleverness—if need be, at fellow workers' expense. Marxist emphasis

32. The stability of Communist regimes in Russia and eastern Europe reflected similar satisfaction of ex-peasants in comparing their encounters with urban life to the rural poverty their parents had experienced.

on impersonal circumstance and social process seemed simply unconvincing to minds committed to the family values and rules for getting ahead that every Greek absorbed in earliest childhood.

To be sure, immediately after the collapse of the Colonels' regime, radicalism, variously colored by Marxist terminology, surged through the highschools and universities of Greece. Memories of the student uprising at the Polytechnic and its part in bringing down the dictatorship remained strong, and the anniversary days have been celebrated ever since with enthusiasm and fierce rhetoric. Student radicalism may of course portend future change in the political climate of Greece; but it is also possible that radical rhetoric and student demonstrations will become (as in time past to some degree) a way by which young persons assert their independence from paternal authority. For such purposes, the more extreme the doctrine the better: and there were signs of such competition in 1976, especially between Andreas Papandreou's Socialist party and the Communists of the interior (those who had broken with the Soviet Union and the presumed control of Communist party policy by an external organization).

It will take time before anyone can tell just what the recent radicalism of educated youth may mean. But the irritable condescension with which youthful ideologues and some foreign observers like to scold the Greeks for failing to produce a political system like that of western Europe, with parties based on social classes and clearly articulated class interests,[33] will do little to weaken the familial and patronage-clientage patterns of real life which have hitherto given shape to urban as well as to rural Greek affairs. And until that familial structure alters in far-reaching ways, one is safe in assuming that Greek public life as well as Greek economic patterns will continue to exhibit systematic differences from patterns familiar in western Europe and the United States.

Modern urbanism may dictate a weakening of family ties. On the other hand, the advantages to be had from their maintenance are undoubted, and it seems at least conceivable that Greeks, starting from a different heritage, will continue indefinitely to

33. See, for example, the otherwise admirable book by Jean Meynaud, *Les forces politiques en Grèce* (Lausanne, 1965).

maintain a distinctive familialism within an urban setting. The payoff in the United States and other lands of diaspora has been spectacular. Tight family solidarity and mutual help against all comers can and does result in very rapid social escalation for those whose energies are focused upon making the best possible career for themselves, because everyone else in the family expects them to do so.[34] The payoff within Greece was less dramatic, for when everyone struggled in the same way, much energy was spent in defeating the maneuvers of others. Yet the remarkable upward movement of the Greek GNP since 1950 registered the net sum of the efforts of more than a million families to improve their income and status. With such success to its credit, surely it is not certain that the Greek family structure will disintegrate, or lose its distinctive, agonistic character.

If one assumes that modern conditions require large-scale bureaucratization, then the inefficiency that familialism, injected into bureaucratic structures, undoubtedly does generate may in future come to outweigh the no less indubitable efficiency Greeks regularly exhibit in managing family enterprises. But the wave of the future may not be solely and simply bureaucratic. Many activities are best performed on a small scale and without the overburden of administrative hierarchy that bureaucracy brings with it. Greeks and other diaspora-prone peoples may perhaps occupy such niches in alien societies indefinitely into the future, and find a very useful and profitable role for themselves by moving betwixt and between the clumsy corporate leviathans modern bureaucracies so often become.

One may also wonder whether social efficiency is inevitably associated with bureaucratization. It seems far from certain that human beings accomplish more or enhance personal satisfaction when they pursue bureaucratic careers within some preexisting

---

34. Phyllis Pease Chock, "Greek-American Ethnicity" (Ph.D. dissertation, University of Chicago, Department of Anthropology, 1969), records the distinctiveness of familial attitudes and customs among Greeks living in and around Chicago with instructive detail and precision. The Greek community she studied was not ghettoized. In externals her subjects were all but indistinguishable from other white Americans, and yet retained family customs little changed from what had been standard in the Greek village whence their ancestors had come.

hierarchy of authority. Yet surely in the long run it is how energetically millions of individuals respond to their life circumstances that defines social efficiency. No one can doubt that the old-fashioned Greek family way, centering around short-range contracts and governed entirely by personal judgment and shrewdness, can often stimulate enormous and extraordinary human effort. Such a mode of life brings uncertainty with it, but when each individual is embedded in a supportive familial structure and can call for help from kindred and patrons in case of need, it is not clear that the balance between psychic gain and loss does not come down on the side of the venturesome independent entrepreneur. People may in fact both work harder and enjoy it more when their economic activity is defined by multiple, short-term contracts personally agreed to, instead of by tables of organization and wage or salary scales negotiated by others on behalf of depersonalized entities called management and labor.

The supposition that there is only one way towards the future and that urban living will inevitably homogenize all the peoples of the earth seems quite unfounded. What is making Greece more like western Europe and the United States is not any inherent quality of urbanism. Greeks have been city folk in fundamental ways for more than twenty-five hundred years. When Latin Christians developed city life about nine hundred years ago, they did not become indistinguishable from the previously urbanized Greeks of Byzantium. Should we expect acculturation to be different in the twentieth century than it was in the tenth? Perhaps so, for communications are far more intense in our time than ever before. On the other hand, cultural conservatism and adaptive capacity are far greater than ethnocentric foreign observers are likely to imagine. As in so many other matters, time alone will tell.

More than anything else, what was pulling Greece towards western norms in the 1970s was the flood of foreign (especially United States) TV programs that have begun to ride the airwaves. Both radio and TV were completely controlled by the national government; and radio programs incorporated only a small amount of foreign material. TV was different. In order to keep signals coming throughout hours of broadcast, a large proportion of time had to be devoted to foreign-produced shows. In 1976, for example, about 40 percent of what was sent out over the two Athens TV stations originated abroad. The officials of the Greek government who decided which programs to broadcast were not particularly concerned about the social implications of what they were offering the Greek public in the way of entertainment. Cheapness and availability, viewer response, and vaguely defined standards of propriety did affect decisions. But even under the Colonels, when defense of Hellenism was central to official ideology, propriety was loosely defined and permitted much that contravened traditional Greek family behavior. As a matter of fact, the Colonels' regime put large resources into setting up relay stations to allow nearly all parts of the country to get a clear signal from Athens. Fascination with the technical virtuosity inherent in this new mode of communication seems to have entirely eclipsed interest in, or concern for, the content of what might be transmitted.

The semiautonomous status enjoyed by the armed forces in Greece was reflected, interestingly enough, in the fact that the armed forces radio network (which dated back to the guerrilla war when it was designed to counteract a Communist station broadcasting from Rumania) branched out into TV within a few weeks of the time when the official government station began to operate in 1966. The two stations continued to broadcast independently. One was a special fief of the minister of defense; the other came under the supervision of the office of the prime minister.

The two ministries systematically used TV and radio to make sure that their own special points of view got attention, both directly in the form of broadcasts of political speeches and more subtly through the way the news was edited and presented. But no one in official position paid much attention to the sociopsychological implications of programs conceived as mere entertainment. Perhaps it was true, as their enemies said later, that the Colonels' regime deliberately fostered sports and sports-consciousness as a way of diverting attention from politics. Certainly, interest in sports, especially football, mounted remarkably. National and international soccer matches, broadcast on TV, commanded intensely enthusiastic audiences. But what was likely to matter most were new ideas about personal behavior that were implied and taken for granted rather than

stated explicitly in the American and European films and TV
serials that made their way onto the Greek networks as a way of
filling in time and attracting viewers.

No one can tell in advance just how old customs and styles of
life will interact with all the novelties thrust before Greek eyes so
suddenly. Aping of western styles—blue jeans were well-nigh
universal in Athens among the young in 1976—has already set in
and may become more far-reaching in time to come. But active
rejection of foreign corruption was also a barely perceptible
undercurrent. In the longer run it seems all but certain that some
aspects of the alien ways will penetrate Greek society and
become normal, while on other matters Greeks will reject the
new and reaffirm more strongly than before aspects of behavior
that make them distinctively different from other peoples.

Thus, for example, Orthodox Christianity is not in any danger
of collapsing or losing its accustomed importance in Greek life,
even though church attendance has diminished sharply. In the
village past, services on a Sunday gave the women of the
community a chance to meet and gossip. Talking during the
service was perfectly all right. What mattered was the ritual
performance itself; and no one had to listen to make the rite
effective. Hence, attendance at church on Sunday played a role
in female lives that the coffeeshop played for their menfolk every
day. In town, on the other hand, women have other places to
meet. Consequently, church services lost their former social
function and attendance dropped accordingly. But rituals for all
the standard crises of human life—birth, marriage, death—
remain vital; and Easter continues, in town as much as in the
country, to serve as the central punctuation of the year—reenact-
ing the relationship between man and God and reaffirming the
community of all Orthodox believers as it has done for centuries. No foreign ideas or attitudes seem in the least likely to
dent the deep attachment Greeks feel to their Orthodox identity.
Anything thought to threaten it would at once be banished from
public showing.

It is not hard to identify some other sacred zones that are
likely to resist any and all challenges inherent in the new pattern
of mass communications. Language, nationality, Hellenism have
often been invoked by patriots and politicians; and nothing
recognized as derogatory to these is likely to be shown on TV or

in any public place. Defense of freedom and of the existing order are also sensitive matters; and even though Greek TV has shown a number of films produced in east European countries, they are carefully chosen so as to eliminate overt Communist propaganda.

Between 1967 and 1974, political debate was banished from the Athens radio and TV. Only the official government line was allowed. But the Greek public recognized at once that half-truths and outright falsehoods were often incorporated into official pronouncements, and quickly developed a profound skepticism about everything Athens had to say. Under the dictatorship, many Greeks relied on foreign radio news broadcasts to correct and contradict what came out of Athens. After 1974, parliamentary debates and set speeches by party leaders found a place on Athens radio and TV; but the government spokesmen got more time and news editors of the two stations (who were, of course, official appointees, serving at the discretion of the ministers) maintained the right to choose which parts of opposition speeches to broadcast. Still, the new arrangement did allow diverse viewpoints to reach the public, and criticism of the government was no longer completely bottled up. In addition, more truthful news broadcasts won back the credence of most of the Greek public, for whom foreign radio ceased to be of much interest.

Nevertheless, the comparative eclipse of newspapers, which used to be the main vehicle of public information, meant that relatively enormous power to shape the patterns of public debate and consciousness rested in the hands of those who controlled TV and radio programming. Athens' influence generally and the influence of the government in particular have been enormously enhanced by this development; and, so far, professionalism among Greek broadcasters seems pretty much confined to imitating the mannerisms of British and American announcers.

In the next couple of decades the really significant impact of foreign entertainment materials on Greek society is almost sure to center on the patterns of family conduct which mark Greeks off from west Europeans and Americans. Courtship and marriage is the point where conflict has been clearest and where changes in Greek custom have come most rapidly. But the whole issue of whether individual self-fulfillment should take precedence over family concerns cannot be far behind. So far, it seems to me, collective solidarity within the nuclear family remains generally firm in spite of the implicit message of hundreds of scenes from foreign films and serials. It may remain so indefinitely, or some further and basic reorganization of Greek society, much more fundamental than anything that has yet occurred with the emptying out of the hill villages, may impend. It will require another thirty years or so before any judgment will become possible.

In this connection it is worth reminding ourselves that tensions between local and national as well as between national and foreign ideas and ideals are nothing new. Such tensions are implicit in the plurality of human cultures. And however such tensions may be resolved or alter across time, the upshot never has been, and is never likely to be, homogeneity. It follows that no one should think that Greek society and economy will soon become a simulacrum of what exists (or will exist) in other parts of the world. Some important elements from old Greek tradition and cultural inheritance are sure to survive and mix with novelties in distinctive, unique ways. Dress, architecture, manners may be modern, cosmopolitan, and indistinguishable from those in a hundred other places in the world. But such outward seeming does not mean that important local differences do not continue to lurk beneath the surface, affecting behavior strongly enough to make the pattern of Greek economic growth, the style of Greek politics, and the texture of Greek urban life distinctive and unique.

Conclusion

If satisfaction of human wants and aspirations is taken as the criterion, then the development of Greece across the last thirty years must be viewed as an extraordinary success story. Things that seemed impossible in 1945 have in fact come true for millions of individual Greeks; and for nearly all of the people involved, whatever has been lost or thrust to the margins of life, while sometimes regretted, does not begin to counterbalance the gains.

The metamorphosis of human life that has been taking place is without historic parallel in Greece's past. It has affected the entire population within a single generation, and worked such a change in the social structure that any return to the old village-centered life has become impossible, short of drastic collapse of urban society and a radical impoverishment that would lead to the death of millions from starvation.

No one can be sure that disruption of urban-centered exchange relationships will not occur. In times past, the Aegean region has more than once seen the decay of city life, with all of its consequences: depopulation, impoverishment, and threadbare survival of a small, locally self-sufficient, rural population. The more elaborate and geographically extensive the exchanges that support human life, the more vulnerable to disruption they become. Yet paradoxically, the increasingly vulnerable fabric of civilized life also becomes increasingly resilient in the face of local and temporary breakdown. This was shown in the effectiveness of relief distribution systems in keeping people alive in Greece during World War II and in the period of guerrilla warfare afterwards. Ever since civilization began, human society has oscillated between mounting intensity of integration and disruptive breakdown of the mutual interdependence such integration creates. The twentieth century thrust towards an intercontinental integration is only the most recent, though by far the most drastic, episode in this ancient seesaw; and the role of Greece in this general global pattern, though modest, has been real.

As it is for the rest of humankind, the fate of the Greek people depends centrally on how the world system evolves. Any prolonged disturbance of global trade, credit, communications, and transport would immediately bring catastrophic consequences for Greece. This, however, is no less true of other societies that have entered into the world network of exchanges. The greatest national structures are almost as vulnerable as the weakest to any prolonged breakdown of the flow of goods and services that keeps us all alive and generates wealth in so remarkable a fashion. What seems unusual about the Greek experience is the ease with which a formerly peasant people have so far accommodated themselves to urbanism. I have suggested that this is due, centrally, to the market aptitudes traditional Greek rural life inculcated across the generations. Certainly from the perspective attainable in 1976 it seems plausible to think that the political storms of 1961–67 may have registered a phase of maximal disorganization, when the strains of urbanization were at a peak, and before continued escalation of living standards and accommodation of in-migrants into the body social of Athens and Salonika had been able to reduce psychic stress among the newcomers.

The experience of dictatorial rule under self-appointed champions of Hellenism may have permanently chastened the spirit of reactionaries who in 1966 and 1967 were confident that a simple cure for the public discord of the times lay within their power. And since the overthrow of the Colonels in 1974, voices on the left have not stirred up wide or deep response, partly because the Communist recipe for social revolution, as displayed in the northern Balkans, exhibited no obvious superiority over what has been achieved within Greece itself. All foreign models, including both the USA and the USSR, lost much of their glamor by the mid-1970s. Certainly neighboring Turkish, Arab, Italian, and Israeli examples of how to navigate the rapids of social change offered little to attract the Greeks. If there was a lodestar towards which Greek attention and aspiration turned it was the European Common Market countries, especially Germany and France. The thought that Greece may now be ready to "join Europe" by becoming a member of the Economic Community has a considerable appeal in a time when Greeks keenly feel the need for external support against the Turks.

But becoming a full-fledged member of the European Economic Community will require extraordinary changes in Greek industry and agriculture, and marked increases in productivity. Perhaps such changes, which in themselves are less incredible than some of the transformations that have already occurred, will prove feasible. Even if that should turn out not to be the case, it is likely that Greek skills in the marketplace, which have served them so well of late, will continue to serve them well as long as the modern megalopolis holds together.

Two potential sources of instability within Greece itself may blight the country's future. If the central institution of the nuclear family should begin to unravel, massive alienation would surely arise among young people, and begin to haunt mature lives as well. In such a case, political extremism may be expected to arise once more and tear the country apart as it seemed to be doing in the middle 1960s. Radicalism of both left and right would then cease to be a phenomenon of youth, and would spread throughout all age groups and social classes. Authoritarian government sustained by police repression of dissidents, of the sort that prevailed from 1967 to 1974, would then almost surely recur, though it is impossible to foresee whether the ruling ideology would be of the left or of the right. The practical difference, if one may hazard a guess, would probably be slight.

The second obvious source of instability is the power of the army to upset any government that betrays the heroic, national ideal too blatantly. The spirit of the professional army officer corps definitely marks it off from the rest of Greek society. For the past thirty years professional army officers have enjoyed a privileged access to foreign aid, so that the patterns of military life have not had to adjust themselves to limits set by Greek civil society and political-economic conditions. The Greeks enjoyed the luxury of letting civilian society maximize market behavior while the military, thanks to NATO support, took off in full-blooded pursuit of its own antithetical ideal. Contradictions and tensions between these styles of behavior have been central to Greek culture for centuries—or so I have argued. Since 1945 they have achieved an institutionalization that gives each pole of Greek life a scope that was unattainable in earlier ages, when the army lacked NATO support and civilian society lacked the access to international loans, gifts, and short-term credits on anything like the recent scale.

How these two poles of Greek reality may continue to fit themselves to their respective international settings, and how they will work out their mutual relationship on Greek soil, remains the critical issue for Greek public life during the next thirty years, just as it has been a central theme of the thirty years past. Greek-Turkish confrontations in Cyprus and in the Aegean put acute strain on the international support systems that the Greek armed forces and the Greek civil government have relied on since the 1940s. NATO planners, clearly, have no wish to supply Greeks to fight Turks and Turks to fight Greeks; international bankers, whether governmental or private, must treat the risks of war between Greece and Turkey as a severe deterrent to making new advances to either protagonist. Yet internal compulsions to defend national interest vigorously, lest some rival political group take power by accusing the regime of betrayal, may at any time lead either Greece or Turkey (more likely the latter, where the disruptions incident to urbanization are far more acute than in Greece) to some act that will lead to war.

War would swiftly undo much of the advance of living standards Greeks (and Turks) have known since 1945. Both governments realize this and intend, presumably, to avoid the precipice even when treading as close to the edge as they dare, so as to deprive domestic rivals of the opportunity to accuse them of craven failure to defend the national interest. This is a dangerous game, but one the world will have to endure, especially in a time when many other countries besides Greece and Turkey are experiencing deep internal strains, and desperately need a foreign enemy to enhance solidarity at home.

Stability and security remain, therefore, unattained and unattainable, for the Greeks as well as for all the rest of the modern world. Greece joined that world after 1949 with élan. Whatever the future may bring, anyone thinking back to the stark poverty that prevailed so widely thirty years ago must admire the way this people has overcome what once seemed insuperable obstacles to achieving a better material standard of living. The symmetries of planning on a national or international scale may be more appealing to technocrats and intellectuals, but the achievements of more than a million Greek families, each acting on its own as an economic unit, have been comparable to anything socialist states have been able to achieve; and it is at least arguable that the inequalities of income and standard of life that Greeks have experienced allow greater net human satisfaction than anything bureaucratically decreed equality (and inequality) has brought to the Communist lands of eastern Europe.

The Greek metamorphosis during the past generation ought to command respect. Those who study it ought also to recognize how new technical and market opportunities interacted with age-old traditional patterns of behavior to make a blend not duplicated elsewhere. The assumption that modernization is an essentially identical worldwide process seems patently false. Greece is not just a few years behind Germany or the USA, nor, for that matter, do the Greeks trail the Soviet Union or China on the path to socialism. Cultural pluralism is as old as humanity, and it seems likely to survive the homogenizing force of modern communications, however great that may be.

One of the purposes of this essay was to illustrate the variety of paths to the present by analyzing the Greek case and emphasizing the general, traditional factors whose persistence has affected the way things developed in the last thirty years. The other aim was to portray as concretely as possible what the metamorphosis of Greek society as a whole has meant for a half dozen villages in one of the smaller countries of the earth where, nevertheless, human wants and aspirations were as intense as anywhere else, and their satisfaction was as difficult. Judicious interplay between the universal and the unique characterizes all intellectual discourse. How well it has here been achieved is for the reader to judge.

Appendix

Table A1   Population Distribution within Greece

Year	Total	Urban	%	Semiurban	%	Rural	%
1920	5,016,889	1,148,341	22.9	760,500	15.2	3,108,048	61.9
1928	6,204,684	1,931,937	31.1	899,466	14.5	3,373,281	54.4
1940	7,377,860	2,411,647	32.8	1,086,079	14.8	3,847,134	52.4
1951	7,632,801	2,879,994	37.7	1,130,188	14.8	3,622,619	47.5
1961	8,388,553	3,628,105	43.3	1,085,856	12.9	3,674,592	43.8
1971	8,768,641	4,667,489	53.2	1,019,421	11.6	3,081,731	35.2

SOURCE   *Statistical Yearbook of Greece, 1975*, table II:5.

Table A2   Emigrants from Greece, 1958–1974

Year	Total	Permanent	Temporary
1958	40,808	24,521	16,287
1959	43,683	23,684	19,999
1960	75,222	47,768	27,454
1961	85,263	58,837	26,426
1962	110,722	84,054	26,668
1963	135,509	100,072	35,437
1964	153,185	105,569	47,616
1965	176,408	117,167	59,241
1966	148,414	86,896	61,518
1967	102,462	42,730	59,732
1968	115,004	50,866	64,138
1969	158,675	91,552	67,123
1970	163,251	92,681	70,570
1971	136,974	61,745	75,229
1972	116,138	43,397	72,741
1973	112,641	27,525	85,116
1974	117,043	24,448	92,595

SOURCE   *Statistical Yearbook of Greece, 1975*, table II:31.

Table A3   Transoceanic Emigration from
                             Greece 1871–1974

Year	Total	To USA
1871–1880	213	210
1881–1890	2,310	2,308
1891–1895	5,790	5,790
1896–1900	11,189	11,189
1901–1905	51,479	49,962
1906–1910	122,034	117,557
1911–1915	128,521	118,916
1916–1920	67,598	65,285
1921–1925	50,531	42,323
1926–1930	40,838	27,352
1931–1935	14,797	11,363
1936–1940	15,703	10,540
1941–1945	—	—
1946*	1,558	1,326
1947	4,901	2,571
1948	4,819	2,047
1949	4,263	1,483
1950	4,635	1,890
1951	14,155	8,930
1952	6,640	2,155
1953	8,820	1,320
1954	18,682	3,487
1955	19,766	6,896
1956	23,147	8,982
1957	14,783	1,807
1958	14,842	3,870
1959	13,871	2,528
1960	17,764	3,561
1961	17,336	3,471
1962	21,959	4,460
1963	24,459	4,564
1964	25,327	2,890
1965	29,035	2,782
1966	33,093	12,193
1967	26,323	11,778
1968	25,891	9,839
1969	28,425	12,716
1970	24,153	11,484
1971	18,690	8,275
1972	13,239	6,613
1973	11,706	6,028
1974	12,380	6,347

SOURCE   *Statistical Yearbook of
                             Greece, 1975*, table II:32.

                             *From 1946, figures do not include
                             tourists in a broader sense and those
                             emigrating for temporary work (less
                             than one year).

Table A4   Repatriation of Greek Citizens

| Year | Grand Total | From overseas countries | |
		Total	From USA
1968*	18,882	4,734	967
1969	18,132	5,156	1,500
1970	22,665	7,112	1,963
1971	24,709	8,226	1,819
1972	27,522	8,484	1,945
1973	22,285	6,326	1,542
1974	24,476	4,793	1,497

SOURCE   *Statistical Yearbook of Greece, 1975*, table II:42–43.

*Repatriation statistics compiled only from 1968.

Index

260 Index